LONDON

LONDON

A CULTURAL HISTORY

Richard Tames

OXFORD
UNIVERSITY PRESS

2006

OXFORD

UNIVERSITY PRESS

Oxford University Press, Inc., publishes works that further
Oxford University's objective of excellence
in research, scholarship, and education.

Oxford   New York
Auckland   Cape Town   Dar es Salaam   Hong Kong   Karachi
Kuala Lumpur   Madrid   Melbourne   Mexico City   Nairobi
New Delhi   Shanghai   Taipei   Toronto

With offices in
Argentina   Austria   Brazil   Chile   Czech Republic   France   Greece
Guatemala   Hungary   Italy   Japan   Poland   Portugal   Singapore
South Korea   Switzerland   Thailand   Turkey   Ukraine   Vietnam

Copyright © 2006 by Richard Tames

Foreword © 2006 by Nigel Williams

Published by Oxford University Press, Inc.
198 Madison Avenue, New York, New York 10016

www.oup.com

Oxford is a registered trademark of Oxford University Press

Co-published in Great Britain by Signal Books

Library of Congress Cataloging-in-Publication Data
Tames, Richard.
London : a cultural history / Richard Tames.
p. cm. — (Cityscapes)
Includes bibliographical references and index.
ISBN-13 978-0-19-530953-9; 978-0-19-530954-6 (pbk.)
ISBN 0-19-530953-7; 0-19-530954-5 (pbk.)
1. London (England)—History. 2. London (England)—Civilization.
3. London (England)—Description and travel. I. Title II. Series.

DA677.T35 2006
942.1—dc22   2006045344

9 8 7 6 5 4 3 2 1

Printed in the United States of America
on acid-free paper

Foreword

My brother has lived for many years in a district of Berlin called Lichterfelde. Nearly twenty years ago, at the end of his garden was the Berlin Wall. One of his neighbours, I recall, once made the mistake of leaning a bag of garden compost up against it—upon which teams of VoPos appeared out of nowhere, brandishing machine guns, taking photographs and keen to assess this new threat from the capitalist West.

And then, in 1989 the Wall came down and, at last, you could see what was on the other side of it. Open country. Suddenly the centre of gravity of the city had shifted, and Lichterfelde, which had been close to the fashionable heart of West Berlin, was transformed into a suburb. It was as if some wizard had cast a spell and translated a Knightsbridge terraced house to Friern Barnet. His house came crashing down in value. Taxi drivers no longer want to take you there. And, even if, at night, he does not have to look at the yellow sodium lights of an odious regime a part of him will always long for the old West Berlin.

Cities change cruelly. And London, as Richard Tames makes clear in this likeable, well-written and delightfully individualistic take on the city where I have lived for the last 58 years, is no exception. Crosby Hall, for example, was originally a fifteenth-century mansion built by a wealthy grocer on Bishopsgate. It was subsequently owned by entities as various as Sir Thomas More and the East India Company and, in 1908, threatened with demolition, was dismantled and rebuilt on a riverside site in Chelsea where it became a dining hall for the British Federation of University Women.

For me, of course (like all natives of the city I am amazingly ignorant about it and could not possibly compete with a qualified guide like Mr. Tames) the changes I regret seem impossibly small to strangers but are none the less potent. I still mourn not being able to drive round Trafalgar Square from the south, turn left just before the National Gallery and sneak through to Charing Cross Road on a weird little road with speed bumps in it that no-one but me and other habitués know about. I still mourn the disappearance of the bus station on the Cromwell Road, where once you could take a coach out to London Airport. To this day I do not know why they built the Brent Cross Shopping Centre—and I am sorry that they did it. Why did they take away Eros for Christ's sake? Why was the BBC, among its many other crimes, allowed to sell the Langham building, that huge mournful, Stalinist tenement in Portland Place, so that it could be turned back into a horrible hotel? Why, as Harold Pinter famously pointed out, is it impossible to drive to Bolsover Street without getting lost in the one-way system? Who turned my favourite restaurant in Notting Hill Gate into a loathsome brasserie, where waiters insult you and charge hundreds of pounds for the privilege?

These are not trivial questions if you live in a city. But the very size and complexity of London reduces you into thinking that they are the most important things about the place. As this book makes clear, it is a very hard town to get a hold of. Even Peter Ackroyd, it appears, left the Strand out of his massive biography of the Smoke. The Strand! Which gave its name to the magazine where Sherlock Holmes first made his appearance! Where, once, the old Savoy Grill, looking out over the river, entertained the likes of Noel Coward, and where once an immigrant policeman, one Peter O'Loughlin, stopped all the traffic with a wave of his hand, in that greatest of all Irish popular songs "The Mountains of Mourne"! Peter, how could you?

One of the many strengths of this book is its appetite for the variousness of the place and the fact that it does not ignore the richness and strangeness of the suburbs. London, as a certain type of bore (now, it appears, including myself) never stops reminding you, is a collection of villages.

I was brought up in West Hampstead (which is estate agent parlance for Kilburn), moved to Mill Hill, then to North Finchley, and, since my father died have lived entirely in south London, mainly in the southwest, ending up halfway up Putney Hill. What has struck me forcibly about all these places is how acutely they are aware of their separate identity. Edmund Leach, the great anthropologist, once told me that all over the world there were people who were absolutely positive that just over the hill were other people who ate human flesh, and that is still more or less what West Putney inhabitants think about East Putney inhabitants or Muswell Hillites believe to be true of Crouch Enders.

If the English talent is for practical individuality, allowing things to grow without apparent system (imagine London zoned into numbered districts like Paris!) then London, from High Barnet to Crystal Palace, is the fullest expression of its genius. This is a book, which in its diversity and sheer joy in the peculiar, is worthy of its subject. If you want to know when billiards first came to town (the sixteenth century apparently) or where cockneys took the word "pal" (from Romany, it seems) or why Osterley is called Osterley (it seems it is because sheep grazed there since eowestre is the Anglo-Saxon for sheep), if you want to . . . well . . . it's all here, read the book. The only thing Richard Tames has not managed to do is to tell me why Camden Town has no character or why the man who designed the Wandsworth one-way traffic system has not being taken out and battered to death in front of a grateful public. But you cannot have everything.

Nigel Williams
April 2006

Contents

Introduction

"There is no civilized part of the world but it hath heard thereof, though many with this mistake, that they conceive London to be the country and England but the city therein."

Thomas Fuller, 1662

City of Superlatives

As a descriptive adjective, London has become paired with fog, clay and gin. "London Pride" is the title of a song by Noel Coward, the web address of an annual gay festival, the name of a pretty pink flower of the saxifrage family and a premium bitter beer brewed by Fullers of Chiswick.

For over a century London was the most populous city in the western world and for half a century the most populous in the whole world. It is still the most populous in Europe. There are more (over 250) direct flights from London to other cities than from anywhere else on the planet. There are more Londoners over 75 years of age than Manchester has residents. More people shop in Selfridges annually than live in Australia. London has 19,000 buildings officially listed as being of architectural or historical interest—and more than half of Britain's homeless. One-fifth of London consists of gardens, parks and open spaces, and on Hackney Marshes there is the largest continuous area of football pitches in the world. Walthamstow has the longest street market in Europe. An Edwardian travel guide boasted that London had "more Scotchmen than in Edinburgh, more Irish than in Dublin, more Jews than in Palestine and more Roman Catholics than in Rome." *The New and Compleat Survey of London*, published in 1762, claimed confidently that London had 322,903 inhabitants more than ancient Nineveh and 237,982 more than Babylon, five times as many as old Jerusalem and 6,093 more than Constantinople and Moscow put together. It was also claimed to have three times as many markets and ovens as Imperial Rome and three times as many houses as Peking. A special sneer was reserved for contemporary Paris, which, if doubled in circumference would still be "Three Quarters of a Mile, One hundred and Thirty-Five Yards, Thirty-One Inches and a half less than London."

Magnet for Talent

For a thousand years London has been a magnet for talent. London scores 23,322 hits in the index of the *Dictionary of National Biography*, ranking it far ahead of the other national capitals, Edinburgh (5,756) Cardiff (430) and Belfast (588). The Edwardian journalist G. R. Sims once asserted that "We have never had a great man who has not lived in London." (I tried that line on a group of visitors once to be greeted with a laconic Scottish rebuttal—"Robert Burns". There *are* a few exceptions, but they are exceptional.) The general rule about drawing talent from across the nation seems to be borne out by the BBC's 2003 poll to choose the ten Great Britons of all time. Of those nominated, Elizabeth I was born in what is now part of London, Greenwich, but it would then have been considered a rural retreat from the city proper. None of the other finalists was born in the capital. Churchill was born in Oxfordshire, Brunel and Dickens in Portsmouth, Darwin in Shrewsbury, Newton in the Lincolnshire village of Woolsthorpe, Cromwell in Huntingdon, Shakespeare in Stratford-upon-Avon, Diana, Princess of Wales in Norfolk and John Lennon in Liverpool. Yet all of them ended up living in London at one point or other in their lives.

As nationally, so globally, at least for the English-speaking world. Culturally London is "Headquarters", the dwelling-place of "Standards" embodied in acronymic authority—GMT, BBC, RA, ICA, TLS . . . London has been a lighthouse drawing in the literary moths of the colonial periphery from Washington Irving and Henry James, through Olive Schreiner and Katherine Mansfield to Clive James, Dom Moraes and V. S. Naipaul. London is where you come to become "a Writer", "an Actor", "a Success". The fact of transition and the possibility of transformation are both reiterated in the very titles chosen by post-war Caribbean writers for the novels and memoirs which draw on this experience: *The Enigma of Arrival, Finding the Centre* (V. S. Naipaul), *Escape to an Autumn Pavement* (Andrew Salkey), *Journey to an Illusion* (Donald Hinds), *The Final Passage, Crossing the River* (Caryl Phillips).

Gifts to the World

London is a crucible of creativity and inventiveness. Shakespeare never wrote a line before he came to London or after he left it. London is responsible for the tuning fork, the concertina, Handel's *Messiah*, Mozart's first symphony and the Rolling Stones; cuff-links, the top hat, the bowler hat, the gymslip and the mini-skirt; the sandwich, the beer-pump, tonic water, soda water, porter and Pimm's No.1. London's contributions to sport include rowing races, boxing, competitive yachting, the rules of cricket, football, tennis, rugby, polo and snooker, the squash court, the gumshield and the FA Cup. As the pioneering centre of global capitalism London gave birth to Lloyd's, numbered bank notes, pre-paid postage stamps, burglary insurance, the desk diary, underground railways, double-decker buses, the railway season ticket, Reuter's, *Das Kapital* and the rubber stamp. In their leisure hours Londoners developed the rock garden, the deckchair, the stamp album, the aquarium and the gardening magazine. In their pursuit of domestic comfort they occasioned the invention of the sprung mattress, the gasworks and the hot water geyser. London's other miscellaneous gifts to the world include the monorail, the hangman's drop, corrugated iron, artificial dyestuffs, rubber gloves, the Salvation Army, the YMCA, the school song, Jack the Ripper, Charlie Chaplin, the destroyer, CT-scanners, penicillin, television—and author's royalties.

What London Isn't
London is self-evidently not the countryside. The English have long celebrated theirs as a "green and pleasant land"—a phrase coined by that quintessential Londoner William Blake. Recruiting posters in both world wars used archetypal images of vales, villas and villages, rather than Big Ben or Buckingham Palace, to evoke the "essential" England. The landscapes of Gainsborough and Constable, the poetry of Wordsworth and Housman and the music of Elgar argue for a deep equation between rusticity and Englishness. Perhaps this is a partial explanation of why some of the creators of enduring images and icons of London have not been English in origin. The fog-shrouded London of Sherlock Holmes and *Dr. Jekyll and Mr. Hyde* was the work of Conan Doyle and Robert Louis Stevenson, both Scotsmen. *Peter Pan* was the creation of Sir James Barrie, another Scot. Eliza Doolittle, the epitome of cockney chippiness, was fashioned by George Bernard Shaw, an Irishman. Australian actress P. L. Travers conjured up Mary Poppins. Celebrated views of London and Londoners in pencil, pastel and paint have been produced by Hollar, a Bohemian, the Dutchmen Hondius and Knyff, Canaletto a Venetian, the Frenchmen Doré, Tissot, Pissaro and Monet, the American Whistler and the Austrian Kokoschka.

Capital Progress

London has not always been the capital and only became so by stages. The Romans initially fixed on Colchester, which consequently claims to be England's oldest city. In fact the notion of a city was unfeasible, not to say inconceivable, to the pre-Roman inhabitants of the British Isles. Colchester was, in effect, a very large cattle enclosure and a symbolically significant place in which the conquering emperor Claudius could, in AD 43, accept the surrender of a dozen tribal chieftains. The Romans, however, soon revised their geographical appreciation of their new colony and relocated their operational headquarters to what became London.

Why? Because of the river. The south-east corner of England is one of the flattest and most fertile parts of the British archipelago. It has a moderate level of rainfall and climate. In terms of sailing it is only a day away from the coastline of mainland Europe and the estuaries of the Rhine, the Scheldt etc., which lead into Europe's heartland. An invader securing the south-east of England has a base which can be reinforced from abroad and from which to annex the rest of the island, as the Romans, Saxons and Normans all did. Bisecting this heartland is the Thames, after the Severn Britain's longest river. Because the Thames is tidal large vessels could be brought more than forty miles inland to the point where Roman military engineers found substantial gravel beds on either side of the river to support the abutments of a bridge. The first London bridge, at London Bridge, seems to have been built around AD 50—and thus London enters history.

With the departure of the Roman legions in the fifth century, history with a capital H left London. The disintegration of a unified, at least partially Romanized, Britannia was accompanied by the collapse of centralized political control and long-distance trade. London had lost its *raisons d'être*—temporarily—but not apparently its reputation as the place that mattered. When St. Augustine arrived in 597 to introduce the Christian faith to the pagan English overlords of the former Roman colony he was ordered by the Pope to base himself in London. He did, indeed, consecrate a bishop for London in 604, which is therefore traditionally taken as the foundation date for St. Paul's Cathedral; but Augustine received such a warm welcome from the King of Kent and his French, Christian wife that Canterbury became England's spiritual epicentre. London defaulted on its intended destiny by rejecting Christianity for half a century rather than offend its pagan trading-partners in Frisia. This was indicative of a great constant in London's history—that it is the place to make money. Writing in the early eighth century the monastic chronicler Bede, the first historian of the English people, who never went within two hundred miles of London, still referred to the crossing-point on the Thames as "the mart of many nations".

The reunification of England was achieved by the royal house of Wessex and its capital, Winchester, therefore became for a while as much the national capital as anywhere could claim to be. Nevertheless in 886 King Alfred of Wessex ordered the reoccupation and refortification of London, primarily as the easternmost anchor-point for the diagonal defensive line of some thirty *burhs* which he had established across England. These were intended to keep the invading Vikings in check by serving as assembly-points for the English militia and as refuges for civilians. By 1016 the official English chronicle established by Alfred could record that Edmund Ironside had been chosen as king by "all the lords who were in London and the citizens". Edmund failed even to see out the year but his successor Knut used London as the capital from which to rule a maritime empire that stretched across the North Sea to Scandinavia and the edge of the Arctic Circle. Half a century later, William the Conqueror was sufficiently wary of the power of London not to attempt a frontal assault on the city and to guarantee its traditional privileges and laws. He, and all subsequent monarchs, would, moreover, be crowned in Westminster Abbey.

The Conqueror's royal successors maintained such a nomadic style of government that the capital was wherever the king happened to be. By the early thirteenth century, however, the volume of governmental business was such that the law courts met continuously at Westminster and the Exchequer became established there as a permanent collection-point for the nation's taxes. Recognition of London's importance was symbolized by the decision of the Archbishop of Canterbury to establish a London residence—Lambeth Palace. In 1215 King John was finally cornered by the leaders of the baronial rebellion against his abuse of royal power. The seals placed on the Great Charter intended to restore rightful government were all those of great magnates—plus one commoner, the Mayor of London. The beginning of London as the nation's capital is synonymous with the assertion of liberty under law.

"Anglobalization"

The historian Niall Ferguson has argued that liberty under law, enshrined in the English language, is Britain's great gift to the world and the central feature of a transformational process he has dubbed "Anglobalization". The driving force of this process was not the urge for conquest but for trade, and trade was centred on London as Britain's leading port. Fuelled by the expansion of global commerce there emerged London's specialized strengths in banking, insurance, accountancy, law, tropical medicine and non-European languages. Ferguson sees this as the great cumulative continuity behind London's eminence: "what makes London so successful as a city is that it combines a huge and variegated service sector with the world's most important international financial market and one of its favourite tourist destinations. It is . . . the quintessential modern megalopolis, multi-tasking its way to ever more jobs and ever higher living standards." Jan Morris put the same point more concisely—London's most characteristic product is expertise.

Industrialization, as significant a transformative process as "Anglobalization", also originated in Britain, though not in London. London was not physically at the heart of the industrialization process but it was to London that surplus capital was despatched from provincial cities and the countryside and from London that it was recycled to finance mills, mines, factories and foundries. London itself always remained a major centre of manufacturing, first in the literal sense of making by hand, as the national centre of excellence for the production of clocks, guns, garments, silverware, navigational instruments and furniture, and second in the sense of possessing early exemplars of the large-scale application of steam-powered technology to brewing, printing, shipbuilding and food-processing. When Blake conjured the image of "dark satanic mills" in his paean to *Jerusalem* he was almost certainly thinking of the monstrous Albion flour mills near his home in Lambeth.

What London Has

The notion of a "hidden history" appeals to me though more, I suspect, on grounds of alliteration than on anything more substantial. In reality the immensity of London's history is not so much hidden as forgotten. London is now dwarfed in population by Shanghai or Mexico City but it retains a depth of history and, within that history, layerings of meanings and resonances which few other cities—perhaps only Rome, Paris, Cairo and Istanbul—can rival. By way of illustration consider the layerings of a single building, a single square and a single locality.

Crosby Hall was once part of a mansion complex on Bishopsgate, built in 1466–75 for a wealthy grocer, Sir John Crosby. In 1483 the future Richard III was living there when the news broke that his nephews had been murdered in the Tower. Shakespeare wrote it into *Richard III* as the scene of the wicked uncle's plotting. In 1532–4 the building was owned by Sir Thomas More, although, as he was by then in disgrace with the king, he may never have lived in it. Sir Walter Raleigh had lodgings there in 1601. From 1621 to 1638 it was the headquarters of the East India Company. From 1672 until 1769 the building served as a Presbyterian meeting-house. It then housed various commercial premises and, from 1842, the Crosby Hall Scientific and Literary Institution. In 1868 it became a restaurant, one of the first to have waitresses and to serve unaccompanied women customers. Threatened with demolition in 1908, the building was dismantled and re-erected on a riverside site at Chelsea which had once been part of Sir Thomas More's garden. From 1926 onwards it was used as the dining hall for residents of the adjacent International Hostel of the British Federation of University Women. In 1988 the building was acquired by TV rental tycoon Christopher Moran, who employed designers from the Historic Royal Palaces Agency to create a £60,000,000 residence with three complementary wings, each modelled on a different house from the fifteenth or sixteenth centuries.

Cavendish Square would not spring to most Londoners' lips first as a location rich in historic associations, but it is. Developed in the reign of George I (1714–27) as a residential *quartier* for aristocrats, it became the home of the portrait painter George Romney. The architect James Gibbs and royal gardener Charles Bridgeman lived in streets leading into the square. Byron was born in one of these. Washington Irving had lodgings in another. Nelson passed his honeymoon there. In 1850 the square was home to a duke, a marquis, three earls, a viscount, a countess, two lords, two ladies, a baronet, a knight, two admirals, a general, a colonel, six members of parliament and the president of the Royal Academy, Sir Martin Archer Shee—an indifferent painter but a first-class committee man. United States President Ulysses S. Grant stayed in Cavendish Square while on his round-the-world tour. Subsequent residents included publisher William Heinemann, who published Galsworthy, Wells and Conrad and introduced the English to the works of Turgenev,

Tolstoy and Ibsen; Nobel Laureate Sir Ronald Ross, who discovered how malaria was spread by the mosquito; Quintin Hogg, founder of Regent Street Polytechnic; G. E. Street, architect of the Royal Courts of Justice; and future Prime Minister H. H. Asquith.

By 1900 Cavendish Square, abutting Harley Street (see pp. 161–2) had become a stronghold of the medical profession, accommodating thirteen dentists, eight physicians, seven surgeons, three ophthalmologists and a "medical galvanist". Today the occupants of the square are institutional, educational or commercial. In the centre of the square still stands an empty plinth, once surmounted by a lead statue of George II's unlovable bully of a son, the rightly named "Butcher" Cumberland. A brutal and untalented military commander, he was, however, an enthusiastic patron of prize-fighting, *de facto* founder of the Royal Yacht Club (originally known as the Cumberland Fleet) and owner of Eclipse, perhaps the greatest thoroughbred sire of the eighteenth century. Nearby still stands a suitably athletic-looking statue of the sporting statesman Lord George Bentinck, who frequently appeared in Parliament in hunting gear and did much to clean up racing as a sport. On the north side of the square hangs Sir Jacob Epstein's mesmerizing statue of the Madonna and Child, which its agnostic creator declared to be his "passport to Heaven".

The name of Clerkenwell itself recalls the water source where in the Middle Ages underemployed clerics put on Bible story pantomimes on "holydays". At that time the area, "in good air out of the press of the City", was dominated by religious institutions, a nunnery, a house of Carthusian monks and the walled and gated precinct of the Knights of the Hospital of St. John of Jerusalem. The area's rural origins are still implicit in its street names—Turnmill Street, Cowcross Street, Vineyard Walk, Saffron Hill, Pear Tree Court—as is its industrial incarnation in Glasshouse Yard, Brewhouse Yard, Timber Street, Mason's Place and Anchor Yard. By the sixteenth century Clerkenwell had become a residential district for aristocrats, commemorated in streets named for the earls of Albemarle and Aylesbury. The French ambassador depicted in Holbein's majestic double portrait, *The Ambassadors*, lived here, as did Henry VIII's last wife, Katherine Parr. In the seventeenth century the area was home to two theatres, the Red Bull and the Fortune. The former had a reputation as a "blood tub", renowned for its rowdy audiences. The Fortune was demolished by Puritan zealots. A century later, Clerkenwell was a byword for criminality, the last stronghold of bull-baiting and the site of the capital's Pest House but also of its first purpose-built swimming pool and its first specialist eye-hospital. In the nineteenth century the district was crowded with clockmakers, jewellers and printers and was a celebrated centre of radicalism. The Swedish mystic Emanuel Swedenborg died in Clerkenwell. The music hall star Marie Lloyd was born there. Other Clerkenwell residents have included Mr. Pickwick, Aaron Burr, Walter Sickert, Aubrey Beardsley and Lenin.

Essential London?

London may have been the capital of England for a thousand years but it has never been solely, or even particularly English. Technically Trafalgar Square, or rather the southern side, historically known as Charing Cross, is the centre and metaphorically, the heart of London. Here Le Sueur's equestrian statue of Charles I points down Whitehall towards the site of the monarch's death outside the Banqueting House—a Frenchman's tribute to a Scottish king executed outside a building designed by a cockney Welshman and decorated by a Fleming. Forty years later the Banqueting House was used to invite a Dutchman to take over the throne of Britain. Very London.

When preoccupied with some task, my father, in his youth a passionate patron of London's many music-halls, would often accompany his labours with a *sotto voce* version of "Let's all go down the Strand!" which, after the briefest of pauses, was followed by the bathetic punchline "'ave a banana!" "Burlington Bertie", who "rose at 10.30" and "walked up the Strand with his gloves on his hand and walked down again with them off" also figured in the paternal repertoire. A century ago, when those songs were newly written and London, the capital of the world's greatest empire, was also the world's most populous and most extensive city, contemporaries often regarded as its heart not Trafalgar Square, but the Strand which led into it. The Strand was once dominated by aristocratic mansions like the Savoy Palace, Somerset House and Bedford House but only the York Watergate survives as a residue of this era. By the eighteenth century the Strand was renowned for its coffee-houses and its whores, hence the extent to which it figures in James Boswell's *London Journal.* Twining's teashop of 1706 (see p. 98) survives as a respectable reminder of that disreputable period.

The major thoroughfare linking the two nuclei of the metropolis— the financial and commercial City of London and royal and political

Westminster—the Strand was so much "improved" by John Nash and Decimus Burton that Disraeli considered it "the finest street in Europe." One doubts he would think it so today—reduced to a jumble of banks, fast-food outlets, pubs, theatres and discount shops, punctuated by occasional points of retail singularity like the Savoy Tailors' Guild or the stamp-dealers Stanley Gibbons.

Peter Ackroyd's best-selling *London: The Biography* does not rate the Strand as worth even a single entry in its index. But for more than a century the Strand seemed to many to epitomize London itself in its vibrancy and glamour. In *Villette* (1853) Charlotte Bronte's heroine Lucy Snowe is drawn to the Strand as if by some mesmeric power: "I got—I know not how—I got into the heart of city life. I saw and felt London at last. I got into the Strand." Sarah Siddons (1755–1831), the greatest tragedienne of her era, had her lodgings on the Strand and so did Coleridge and George Eliot. The side-streets to the south, leading down to the river, were once home to Samuel Pepys, Benjamin Franklin and Robert Adam. On the Strand itself Ackermann's print-shop, the first retail establishment to be gas-lit, was a favoured rendezvous for literary intellectuals. There was a German restaurant where mid-Victorian "asylum-seekers" met to rant and plot. Later the radio pioneer Guglielmo Marconi had his head office there. Nearby his fellow Italian Charles Forte opened a milk bar which grew into an hotel and catering empire. In its 1890s heyday the Strand had more theatres and music-halls than any other street in London. The Savoy Theatre was the first public building in the capital to be lit by electricity. The Savoy Hotel had Cesar Ritz as its manager and Auguste Escoffier as its chef. Romano's and Simpson's restaurants represented the ultimate in gastronomic chic.

The Strand Magazine was launched by the astute George Newnes in 1891, when the street was at the height of its fame. Produced to unprecedented standards of glossiness and design, it soon attracted a wide readership eager to devour the adventures of Sherlock Holmes or the "gentleman cracksman" Raffles and the short stories of H. G. Wells and P. G. Wodehouse. Newnes' editorial office was actually in Burleigh Street, just *off* the Strand, but he regarded not calling it *The Burleigh Street Magazine* as proof of his marketing instinct, remarking complacently in the celebratory pages of the hundredth issue, "now this celebrated street—perhaps the most widely known of any in the world—is permanently associated with this pioneer magazine." Writing for *The Strand Magazine* in 1907, the Canadian historian Beckles Willson (1869–1942) asserted that for him the Strand was "the face of London. No street seems to me less cosmopolitan, more characteristic." Invoking the memory of the episcopal and aristocratic palaces which once lined it, he conjured up the ghosts of "pageants, cavalcades and processions", quoting John Evelyn's reaction to the triumphant entry of Charles II at his Restoration: "I stood in the Strand and beheld it and blessed God!" Surely, Willson concluded, "it is the homely Strand that so often greets the English home-comer after his exile and the look and the smell and the gentle roar of it brings the lump to this throat."

Past into Future

If the Strand shows how parts of London can lose their accustomed *cachet*, Stratford at the time of writing is set to show how others can acquire—or re-acquire—it. At 12.46 p.m. on Wednesday 6 July 2005 it was announced that London would be invited to host the Olympic Games of 2012. London's bid had emphasized that the designated site, lying along the lower reaches of the River Lea, between Stratford in the east and Bow to the west, was characterized by massive deprivation and decay, a wasteland of scruffy industrial premises, fringed by truncated terraces of Victorian houses and relieved by a few obtrusively new steel and glass structures and the dilapidated monuments of vanished communities—a Victorian church in grimy Gothic, a towering Edwardian elementary school, a derelict dog-track and a cluster of rusting gas-holders. This *terra nulla* was to be reclaimed, revitalized and reinvented. A new station, Stratford International, serving the Channel Tunnel link, will open in 2007. Nearby, a massive new development, Stratford City, will be built, providing 5,000,000 square feet of office space, 5,000 new homes and a shopping precinct which aims to rival Knightsbridge. These initiatives would have happened anyway, regardless of the Olympics.

Part of the process of reinventing the Lower Lea Valley must involve the reclamation of the locality's past. Appearances notwithstanding, this *is* a locale rich in history. The Blackwall Tunnel Approach Road, which defines the western edge of the Olympic site, slices through what were once the gardens of the priory of St. Leonard, immortalized by Chaucer's *Canterbury Tales* in the person of its coquettish prioress, Madame Eglantyne, whose pretentious attempts at speaking French were undone by her cockney accent. Her priory existed in the shadow of the mighty Cistercian abbey of Stratford Langthorne, for four hundred years one of the richest in England, now utterly lost beneath a tangle of railway tracks. The religious turmoil that swept away that great abbey also brought thirteen local Protestants to the stake at Stratford, the largest single mass-execution of Bloody Mary's campaign to re-impose the old faith by force.

In the seventeenth century the lower Lea was still unpolluted enough to be a favourite fishing spot for Izaak Walton, the author of *The Compleat Angler*. On summer evenings Samuel Pepys would bowl out to Bow for a bowl of cherries and cream and a game of bowls. But by then the river's banks had already begun to attract Dutch dyers and they were followed by printers of calico and millers of flour. The transformation to industry had begun. For over a quarter of a century the Bow porcelain factory stood on the Stratford side of Bow Bridge. Cheekily called the New Canton Works, it produced not only blue and white wares in imitation of Chinese imports but also turned out figurines of the famous like the style-setting actor David Garrick. Porcelain production shifted away in the 1770s, but from that decade there still remains the tidemill which has been variously used to manufacture both gin and gunpowder. The gaunt gas-holders to the south of the mill mark where Colonel Congreve's rockets were made for use against Napoleon's cavalry at the Battle of the Nations. Downstream from there once stood the Thames Ironworks which built the Royal Navy's first ironclad, HMS *Warrior* as well as the Dreadnought HMS *Thunderer*. The Thames Ironworks' football team evolved into West Ham United football club. West of the gas-holders, rearing up in isolation, stands Abbey Mills Pumping Station, a miracle of mid-Victorian high-tech. Looking for all the world like a Byzantine cathedral, it was built by Sir Joseph Bazalgette to process the waste collected by the world's first modern sewerage system. To the east at Stratford once stood the engineering workshops which served the railway lines of eastern England. The solid prosperity of the artisans who laboured there gave birth to the London Co-operative Society. A roadside monument perpetuates the memory of the poet Gerard Manley Hopkins, who was born in Stratford. Under Joan Littlewood's inspiration the Theatre Royal gave birth to *The Hostage, Sparrers Can't Sing, A Taste of Honey, Oh, What a Lovely War!* and *Fings Ain't Wot They Used t'Be*. For London "Fings" never are.

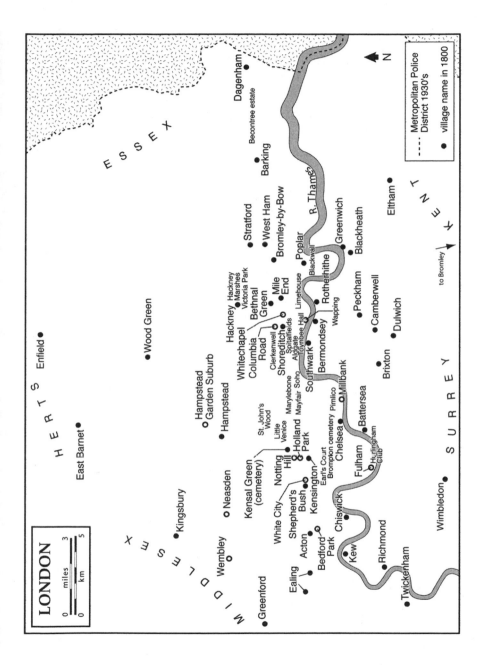

LONDON

miles 0 — 3
km 0 — 5

N

----- Metropolitan Police District 1930's

• village name in 1800

HERTS

ESSEX

MIDDLESEX

SURREY

KENT

R. Thames

Enfield

East Barnet

Wood Green

Kingsbury

Wembley

Neasden

Hampstead Garden Suburb

Hampstead

St. John's Wood

Little Venice

Greenford

Ealing

Acton

Bedford Park

Kew

Richmond

Twickenham

Wimbledon

White City

Shepherd's Bush

Kensington

Earl's Court

Brompton cemetery

Chiswick

Kensal Green (cemetery)

Notting Hill

Holland Park

Fulham

Hurlingham Club

Chelsea

Battersea

Millbank

Pimlico

Mayfair Soho

Marylebone

Clerkenwell

Spitalfields

Aldgate

Toynbee Hall

Southwark

Bermondsey

Wapping

Shoreditch

Columbia Road

Whitechapel

Bethnal Green

Hackney

Hackney Marshes

Victoria Park

Mile End

Limehouse

Blackwall

Poplar

Rotherhithe

Blackwall

Greenwich

Blackheath

Eltham

Peckham

Camberwell

Dulwich

Brixton

to Bromley

Stratford

West Ham

Bromley-by-Bow

Barking

Becontree estate

Dagenham

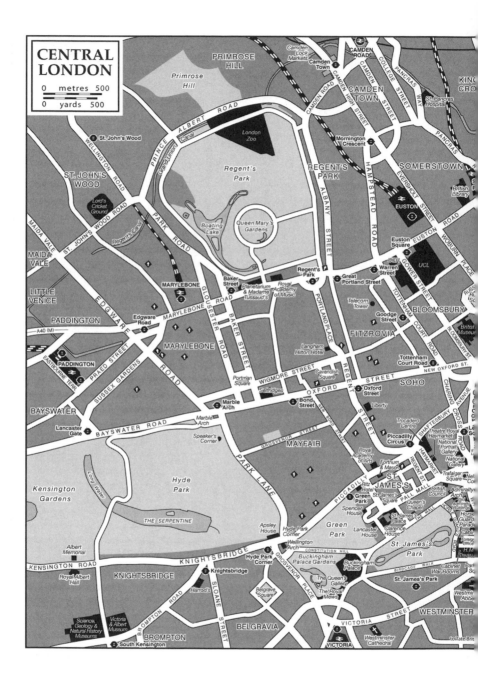

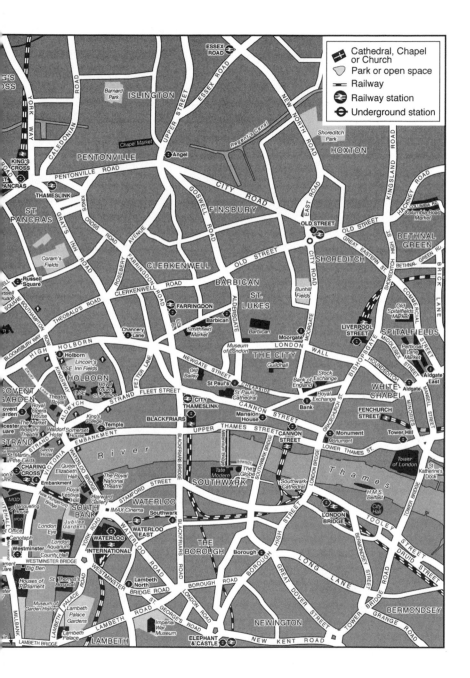

LONDON

Chapter One
SIGHTS AND SITES: ICONIC LONDON

"... when a Londoner says 'Have you seen the Tower of London?' the answer is 'No, and neither have you.'"
Stephen Leacock, *My Discovery of England,* 1922

The Millennium Eye

Londoners are probably the last people to bother themselves with the world-class wonders that litter their city, but they do at least habitually refer to them with unassuming arrogance as "*The* Abbey", "*The* Monument" and "*The* Tower", as though there weren't any others—that count. And they do have something of a point. UNESCO has granted World Heritage Site status to four London locations. One is constituted by what it calls "Westminster Palace" (i.e. the New Palace of Westminster = Houses of Parliament) plus Westminster Abbey and the adjacent church of St. Margaret. The others are the Tower of London, the Royal Botanic Gardens at Kew and "Maritime Greenwich". If roused to the task, Londoners could readily nominate more than a few more; but let us examine UNESCO's endorsements first.

Westminster Abbey

"Holy Moses! Take a look!
Flesh decayed in every nook."
Amanda Ros, *Verses on Visiting Westminster Abbey,* 1933

Dismissed by G. K. Chesterton as a "lumber-room of the larger and less successful statuary of the eighteenth century", the Abbey has been praised by the equally judgmental Ian Nairn as "the unexpected case of an impersonal building with a lot of personality". Despite the dissolution of its monastic community in 1540, Westminster Abbey's royal associations saved its statuary and art treasures from extensive damage during the Reformation. The loss of traditional revenues from pilgrims and chantries encouraged the practice of burying those who could afford to pay for the privilege of lying among kings—hence the ornate clutter of imposing memorials that fill the former chantry chapels.

What is, strictly speaking, "The Collegiate Church of St. Peter at Westminster" is one of a dozen "Royal Peculiars", whose Dean is answerable directly to the sovereign rather than to a bishop. There are only a dozen of these, eight of them in London. Westminster Abbey is both the coronation church of Britain's monarchy and additionally serves as "the parish church of the Commonwealth", organizing ecumenical services to embrace non-Christian faiths as well as the various strands of Christianity. Tradition credits the establishment of a church on this site, then Thorney Island in the marshy delta of the river Tyburn, to Saebehrt, king of Essex, in the early seventh century. St. Dunstan certainly re-established a Benedictine monastery here in the tenth century. Edward the Confessor built a Romanesque abbey church, modelled on that of Jumièges in Normandy. His successor, Harold II Godwineson, initiated the tradition of royal coronation, confirmed on Christmas Day 1066 by his vanquisher, William the Conqueror. Edward's state-of-the-art building was demolished and partly replaced by Henry III, a devotee of the Confessor's cult, between 1245 and 1269. Henry himself helped carry the saint's bones to their present position in the chapel behind the high altar. Around the Confessor's shrine now lies "a royal fellowship of death", of English kings and their foreign consorts. The tomb of Edward I, "Hammer of the Scots", has a sliding lid so that his bones could be exhumed to lead his men once more northwards. The tomb of his beloved consort, Eleanor of Castile, is guarded still by a stupendous medieval iron screen. Her heart was buried at long-vanished Blackfriars monastery. Her memory is enshrined in the elaborate Eleanor Crosses erected to mark the passage of her corpse from Lincolnshire to its last resting-place. The effigy of Edward III, founder of the Order of the Garter, depicts the sunken cheek of a stroke victim. Richard II and Anne of Bohemia once held hands but vandalism has deprived their wooden reincarnations of this intimacy. Henry V, victor of Agincourt, lies beneath and at right angles to his French wife Katherine of Troyes. At the entrance to the chapel stands the sturdy but battered coronation chair in which every monarch has been crowned since Edward II in 1308.

Henry III's abbey, neatly characterized by Pevsner as "the most French of all English Gothic churches", consisted of the present choir, transepts and chapter house, plus parts of the cloisters and one bay of the nave. A spacious "theatre" for coronation rituals was provided at the junction of choir and transepts. The nave was completed in the reign of Richard II under the direction of Henry Yevele, who faithfully followed the aesthetic of his predecessor, Henry de Reyns. Later additions include the stupendous Henry VII chapel and Wren and Hawksmoor's imposing West Towers, blending Gothic form with classical detail to give the building its best-known aspect. An extensive restoration was undertaken by Sir George Gilbert Scott, during which the wall paintings in the Chapter House were re-discovered. The embellishment of the interior continued with the addition of Blore's gilded pseudo-medieval screen, Sir George Gilbert Scott's reredos, much Victorian stained-glass and the striking Waterford crystal chandeliers gifted by the Guinness family to mark the Abbey's 900th anniversary in 1965.

Henry VII's chapel, originally intended to honour the saintly Henry VI, is dominated by the remains of the founder of the Tudor dynasty, lying beneath a fine effigy modelled by Pietro Torrigiano, the man who broke Michelangelo's nose with a single punch. Nearby lie Edward VI, James I and George II, the last monarch to be buried here. To most a boorish martinet, George II had a softer aspect, requesting that the side of his coffin be broken open that his dust might mix with that of his consort, blonde, buxom, wily, sexy, clever Caroline of Anspach. (*Her* monument is Kensington Gardens.) A floor slab marks where Cromwell briefly lay before his corpse was disinterred, decapitated and discarded. Nearby, undisturbed, lie the ashes of air force commanders Trenchard and Dowding beneath the luminous stained-glass memorial windows honouring RAF squadrons of the Battle of Britain. Since 1725 Henry VII's chapel has served as the ceremonial focus of the revived Order of the Bath. Side-chapels contain the remains of Elizabeth I and Mary Tudor, Mary, Queen of Scots, Charles II, William and Mary and Anne.

Themed "cluster burials", of which Poets' Corner is the most celebrated, exemplify the Abbey's role as a showcase of the national heritage. Dryden, Johnson, Sheridan, Browning and Tennyson are all buried here, alongside Dickens, who was denied the spot he had already chosen for himself in Rochester. Memorials honour Shakespeare, the "War Poets", W. H. Auden and others who lie elsewhere, including, belatedly, such nonconformists, unacceptable to previous generations, as William Blake and Oscar Wilde. Nearby, recent memorials honour such modern cultural icons as Noel Coward and Richard Dimbleby, whose masterly single-handed commentary on the Queen's coronation in 1953 was a milestone in broadcasting history.

The north transept is given over to past political giants: Pitt the Elder, Peel, Palmerston, Gladstone and Disraeli. In a nearby aisle, appropriately in the shadow of the organ, are memorials to Abbey organists Orlando Gibbons and Henry Purcell, complemented by later luminaries like Edward Elgar and Benjamin Britten. In the nave is an eternal, international conclave of scientists and medical men: the Englishmen Sir Isaac Newton, Charles Darwin and Joseph Lister, the Scottish physicist William Thomson Kelvin, the German astronomer Sir William Herschel, discoverer of Uranus, New Zealander Ernest Rutherford, pioneer of atomic theory and Australian Howard Walter Florey, perfecter of penicillin. Beyond them lie master clock-maker Thomas Tompion, explorer-missionary David Livingstone, Thomas Cochrane, the model for C. S. Forester's Hornblower, railway pioneer Robert Stephenson and Charles Barry, architect of the Houses of Parliament.

The centre of the nave is dominated by the Tomb of the Unknown Warrior, an anonymous serviceman, buried in English oak under a Belgian marble slab perpetually framed with poppy leaves, the only spot in the Abbey where no one ever treads. Nearby are memorials to

Churchill, the American financier-philanthropist George Peabody and
Robert Baden-Powell, founder of the Boy Scout movement, Lord Louis
Mountbatten and Franklin D. Roosevelt. Above the great west doorway
the younger Pitt ostentatiously gestures the onlooker's gaze away from
"Radicals' Corner" where Fox, Lloyd George and Attlee are honoured.
Outside in the cloisters lie Restoration dramatist and spy Aphra Behn
and Museo Clementi, "father of the piano". Other memorials honour
Edmund Halley of comet fame and the circumnavigators Drake, Cook
and Chichester. The cloisters also give access to the luminescent
Chapter House with its remarkably preserved medieval tile floor and to
the museum housing wax effigies used in royal funerals. Beyond,
through a magical courtyard centred on a murmuring fountain, lies
London's oldest garden, cultivated for perhaps a thousand years and still
enclosed by a wall dating from Chaucer's day.

The Houses of Parliament
  *"Like the Gothic Revival itself... a vast hallucination, set down in
  Westminster to bewitch and enchant..."*
                                                          Ian Nairn

What is more properly called "The New Palace of Westminster"
occupies the site of the medieval palace begun by Edward the Confessor
and extended by his successors. Of that only Westminster Hall remains.
Only! Built by William Rufus, it has accommodated coronation
banquets, housed the Law Courts and witnessed the trial of Charles I
and the lying-in-state of Winston Churchill. Its stupendous fourteenth-
century hammerbeam roof means that it is also, according to the Royal
Commission on Historical Monuments (a body not prone to
hyperbole), "probably the finest timber-framed building in Europe".
Almost all of the rest of the old palace, with the exception of the Jewel
Tower, now an isolated residuum on the far side of College Green, went
up in flames in 1834. The competition to design a replacement
building, specified to be in the Gothic or "Elizabethan" style, attracted
almost a hundred entries. (Some prize flops are on display in the Jewel
Tower.) The job went to Charles Barry, architect of the Reform Club
and Trafalgar Square. The decorative aspects were delegated to the
workaholic Augustus Pugin. The project went wildly over budget, took
three times as long as originally envisaged, and killed both men. But it

was a triumph, since praised unreservedly by Pevsner as "the most imaginatively planned and the most excellently executed major secular building of the Gothic Revival anywhere in the world."

St. Margaret's, Westminster, now in its fourth incarnation, dating from 1482-1523, has been "the parish church of the House of Commons" since 1614. Churchill led his fellow Members here to give thanks for victory in 1945. It was also where he had himself been married. Dominated by an east window featuring Henry VIII and a west window featuring Raleigh, who was buried here, as was Caxton, the church also has another showing the blind Milton dictating *Paradise Lost* to his daughter. (He lived nearby on Tothill Street.) A wall plaque acknowledges the generosity of Francis Albert (Frank) Sinatra and others in supporting the post-war restoration of the church.

Tower of London
Even without its wealth of historical associations the Tower of London might well have qualified for World Heritage status simply by being— as Pevsner reminds us at the risk of stating an obvious, though often overlooked, truth—"the most important work of military architecture in England". The Tower (actually towers, there are twenty of them) is perhaps less famed for its architecture than as a place of imprisonment, torture and execution. Involuntary residents have included Sir Thomas More, Elizabeth I, Sir Walter Raleigh, Samuel Pepys, Rudolf Hess and the Kray brothers. Edward V and Henry VI were both murdered here. The death-roll is as distinguished as it is lengthy, though execution within the Tower, rather than up on Tower Hill, was the exception rather than the rule. The last execution—of a German spy, shot in a rifle range then located in the moat—took place as recently as 1941. Trainee guides use the mnemonic MOZART to remind themselves that Her Majesty's Palace and Fortress the Tower of London has performed many other functions in its nine hundred-year history: Mint, Observatory, Zoo, Armoury, Royal Residence and Treasury, not to mention National Archive and Tourist Attraction. Yeoman Warders (a.k.a. "Beefeaters") have been taking tips and teasing tourists with tall tales since at least the sixteenth century. Nathaniel Hawthorne in 1855 thought they "looked very much like the kings on a pack of cards, or regular trumps," but, despite his amusement, observed that to foreigners the Tower had the magic of "a haunted castle in dream-land".

He had brought his family to see the Crown Jewels, which are even more fabulous now than they were then. The three-thousand carat Cullinan diamond, discovered in South Africa in 1907, yielded no fewer than ninety-six stones, including the First Star of Africa adorning the royal sceptre, which, at 531 carats is the largest cut diamond in the world. The crown made in 1911 for George V to wear at the Delhi Durbar (and never worn since) consists almost entirely of diamonds. The fabled Koh-i-Noor ("Mountain of Light") diamond, which has allegedly brought death to every male who ever owned it, has been neutralized by setting it in the crown made for the late Queen Mother to wear at the coronation of George VI in 1937. Were it not for the dazzling presence of the royal regalia, the superbly crafted armours housed in the White Tower might be better appreciated as treasures in their own right. Were it not for the fact that there is so much else to see more visitors might discover the museum which presents the history of London's own regiment, the Royal Fusiliers.

Given UNESCO's linkage between Westminster Abbey and the Houses of Parliament, it seems legitimate to associate Tower Bridge with the Tower. Although it only dates from 1894 Tower Bridge has been chosen as *the* London icon to adorn the Blue Badge worn by guides who have passed the rigorous examinations required to attain official registration with the London Tourist Board.

The Royal Botanic Gardens at Kew

"So sits enthroned in vegetable pride
Imperial Kew by Thames's glittering side..."
Thomas Chatterton, *Kew Gardens*, 1770

Imperial indeed. When I was an undergraduate it was explained to me that the entire British empire was the product of an immense botanical conspiracy by means of which our green-fingered forefathers had taken plants from one place on the planet to exploit them *in extenso* at another, thereby creating the rubber industry of Malaya, the tea industry of Assam, the coffee industries of Kenya and Jamaica, etc. And all this revolved around Kew where the theory and practice of botany achieved what Marxists were wont to call a *praxis* which proved, if the pun be allowed, uniquely fruitful. We owe the gardens to Augusta, Dowager Princess of Wales, relict of the unlamented Fred, whose few worldly distinctions included dying as a result of a cricketing mishap. Encouraged by her son's Scottish tutor, Lord Bute, from 1759 onwards Augusta began to build on the previous (literal) groundwork of Caroline of Anspach. Lancelot "Capability" Brown contributed his customary "improvements" ca. 1770 and under the unofficial directorship of the tyrannical President of the Royal Society, Sir Joseph Banks, the gardens developed a strongly scientific sense of mission to undertake pioneering work in the collection, classification and conservation of plant species world-wide. The royal family's pet architect, Sir William Chambers, meanwhile littered the grounds with pseudo-classical confections in the shape of temples, bridges, alcoves and purpose-built ruins, much to the scorn of local resident, Horace Walpole (see p.46). Of Chambers' surviving creations the most impressive are the Orangery and a ten-storey Chinese pagoda. Other features of Kew include the *cottage ornée* used by Queen Charlotte for summer tea-parties, the immense glasshouses engineered by Decimus Burton, a flagstaff 225 feet high, made from a single trunk of Douglas Fir, a Japanese gateway from the White City exhibition of 1910 and the astonishing 848 botanical paintings donated by their creator, Marianne North.

Maritime Greenwich
Daniel Defoe rhapsodized that Greenwich was "the most delightful spot of ground in Great Britain; pleasant by situation, those pleasures encreas'd by art, and all made completely agreeable by the accident of fine buildings, the continual passing of fleets of ships up and down the most beautiful river in Europe; the best air, the best prospect and the best conversation in England." Much that Defoe would have known remains. The Queen's House, the first neoclassical building in England, designed by Inigo Jones for Anne of Denmark, has been delicately restored to reflect its condition in 1662 when it was occupied by Charles I's widow, the Queen Dowager, Henriette Marie. Consisting of symmetrical suites of apartments and originally built to span the main road, it features a hallway with the dimensions of a perfect cube, a *trompe l'oeil* geometrical staircase with no apparent means of support and an elegant loggia from which the ladies of the court could watch the gentlemen disport themselves in the enclosed hunting park to the rear. The descendants of their quarry, a small herd of deer, still shelter shyly in a discreetly hedged "Wilderness".

The handsome parish church of St. Alfege, designed by Wren's lieutenant, Nicholas Hawksmoor, was newly rebuilt in Defoe's day. Dedicated to an Archbishop of Canterbury who refused to be ransomed from the Vikings and was martyred here in 1012, the previous church had witnessed the baptism of Henry VIII and the burial of Thomas Tallis, the "father of English church music". General Wolfe, whose conquest of Quebec assured Canada for Britain but cost him his life in the hour of victory, was brought to St. Alfege's for burial. General Gordon "of Khartoum", whose portrait adorned the wall of Sherlock Holmes' study, was baptized here. A time-travelling Defoe would also recognize Wren's Royal Observatory—"Time's Headquarters"—and the intended Stuart palace which became a retirement home for naval veterans. The dining hall for which Hogarth's father-in-law Sir James Thornhill supplied a stupendous painted ceiling in honour of George I, is open to visitors, as is the wonderfully light chapel with its delicately coffered ceiling, rebuilt by James "Athenian" Stuart.

History has erased other landmarks. The Observatory occupies the site of the watch tower of the riverside royal residence built (1432-7) by Duke Humphrey, Henry V's learned, lascivious brother; his famed collection of books went to Oxford to become the nucleus of the Bodleian Library. The German armourers brought in by Henry VIII are long gone; but their work finds a resonant echo in the museum of artillery, "Firepower", at Woolwich nearby.

Wind-blown Blackheath, abutting Greenwich Park, is now beloved of London children for kite-flying and donkey-rides but it has had its darker side. This was where Kentish rebels massed during the Peasants' Revolt of 1381. In 1450 part of the quartered corpse of rebel leader Jack Cade was displayed here after his rag-tag contingents lost the Londoners' support by threatening to loot their homes. A generation later Henry VII bloodily crushed a host of discontented Cornishmen at Blackheath. A century after that James VI of Scotland, on becoming James I of England, is supposed to have introduced his new subjects to a new pastime—golf. Blackheath does, indeed, lay claim to England's oldest golf club, as well as its oldest clubs for athletics, rugby and hockey, too.

If Greenwich is no longer the most favoured royal residence, as it was under the Tudors, it has continued to bear witness to history. Dramatist and self-taught architect Sir John Vanbrugh built himself a pioneering neo-Gothic residence, modelled on the Bastille, in which he had been imprisoned as a spy. Nelson's body lay in state at Greenwich before being borne upriver for burial in St. Paul's. Slovenly, scandalous Princess Caroline of Brunswick found a semi-rural retreat hereabouts prior to attempting her claim on the royal throne. In Dickens' day Greenwich Fair became notorious as a rollicking excursion for cockneys, what he called "a sort of spring rash". In sinister contrast, Joseph Conrad chose the Observatory as the setting for the bloody climax to his dark novella *The Secret Agent*, after a real, live anarchist had blown off his own arm there when the detonator of the bomb he was carrying malfunctioned. A statue of General Wolfe, the gift of Canada, now gazes at Canada Tower, Britain's tallest building, which towers over Canary Wharf on the Isle of Dogs. The China tea-clipper *Cutty Sark*, launched at Dumbarton in 1869, has found a final berth by the foot-tunnel which has run under the river since 1904. Downriver a little, gleams the mighty Millennium Dome and the tidal barrier at Woolwich, rearing up from the river-bed like so many Spanish helmets of shining steel.

Places to Ponder

Where else might merit the UNESCO accolade? In terms of an assemblage of architecture, none of it perhaps individually outstanding, but collectively quite as meaningful as any of the above, Trafalgar Square takes some beating. It is, after all, the centre of London; and that is official. And I would guess that to many Londoners it *feels* like it—unlike Piccadilly Circus, which many tourists mistakenly take to be London's hub. Nelson's Column, Le Sueur's equestrian statue of Charles I, the National Gallery, South Africa House and Canada House, Gibbs' soaring church of St. Martin-in-the-Fields, the Admiralty Arch with its glimpse of the Mall and Buckingham Palace beyond add up to a panorama of British and Imperial history. Since the north side has been re-pedestrianized the Square has even begun to resume the attributes of a public space rather than a traffic roundabout. Perhaps, however, there are too many whiskered generals and jaunty admirals—altogether too nationalist to be international? Ditto Whitehall, the epicentre of the British state—sequestered Downing Street, Lutyens' austere Cenotaph, Inigo Jones' majestic Banqueting House, Horse Guards with its plumed and cuirassed guardians, more generals...

If "Maritime Greenwich" can qualify, what about the Thames itself? Recent tourist promotion has lauded the attractions on either side of the river as a "string of pearls". From Boadicea's chariot at Westminster Bridge a procession of statues and monuments unfolds to the east, commemorating the pilots of the Battle of Britain and their commanders, half-forgotten heroes of empire like General Gordon, makers of national culture like William Tyndale, translator of the Bible, Robert Burns and Gilbert and Sullivan, Sir Joseph Bazalgette, who masterminded the building of London's sewers, Robert Raikes (the man who invented Sunday Schools), Michael Faraday, Isambard Kingdom Brunel, John Stuart Mill... Even the Cinderella South Bank has smartened itself up since the real-life business of landing cargo has moved downstream. The London Eye Millennium Wheel has swiftly established itself as a skyline fixture to match Big Ben and has been granted the ultimate touristic accolade of fridge-magnet status. Downstream are the tautly elegant Millennium Bridge and the towering brick bulk of Tate Modern, Sam Wanamaker's monument, the reconstructed Globe Theatre, the view from the Oxo Tower, the smells of the Borough farmers' market on a Friday, HMS *Belfast*, Humpty Dumpty City Hall and the surreal, cobbled wharfside passageway that is Shad Thames, all leading down to the glitter and glitz of renascent Docklands.

If Westminster Abbey can qualify, why not St. Paul's? Supreme symbol of London's wartime endurance, it also serves as Britain's Pantheon, the last resting-place of Wellington and Nelson, Wren and Reynolds, Turner and Fleming, Donne and Van Dyck, John of Gaunt and Ethelred the Unready. A chapel of restrained extravagance honours that moustachioed titan of the recruiting-poster, Lord Kitchener, who lies beneath the waves of the North Sea. A life-size bronze effigy stands in for General Gordon, chopped to pieces in the Sudan. Behind the High Altar, dedicated to the war dead of the Commonwealth, the American Memorial Chapel symbolizes in stained-glass, carved limewood, wrought iron and polished marble a shared heritage of sacrifice.

Here Dr. Martin Luther King preached, Churchill was mourned and the victims of terrorism in New York and London remembered. If Westminster Abbey is "the parish church of the Commonwealth", St. Paul's stands at London's spiritual heart.

Top Twelve

As UNESCO is unlikely to be much moved by my arguments or
opinions, I may as well close with a purely personal selection of London
must-sees. Not World Heritage, perhaps, but Worthwhile. In no
particular order:

1. The Great Court and Reading Room of the British Museum—
   memorable enclosed spaces to lift the spirit on even the dullest
   day. Where else can you have a coffee beneath a stele of an
   Assyrian king plus "eye-opener" tours of specific rooms with
   volunteer guides, extended evening opening hours and, upstairs at
   the front where visitors, sated on the traditional museum
   "highlights"(Parthenon marbles, mummies, Portland Vase,
   Rosetta Stone etc.) rarely penetrate, dazzling collections of clocks,
   medieval artwork, Huguenot silverware, Bow and Chelsea
   porcelain, Napoleonic memorabilia, an entire gallery devoted to
   the history of money—all free?

2. The British Galleries of the Victoria and Albert Museum, a plethora
   of pleasures laid out as a corridor through time: Hilliard
   miniatures, the Drake Jewel, the golden Music Room from Norfolk
   House, a fantastical Chinoiserie bed, the finest craftsmanship in the
   creations of Adam and Chippendale and Wedgwood, the ideals of
   craftsmanship in the designs of Pugin and Dresser, Morris and
   Mackintosh—free again. At the top of Exhibition Road stands the
   Albert Memorial, a super-sized Victorian reliquary to honour the
   man whose vision the Museum exemplifies.

3. The Cabinet War Rooms and Churchill Museum, where the world
   was saved and the life of the man who did it is remembered
   through seventy displays, one hundred and fifty original artefacts,
   two hundred facsimile documents, a thousand photographs.

4. Guildhall, the second greatest Gothic space in London, focal point
   of the government of the Square Mile; flanking it on one side is
   the City's own art gallery, which many have yet to discover, and on
   the other the best library for London history, with open access
   shelves and a vast online database (COLLAGE) of paintings,
   prints and drawings of London topography.

5. The Gherkin. Designed by Norman Foster as a headquarters for
   the Swiss Reinsurance Company, this instant icon of the London
   skyline was awarded the Royal Institute of British Architect's

prestigious Stirling Award when it was completed in 2004; with its novel system of natural ventilation this ecologically advanced structure is not only spectacular but very, very clever. Located at 30 St. Mary Axe, it can be viewed to advantage from Bishopsgate, looming over the tiny medieval church of St. Ethelburga.

6. The Foundling Hospital—established in then rural Bloomsbury in 1739 as London's first orphanage, the surviving remnant now houses state-of-the-art displays recalling the support of such benefactors as Handel, Hogarth, Reynolds and Dickens.

7. Little Venice—an unsuspected *quartier* of boulevards, trees and canals lined with flower-bedecked narrow-boats, hidden away beyond the thunderous traffic of Westway; ideal for a summer evening stroll and only a few minutes' walk from Warwick Avenue on the Bakerloo line.

8. Columbia Road market: an East Ender's delight, this literally colourful flower market is a Sunday morning treat which has attracted a coterie of cafés, designer and deli shops.

9. Spencer House, St. James'—built (1756-66) by a direct ancestor of the late Diana, Princess of Wales, this was the most ambitious central London palazzo of its period and the only on to survive intact and remain open to the public. Contemporary Arthur Young thought it "in richness, elegance and taste superior to any house I have seen." Its fantastical Palm Room is arguably the finest interior ever created by James "Athenian" Stuart. After a chequered history it has been skilfully restored. President Putin of Russia hired it to entertain the Queen. Very, very grand.

10. St. Etheldreda's, Ely Place: restored to Catholic worship, this last surviving remnant of a medieval episcopal palace dates from ca. 1270 and features statues and striking stained-glass memorializing English martyrs as well as an atmospheric crypt. St. Andrew's, Holborn, two minutes away provides a powerful contrast.

11. Shri Swaminarayan Mandir. Most Londoners would need convincing that there is anything worth seeing in Neasden but this, the largest Hindu temple outside India, is simply spectacular in both style and scale. Completed in 1995, the complex incorporates some five thousand tons of Bulgarian limestone and Italian marble and represents the labours of over fifteen hundred Indian craftsmen. Visitors are welcome.

12. The Museum of London: the largest museum in the world devoted to the history of a single city. If you're serious about knowing your London this has to be on your list.

I do have other favourite places: St. Katharine's Dock just beyond the Tower, The Italian Garden in Kensington Gardens, St. John's Gateway in Clerkenwell, Eel Pie Island at Twickenham, the House of St. Barnabas in Soho, the Percival David Foundation of Chinese Art in Bloomsbury—but I would put these in Dr. Johnson's apt category of worth seeing but not necessarily worth going to see.

No Buckingham Palace? Not really. Access is, of course, restricted to the summer, when the Queen is elsewhere. There are many excellent paintings but for historical interest it cannot really hold a candle to Windsor Castle or even Hampton Court. As for the decor, reminiscent of a grand Edwardian hotel, it is hard to improve on the memorable verdict of a photographer from the *Sun* newspaper: "They call it the Red Room or the White Room—but they're all bleedin' gold."

OF BARDS AND BUSINESS
A Poetic Interlude

Robert Herrick

"...poetry which is in Oxford made An art, in London only is a trade."

John Dryden, 1673

The great attraction of London to a novelist like Henry James was its endless stimulus to the writer's imagination. The same need not apply to poetry. Nature and landscape have played such a large part in shaping the English poetic imagination that London has had some competition to look to. Many of the greatest English poets are associated with particular regions or counties, like Tennyson with Lincolnshire and Hardy with Dorset respectively. Swinburne, born a Londoner, preferred to live in the "crowning county", Northumberland. A. E. Housman taught classics at University College, London but wrote of Shropshire.

Robert Herrick is an example of the contrary tendency. Born on Cheapside, as a young man he adored just being in the same city as roistering Ben Jonson. But the necessity of earning a living obliged him to take the cloth and to accept the living of Dean Prior in distant Devonshire. When relieved of his benefice as a Royalist, Herrick was positively overjoyed to return to London:

> *O Place! O People! Manners! Fram'd to please*
> *All Nations, Customs, Kindreds, Languages!*
> *I am a free-born Roman; suffer then,*
> *That I amongst you live a Citizen.*
> *London my home is; though by hard fate sent*
> *Into a long and irksome banishment;*
> *Yet since call'd back; henceforward let me be,*
> *O native country, repossest by thee!*

It did not last. If the Restoration delighted Herrick the Royalist, it doomed Herrick the Londoner. Reinstated in his living, it was back to "the dull confines of the drooping West".

Moving in the opposite direction, from provincial Lichfield to the capital, a youthful Samuel Johnson experienced a distasteful disorientation from the hazards of his new home:

> *Here Malice, Rapine, Accident, conspire*
> *And now a Rabble rages, now a Fire.*
> *Their Ambush here relentless Ruffians lay,*
> *And here the fell Attorney prowls for Prey.*
> *Here falling Houses thunder on your Head,*
> *And here a female Atheist talks you dead.*

Johnson endured twenty years of hand-to-mouth hack drudgery for

"Grub Street" before his *Dictionary* brought him celebrity and the cushion of a Civil List pension.

Rare the poet who could make a living from poetry alone. The glitterati of the Elizabethan Court lived off royal favour. Byron and Shelley were both from wealthy, aristocratic backgrounds and could be careless of cash until their own extravagance and negligence pulled them up from time to time. One reason why they and Robert Browning left London to live in Italy was that it was so cheap. Dylan Thomas quit his native Wales ("land of my fathers—my fathers can have it") to base his economic survival largely on sponging off others in the pubs of Fitzrovia. Like many other poets, Dylan Thomas got the occasional fee from nearby Broadcasting House, the twentieth-century equivalent of the royal Court as a source of patronage. Louis MacNeice worked as a BBC producer. A wartime photograph of George Orwell, in his then capacity as a producer of "Talks", shows him flanked by T. S. Eliot and the Sri Lankan poet J. M. Tambimuttu, editor of the influential magazine *Poetry London* and another Soho pub-dweller.

The working poet, then, has a long London tradition behind him. Chaucer had a multiplicity of employments. One was supervising the repair of the highways in Kent, which meant that he knew in very great detail the route over which his Canterbury pilgrims would travel. His burial in Westminster Abbey predated the establishment of Poets' Corner by a century and a half and was justified on the grounds that he had supervised building work on the Abbey and had retired to and died in a cottage in its grounds. John Milton worked as a political secretary for the Cromwellian regime. Andrew Marvell worked as Milton's assistant. John Dryden subsidized his poetry by means of his plays until his talents for flattery and invective brought him the posts of Poet Laureate, Historiographer Royal and a sinecure in the Customs service. A change of monarch, however, drove him back to living by his pen. Alexander Pope was disbarred from public office because he was a Catholic but did well enough out of his translation of the *Iliad* to set up in some style at Twickenham.

The necessity of making a living created a unique fusion of the verbal and the visual in the illustrated poetry books self-published by William Blake. Few Londoners have inhabited the city more imaginatively than Blake; seeing angels in an oak tree on Peckham Rye takes some beating. Blake's conviction of the immanence of the spiritual in the everyday was strengthened in adult life by his early adherence to the teachings of the Swedish mystic Emanuel Swedenborg. Born in Soho, the son of a prosperous hosier who could indulge his son's precocious talent for art, Blake was at ten "put to Mr. Pars' drawing-school in the Strand." Apprenticed to James Basire, engraver to the Society of Antiquaries, he was set to drawing the monuments of Westminster Abbey, where Epstein's arresting bust of Blake himself can now be seen. In 1778 Blake became a student at the recently-established Royal Academy Schools but soon dropped out. In 1782 he married Catherine Boucher, daughter of a market-gardener, who signed the register with an X but was, despite her illiteracy, to prove an ideal wife to the wayward genius. By 1785 they were living at 28 Poland Street in Soho, where Blake composed, engraved and printed his *Songs of Innocence*. A decade later the Blakes were living in "a pretty, clean house" in what is now Hercules Road, Lambeth, where a visitor came upon them sitting naked in the summer house, reciting passages from *Paradise Lost*. In 1803 Blake and his wife moved into second-floor rooms at 17 South Molton Street, Mayfair, "still poor and dirtier than ever" but rich in the regard of fellow-artists and disciples like Flaxman, Fuseli, Linnell and Samuel Palmer.

William Morris, for much of his life better known as a poet than as an artist-designer, inherited a private income and by the time his dividends dried up had established a successful artwork business, supplying stained-glass windows for the mid-Victorian church-building boom. Morris could afford to indulge a passion for medieval manuscripts and missals and to spend thousands of pounds painstakingly experimenting with papers, inks and type-faces to revive the art of fine printing—and still to die the equivalent of a modern millionaire. Besides which, Morris, who turned down both the Laureateship and the Professorship of Poetry at Oxford, thought that anyone who could not compose verse while weaving a wall-hanging at the same time was not worth much; Morris had himself once composed seven hundred lines in a single night while doing so.

Rudyard Kipling could live well from his journalism and found fame with rollicking rhymes that proved popular with the sort of people who did not think they liked poetry. Thanks to Kipling's youthful success in India, he had come to London with no shortage of self-confidence, taking rooms in Villiers Street and putting a notice on the door "Masterpieces written to Order". In 1895 Kipling, still only thirty, refused the Laureateship which had been vacant since the death of Tennyson. He would later be offered, and refuse, the Order of Merit three times. In 1907 he became the first English-language writer to be awarded the Nobel Prize for Literature. Kipling's writings proved not only popular but in one unforeseen respect unexpectedly influential. The strenuous morality of *The Jungle Book* was adapted by Boer War hero Robert Baden-Powell to serve as the ideological underpinning of his newly-established Boy Scout movement. Kipling's reputation nose-dived in the closing decade of his life, when he was denounced as a jingo and an imperialist. Ironically, his sheer craftsmanship would later be praised by writers who considered his politics irrelevant to his achievement, most notably T. S. Eliot and George Orwell.

Like Kipling, Sir John Betjeman, Laureate of the Suburbs, found many admirers among readers normally indifferent to poetry. A Londoner by birth and briefly taught by T. S. Eliot as a child, Betjeman later versified with topographic precision his Highgate childhood. It was as a writer on architecture, however, that he first came to public attention. Escaping (like Eliot) from schoolmastering, he became assistant editor of the *Architectural Review* and in 1933 published *Ghastly Good Taste*, subtitled "a depressing story of the rise and fall of English architecture". Film critic for the *Evening Standard*, publicist for the Shell oil company, war-time censor in the Ministry of Information, broadcaster for the BBC, Betjeman became a national figure in a way that no poet since Kipling had. In later life he was able to use his personal popularity to campaign to save buildings as diverse as St. Pancras Station and Sweeting's fish restaurant in the City. Betjeman long retained a *pied-à-terre* in the heart of Smithfield, overlooking the churchyard of medieval St. Bartholomew-the-Great. In the long run he will be remembered as the bard of rural Middlesex as it was transformed into "Metro-land", a designation now indelibly associated with his name.

CHELSEA

Royal Hospital, Chelsea—home for army veterans, founded by Charles II in 1682, housed in a Wren masterpiece and still in the same business. Chelsea buns—a sugar-drenched eighteenth-century treat. Chelsea

Peter Jones department store

porcelain—produced 1743-85 and good enough to be extensively faked. Chelsea boots—1960s elastic-sided men's footwear. "Chelsea Tractor"—an immaculate, oversized cross-country vehicle for the private school run. Chelsea FC—Premiership team of foreign footballers. Chelsea Flower Show—top national plant-fest, held in May. Chelsea—probably London's largest concentration of rich residents, where pastel-painted artisan cottages sell for seven figure sums.

Chelsea is usually approached from Sloane Square station at its eastern edge. Named for Sir Hans Sloane (see p.157), once Lord of the Manor and now buried in historic Chelsea Old Church, Sloane Square is overlooked by the Royal Court Theatre, traditional home of challenging drama (Shaw, *Look Back in Anger*, English Stage Company), and by Peter Jones department store, a 1936 modernist icon. To the north is J. D. Sedding's Holy Trinity, seemingly twice as wide inside as outside, an unrestrained celebration of Arts and Crafts virtuosity. Leading south-west, the King's Road, built as Charles II's private weekend getaway route, is lined with fashion, food and antique shops. In contrast, the National Army Museum records a sterner side of life. Especially strong on the Napoleonic period and colonial warfare, its programme of special activities reminds us that, as well as fighting, soldiers also travelled, wrote, sang, sketched and cooked.

Sir Thomas More had his riverside retreat at Chelsea. The Moravians, persecuted Protestants from Germany, also found refuge here, as their cemetery testifies. Thanks to Sloane, Chelsea's Physick Garden was secured for the Society of Apothecaries. Here grew England's first cedar and from here the first cotton seeds were taken to Georgia. At Ranelagh, beside the Royal Hospital, flourished the most brilliant of Georgian pleasure-grounds. Dickens was married at St. Luke's, one of London's earliest Gothic Revival churches. In old age Turner hid away in a riverside cottage to paint nudes while passing himself off as a sea-captain. A few minutes' walk away lived a real one, "Scott of the Antarctic". At Lindsey House the Brunels designed their engineering wonders and Whistler created his famous profile portrait of his mother. John Singer Sargent had his studio in Tite Street, with Oscar Wilde for a neighbour. Philip Webb, Walter Greaves, Wilson Steer, Frank Brangwyn, C. R. Ashbee and Charles Rennie Mackintosh all worked in Chelsea. With Carlyle (see p.222) as its presiding literary *genius loci*, the area subsequently attracted Swinburne and Rossetti, who kept wombats as pets, and William de Morgan, who in his sixties switched successfully from making tiles to telling tales. Henry James and T. S. Eliot both lived in Carlyle Mansions. Ian Fleming imagined James Bond as living on Royal Avenue, where film director Joseph Losey actually did. Bram Stoker wrote *Dracula* just round the corner. Carol Reed, director of *The Third Man*, lived next to the former home of Ellen Terry. Ralph Vaughan Williams, Sir Alexander Fleming, Joyce Grenfell... Chelsea has had plenty of talent among the smart.

Chapter Two
LONDON DESCRIBED

"... how different a place London is to different people... A politician thinks of it merely as the seat of government... a grazier, as a vast market for cattle; a mercantile man as a place where a prodigious deal of business is done... a dramatick enthusiast as the grand scene of theatrical entertainment; a man of pleasure, as an assemblage of taverns and the great emporium of ladies of easy virtue."

James Boswell, 1763

Anthony Trollope

The Chroniclers

The first Londoner to write about London was William FitzStephen, former chaplain to, and self-appointed biographer of, Thomas à Becket. Becket, son of Gilbert Becket, a wealthy London mercer, was born in his father's house at the corner of Ironmonger Lane and Cheapside. This location is now occupied by a shoe-shop bearing a giant reproduction of the sort of cheap lead badge, depicting the martyr in a mitre, which would have been bought as a souvenir by visitors who, like Chaucer's pilgrims, had made the trek to Becket's shrine at Canterbury. Just behind the shoe-shop, appropriately enough, is the livery hall of the Mercers' Company. Becket, who actually styled himself Thomas of London, was adopted by Londoners as a second patron saint, alongside St. Paul. His image appeared on official seals and a chapel dedicated to his memory was erected in the middle of London Bridge. FitzStephen's biography of Becket is prefaced by an enthusiastic description of the saint's native city. Considering the author was a cleric, the emphasis is remarkably secular, dwelling on the delights available in the wealthy, bustling city. Down by the river were 24-hour cook-shops where spitted sparrows could be bought for ten a penny. Outside the walls to the north was the marshy expanse of Moorfields where the city's youth would wrestle in summer and skate in winter. Londoners themselves, according to FitzStephen, "are universally held up for admiration for the elegance of their manners and dress. Other cities have citizens, London's are called barons." The only drawbacks to the city that FitzStephen would concede were the frequency of fires and "the immoderate drinking of fools".

A contrasting view from the provinces was offered by FitzStephen's contemporary, Richard of Devizes, a monk of Winchester:

> *All sorts of men crowd together there from every country under the heavens. Each race brings its own vices... No one lives in it without falling into some sort of crimes. Every quarter of it abounds in grave obscenities... You will meet with more braggarts there than in all France.*

According to the censorious cleric, London's typical inhabitants consisted of "actors, jesters, smooth-skinned lads, Moors, flatterers, pretty boys, effeminates, pederasts, singing and dancing girls, quacks, belly-dancers, sorceresses, extortioners, night-wanderers, magicians, mimes, beggars, buffoons; all this tribe fill all the houses."

FitzStephen's account, although vivid and informative, was essentially a snap-shot of the city's main features rather than even a bare sketch of its history. The next attempt to chronicle London as a whole would not occur for another four centuries. Aldgate tailor John Stow was partly motivated by his own personal experience of the tremendous changes that had transformed London in his own lifetime. Old enough to remember the devastations unleashed by the dissolution of the monastic houses, Stow was also aware of the sprawling expansion of the city outside the walls as its population quadrupled to 200,000. Remembering what is now Petticoat Lane as a rural pathway lined with hedges and elms where one could pick wild berries and buy milk warm from the cow, he deplored the squalid tenements proliferating over reclaimed marshland at Wapping and encroaching on Mile End Waste. Stow therefore "attempted the discovery of London, my native soil and country."

Stow's odyssey was intellectual as well as topographical. The pioneering *Survey of London* (1598) he composed is a true work of historical scholarship, based on careful scrutiny of original documents held in parish churches or by livery companies, and supplemented by painstaking perambulations of the entire city, ward by ward; in Stow's own words his erudition "hath cost me many a weary mile's travel... and many a cold winter night's study." And, he might have added, his personal prosperity as well. William FitzStephen's "Description" was printed by Stow as an appendix to the *Survey*, thus making it known to a general readership for the first time. Stow also rescued many manuscripts that would almost certainly have been lost by decay or destruction in the aftermath of the dissolution of religious houses and so deserves to be recognized twice-over, as the father of London historiography and as a pioneer of manuscript conservation. Because many of these items by definition dated from the days of Catholic orthodoxy Stow was periodically arraigned by the authorities for possessing "foolish fabulous books of old print". He spent up to two hundred pounds a year on books and manuscripts and virtually abandoned his trade as a tailor, his sole reward in old age being a license to beg alms. Posterity belatedly acknowledged his merits with an annual ceremony in which the Lord Mayor of the day equipped Stow's effigy in St. Andrew Undershaft with a new quill pen.

Stow's *Survey* was updated most extensively in 1720 by the Reverend John Strype of Leyton, who added in new material based on his own consultation of parish materials, records in the Tower and the library of Robert Cotton, shortly to become one of the core manuscript collections of the British Museum. Strype also added a detailed account of changes in the physical fabric of London since Stow's death, doubtless made aware of their scale by the post-Fire reconstruction of the capital, as Stow had been by the destruction that accompanied the dissolution. Strype not only illustrated his revision of Stow with detailed ward maps but also with engraved plates of churches, hospitals and other public buildings and the only known drawings of the city gates, which would be swept away in 1760-61. For all his diligence, labouring for the best part of twenty years over the revision, Strype lacked Stow's vigorous style, made numerous errors and was so clumsy in his arrangement of the materials he piled up that he was nicknamed "the appendix-monger".

Strype was an Oxford graduate and as the vicar of a relatively undemanding semi-rural parish within convenient reach of London had the training, means and leisure for scholarship. William Maitland was an unschooled Scottish hair merchant whose business success enabled him to indulge a personal passion for the past and in 1739 to publish the ponderously titled *History of London from its Foundation by the Romans to the Present Time, with Several Accounts of Westminster, Middlesex and Southwark and other parts within the Bills of Mortality*. Maitland thus recognized the significance of what would be called "greater London" and not only gave an account of the city's government, commerce, schools and hospitals but also illustrated his description profusely with engravings and, unusually, with many tables of statistics.

The Guides

In *The London Spy* the entrepreneurial Ned Ward offered the reading public a very different take on metropolitan lifestyles. The personification of the cocky cockney, streetwise and pleasure-loving, Ward was in fact a provincial both by birth (Leicestershire) and by upbringing (Oxfordshire) and deftly used this background to mould his self-invention. *The London Spy*, which began to appear in parts in 1698, is a schizophrenic autobiography in which newly cocknified Ned introduces his former self, an innocent from the shires, to the dubious delights of the big city, from a brothel specializing in flagellation to spectating at the dissection of a criminal's corpse. Ward took a cheerily pragmatic view of the literary life: "the Condition of an Author is much like that of a Strumpet, Both exposing our reputations to supply our

Necessities." In 1712 he settled down to become a publican and saloon-bar sage, regaling his clientele with pungent reminiscences of:

Old Dunghills, Night-Men, Slaughterers, Jayls, Butchers, Dogs and Hogs that dwell In sweet St. James's, Clerkenwell

Ward's lineal descendant in Regency times was Pierce Egan, creator of the original Tom and Jerry, the gadabout protagonists of *Life in London: or the Day and Night Scenes of Jerry Hawthorn Esq. and his elegant friend Corinthian Tom, accompanied by Bob Logic, the Oxonian, in their Rambles and Sprees through the Metropolis.* Published in 1821, the book was illustrated by George Cruikshank and dedicated to George IV, who was rather sporting in accepting the dedication since both author and illustrator had mercilessly satirized and caricatured his love-life in print. Egan was a pioneer sports reporter, travelling the country to witness and report on horse races, prize fights and athletic contests of all kinds. Sport at that time being a pretty rough business, with gambling almost invariably involved, Egan had acquired an extensive familiarity with the manners, dress and argot of "the Fancy", that motley crew of toffs, tipsters and low-life whose passions were the prize-ring and the race-track. The success of *Tom and Jerry* was instant and immense, inspiring a host of pirated and plagiarized imitations, in prose, print and stage versions. Egan's own stage version, for Sadler's Wells, ran for 191 nights, a massive hit when a month was thought of as a good run. A recent scholarly interpretation attributes the popularity of Tom and Jerry to the very fact that they are not real Regency rakes or roués but lower middle-class chancers passing themselves off as such— hence their appeal to a reading and viewing audience of the same ilk. Mastery of current slang, "Flash Style", confers a classlessness which is the passport to universal acceptance. The isolation and insecurity of life in the cauldron of Regency London is given a positive spin as an invitation to self-reinvention.

Dickens' London

The picaresque vivacity of Tom and Jerry was reiterated more subtly and with even greater success in Dickens' *Pickwick Papers*. Pickwick, as a contemporary reviewer remarked, catapulted its author to fame "like a skyrocket", and it was Mr. Pickwick's street savant servant, Sam

Weller, who made *Pickwick* a sensation. Of the thousand copies printed of the first episode, published in March 1836, fewer than half were sold. Sales of the second and third were also discouraging. But the fourth, appearing in June, marked a clear turning-point, thanks to the introduction of Sam and the appointment of a third successive illustrator, Hablot Browne ("Phiz"), who would remain Dickens' collaborator for the next twenty-three years. By February 1837 monthly sales had climbed to 14,000 copies, and by the novel's conclusion in October 1837, to 40,000. Even before that conclusion five theatrical versions had appeared, as well as Pickwick figurines, hats, cigars and joke books. Over the following forty years the book sold 1,600,000 copies on both sides of the Atlantic.

Charles Dickens' position as the chronicler of London life should not disguise the fact that if his knowledge of the city was, like Sam Weller's, "extensive", it was also like Sam's "peculiar", with distinctive emphases and lacunae. Dickens had been born in Portsmouth, not London, moving to the capital as a lively and impressionable boy, and it is the essentially Georgian London of his youth, rather than the Victorian metropolis of his adult years, which framed the way that he saw and wrote about London.

Dickens' London was defined on the south by the brooding presence of the mighty Thames, a recurrent motif in so many works but perhaps most clearly in *Our Mutual Friend*, and on the north by the line of the New (now Marylebone) Road. Along either side of this great thoroughfare, first by fate and later by choice, Dickens would himself live, though only his first marital home, at 48 Doughty Street, now survives, fittingly preserved as his museum. Outside this central corridor he knew Southwark well from painful personal experience. He explored the docks and riverside areas of the East End, sometimes with a prudential police escort. West of Belgravia lies *terra incognita*, socially, if not topographically speaking. In *Nicholas Nickleby* the Witterleys of Cadogan Place know that they rank below the residents of Grosvenor Place but "look down upon Sloane Street and think Brompton low. They affect fashion too, and wonder where the New Road is"—this last reference a little joke by the author at his own expense.

In literary terms Dickens virtually ignored the prestigious building projects transforming the capital throughout his lifetime, although he can scarcely have been unaware of the laying out of Trafalgar Square in the 1840s, the reconstruction of the Houses of Parliament from the 1830s to the 1860s, the advent of the London Underground or the construction of the Embankment. Despite having been in a serious railway smash himself, he has little to say about railways, apart from the memorable passage describing the construction of the London-Birmingham line, which obliterated both the imaginary "Stagg's Gardens" and his own real-life former school. The suburbs are largely treated as a refuge or a dumping-ground for minor or inconvenient characters and the suburbs he does describe are usually the new growths of his teenage years, like Pentonville or Pimlico. Marylebone is dismissed as "Stucconia". Kensington, essentially a creation of the period after the Great Exhibition, he scarcely mentions.

Like a typical Londoner Dickens refers casually to St. Paul's, the Monument, the Tower and the Abbey, but only as landmarks, not as great historic entities to be explored or exploited. What Dickens emphasizes is the London destroyed by the projects of the Metropolitan Board of Works rather than the London it was trying to create—the slums and rookeries of St. Giles and Seven Dials, rather than the Charing Cross Road which sliced through the one and the New Oxford Street which swept away the other. Prisons figure prominently in Dickens' London, as do the Inns of Court, the former recalling his father's imprisonment in the Marshalsea for debt, the latter Dickens' own stupefyingly boring teenage employment as a clerk in Gray's Inn. More cheerfully there is the world of entertainment that provides so much of the material for *Sketches by Boz*—Vauxhall Gardens, Astley's equestrian circus, the Eagle music-hall, theatres, dinners and river excursions. This often tawdry world of "penny gaffs", waxworks, painted panoramas and itinerant street-performers reflected both the youthful Dickens' own leisure hours and the frustrated actor in him. Complementing this chiaroscuro of colourful characters were the streets which afforded "inexhaustible food for speculations" and supported some forty thousand traders and untold thousands more scavengers.

Markets supply another recurrent setting. The editorial offices of Dickens' own periodical, *All the Year Round*, were in Wellington Street right by Covent Garden, which figures in no fewer than eight of his novels. Dickens himself ran a successful journalistic campaign to have the bloody shambles of Smithfield's livestock market removed to a new and hygienic site at Caledonian Road but, typically, regretted its passing. Like the grotesques, victims and casualties he encountered on nocturnal excursions to Ratcliff Highway or Jacob's Island it held for him "the attraction of repulsion".

Trollope: "The Supreme of Power"

Although best known for novels set in an imaginary Barsetshire or the real Ireland, Anthony Trollope was also a metropolitan novelist. Only one of Trollope's novels, *The Struggles of Brown, Jones and Robinson*, is set entirely in London, but the city figures in two-thirds of the three dozen novels and eight of the seventeen short stories he set in England. As the critic R. H. Hutton observed, "in Miss Austen's world, how little you see of London.... in Mr. Trollope's novels... nothing can be done without London." Done is the operative word. London is the key to what can be done because London is, in Trollope's own words, "the supreme of power" and of its expressions and instruments—money, fashion, the "Season", "Clubland", violence and vice.

Political power, its acquisition and manipulation, is the preoccupation of Trollope's *Palliser* novels, and the country-house machinations that fill so many of their pages are essentially the off-stage continuations of what is happening in Westminster. The financial power of the City and the persuasive power of the London press, their moral corrosiveness and abuses, provide subsidiary themes and occasionally, as in the persona of the monstrous swindler Augustus Melmotte in *The Way We Live Now*, take centre stage.

Although he was based for almost twenty years in Ireland, Trollope was the only one of the great mid-Victorian novelists to have been born and to die in London. As a lifelong Post Office official he not only had as detailed a knowledge of London's streets as Dickens but a much more extensive and systematic one. In 1866 Trollope was appointed Surveyor for North and West London with the task of reorganizing postal delivery schedules. Familiarity with suburbs unknown to Dickens enabled him to locate the heroine of Marion Fay in a Holloway street aspirationally dubbed "Paradise Row". Dickens' antagonism towards the world of London politics and, in Trollope's view, his profound ignorance of it, puzzled him. As a civil servant who was proud of his work and its contribution to the better ordering of society, Trollope was angered by Dickens' caricature of the bumbling and obstructive Circumlocution Office in *Little Dorrit*. Like Dickens

Trollope belonged to both the Garrick and the Athenaeum. Unlike Dickens he not only knew Clubland but wrote about it. Trollope also belonged to the Cosmopolitan Club, which offered a meeting-ground between literary men and politicians; portrayed as "the Universe" in *Phineas Redux*, it supplied him with much background material for the Pallisers.

Gissing: Grub Street

The life of George Gissing was almost as depressing as his novels. A bookish, prickly, prize-winning prodigy at school, Gissing was then and repeatedly thrown off course by what the *Dictionary of National Biography* refers to delicately as his "amorous propensities". He also lost nearly all his savings on publishing his first novel. Scorning both the journalism and tutoring that were his main sources of livelihood, Gissing was nevertheless obliged to earn money to support the wife from whom he was separated, before she died of a combination of alcoholism, syphilis and malnutrition. Of the novels which gained him the sobriquet of "spokesman of despair" (suicide, destitution and estranged wives tend to recur) the most enduring have proved to be *The Nether World* (1889), set in industrial Clerkenwell, and *New Grub Street* (1891), which, appropriately enough, delineates the desperate straits of an exploited writer. Gissing's description of a train passing through—or rather over—the East End gives the reader a cautionary whiff of an authorial tone which can turn even a summer's day to gloom:

> *Over the pest-stricken regions of East London, sweltering in sunshine which served only to reveal the intimacies of abomination: across miles of a city of the damned, such as thought never conceived before this age of ours; above streets swarming with a nameless populace, cruelly exposed by the unwonted light of heaven; stopping at stations which it crushes the heart to think should be the destination of any mortal, the train made its way at length beyond the utmost limits of dread...*

Nether World and no mistake.

Cunningham's *Handbook of London*

Like Trollope, Peter Cunningham was a civil servant who ran his literary career in parallel to his office life. Cunningham's prolific output included biographies of Inigo Jones and Nell Gwyn and a guide-book to Westminster Abbey. Like Stow, whose work he knew expertly, he had a passion for manuscripts. On his very first excursion into the neglected archives of the Audit Office where he was employed he uncovered three rolls of expenses for Henry, Prince of Wales, covering the years 1610-12 and including payments naming Inigo Jones and Ben Jonson. In 1849 John Murray published the fruit of seven years of Cunningham's labour as an alphabetical *Handbook of London Past and Present*. A second edition, with a much-needed index, appeared in 1850. In 1851 Murray shrewdly produced a greatly abridged, pocket-sized version to cash in on the unique commercial opportunity created by the Great Exhibition.

Although London's first railway had opened in 1836, carrying a line from London Bridge to Dartford, and railways had connected London with other major cities by the time Cunningham's *Handbook* first appeared, they had not yet dramatically changed the dimensions of the capital itself. London was therefore, to Cunningham, defined on the north by Hampstead and Kilburn, on the south by Camberwell and Norwood, to the east by Blackwall and Greenwich and to the west by Hammersmith and Battersea. Kensington was included "on account of its Gardens" but is described as "a village... almost a part of London". The entries reflect Cunningham's diligence in sifting through the archives of ten parishes and in their illustrative quotations reveal his extensive knowledge of seventeenth- and eighteenth-century literature, further reflected in his expertise on the development of London theatre and the world of the coffee-houses. Much curious or useful information is further imparted on topics as various as where to get the best coffee, ices and buns, how to keep turtles tasty and the identities of all the people who had thrown themselves off the Monument. For the contemporary visitor Cunningham offered must-see lists of sights. The fifty-three "recommended for the Stranger" start with, in order, the Tower, the Abbey, St. Paul's, the British Museum, the National Gallery and the Houses of Parliament—not much change from any modern list. They also include, however, "Hyde Park between half past five and half past six p.m. in May and June", the engineering wonder (and commercial white elephant) that was the Brunels' Thames Tunnel between Wapping and Rotherhithe, five docks, four parks, three churches and three palaces, two each of bridges, zoos and markets and such commercial operations as Barclay's Brewhouse and Clowes' Printing Works in Stamford Street. He also offered other selective lists for connoisseurs of paintings, architecture, sculpture and archaeology. Evidently assured of the immense superiority of London to all other cities, Cunningham introduces no comparisons beyond a single mention of Poissy, near Paris, in the course of explaining the overcrowdedness of Smithfield market.

Mayhew: Categorizing the Capital

The career of Henry Mayhew demonstrated an immense capacity for hard work and an inability to focus it to his advantage. He started numerous periodicals, including *Punch*, and wrote unflattering books about Germany, "improving" works for children and half a dozen plays but he is best remembered, in the words of the *Dictionary of National Biography*, as being "the first to strike out the line of philanthropic journalism which takes the poor of London as its theme." Mayhew's interest was sparked by reporting the impact of the 1849 cholera outbreak. He persuaded the editor of the *Morning Chronicle* to run an on-going series of investigations into the condition of the poor. Over the best part of two years Mayhew produced some 800,000 words, republished in volume form as *London Labour and the London Poor* in 1851. Mayhew divided the poor into three categories: those who were willing to work, those who were, through age, illness or disability, unable to work and those who refused to work. Although the great majority of London's poor consisted of semi-skilled or unskilled labourers, Mayhew became increasingly interested in those who survived at the margins of economic life. A compulsive quantifier, Mayhew worked out how much horse-dung was dropped on the streets of London daily and how many pounds of used tea-leaves were sold by servants in middle-class households weekly for re-sale to the poor. He was equally driven by the urge to categorize and devised, for example, a hierarchy of scavengers, ranging from the elite "toshers", who hazarded noxious fumes and packs of rats to grope in the sewers for dropped coins and cutlery, to "mudlarks" who recovered scraps of rope and metal from the foreshore at low tide and "pure finders" who collected canine droppings for the tanners of Bermondsey.

By attempting to record and reproduce the speech of his informants Mayhew also accumulated much data regarding mid-Victorian cockney accents and idioms. At times we share his scarcely concealed amazement at the ignorance of the unlettered or the daily humiliations of the marginalized. Thus he was told that the moon was certainly further away than the height of St. Paul's because it could often be seen above it at night. And a pie-seller informed him that customers in pubs routinely tossed a coin with him for the pie rather than simply buy it—and when they won quite often broke it up to pelt him with the pieces rather than eat it. Mayhew's achievement as a social investigator, rather than a mere reporter, has been underestimated. He came close to defining the notion of a "poverty line", albeit crudely:

> *Under the term... "poor" I shall include all those persons whose incomings are insufficient for the satisfaction of their wants—a want being, according to my idea, contra-distinguished from a mere desire by positive physical pain, instead of mental uneasiness accompanying it.*

He also neatly encapsulated a formulation that later investigators were to confirm and elaborate: "regularity of habits is incompatible with irregularity of income." Dockers might earn good money but as they could never know from day to day when they would be "called on" to work their potential earning-power was invariably corroded by drink and debt. Mayhew's concern to uncover the causes of poverty, i.e. exploitation, led to court proceedings and a break with the *Morning Chronicle*. He returned repeatedly to the problems of London poverty, investigating prostitution, producing books on prisons and shops and a brief study of working-men's clubs but his latter years were blighted by insolvency and the necessity of living abroad for long periods to escape his creditors.

In Darkest London

Although the term "East End" appears to have been first coined in the 1840s, it was in the 1880s that it gained general currency. The 1840s had been preoccupied with the "condition of England question"—the growing and potentially explosive divergence between the lives of rich and poor produced by industrialization, and reflected in Carlyle's polemical *Past and Present* (1843) and Disraeli's novel *Sybil: or The Two Nations* (1845). In the 1880s the contrasts between London's West End and East End inspired similar anxiety, leading to new philanthropic initiatives and a burgeoning literary genre of imaginative concern.

In 1880-81 Sir Walter Besant, a prolific novelist and diligent philanthropist, "spent a great deal of time walking about the mean monotony of the East End of London... And presently I understood that one of the things very much wanted in this great place was a centre of organized recreation, orderly amusement and intellectual and artistic culture. So I pictured an heiress going down to the place under the disguise of a dressmaker..." Besant's resulting novel, *All Sorts and Conditions of Men*, prudently carried the sub-title *An Impossible Story* but five years after its publication Queen Victoria herself came down to the Mile End Road to open the People's Palace as the realization of his vision. Its existence as a high-minded leisure centre, however, was brief, as its vocational provision outweighed its cultural mission and it evolved into the East London Technical College and eventually Queen Mary College of the University of London. Yet the novel proved to be Besant's best-selling effort, notching up a quarter of a million copies by 1918.

In 1882 *The Pictorial World* commissioned from George R. Sims a series of articles on a topic of his own choosing, provided only that it would lend itself to illustration. Sims had recently been exploring some of south London's most deprived areas under the guidance of School Board officer Arthur Moss and decided therefore to introduce readers to "a dark continent that is within easy walking distance of the General Post Office". Sims' articles, accompanied by pictures by Besant's illustrator, Frederick Barnard, were reprinted in volume form in 1883 as *How the Poor Live*. He later wrote a *Daily News* series on housing conditions (republished in 1889 as *Horrible London*), which led to his being called as an expert witness before the Royal Commission on the Housing of the Working Classes in 1884. Sims' *Daily Telegraph* attacks on what would now be called sex slavery were reprinted as *London by Night* (1906) and *Watches of the Night* (1907). Despite his influence as a social crusader, Sims also wrote novels, detective stories, three dozen plays, seventeen musicals, dozens of comic and sentimental ballads and memoirs entitled *My Life: Sixty Years Recollections of Bohemian London*. He also claimed to have invented a cure for baldness and to know the identity of Jack the Ripper but is best remembered for his much parodied tear-jerker, *In the Workhouse: Christmas Day*.

Published in 1883 by the London Congregational Union as a penny pamphlet, *The Bitter Cry of Outcast London*, sub-titled *An Inquiry Into the Condition of the Abject Poor*, appeared anonymously. Its author, the Reverend Andrew Mearns of Orange Street chapel, Leicester Square, acknowledged his debt to Sims' *Pictorial World* series but made even larger claims:

> *Seething in the very centre of our great cities, concealed by the thinnest crust of civilization and decency, is a vast mass of moral corruption, of heart-breaking misery and absolute godlessness and... scarcely anything has been done to take into this awful slough the only influences that can purify or remove it.*

The existence of urban poverty and depravity was scarcely unknown to the Victorian establishment; what shocked readers were Mearns' claims that despite the great mid-century church-building boom and an apparent plethora of philanthropic initiatives, the sheer scale of the challenge had simply not been grasped: "we are simply living in a fool's paradise if we suppose that all these agencies combined are doing a thousandth part of what needs to be done." Mearns then supported his assertion, abetted by evidence he claimed to be neither misleadingly selective nor exaggerated, with a relentlessly grim account of non-attendance at worship, vile overcrowding, homelessness, prostitution, incest, alcoholism, sweated labour, pollution and chronic malnutrition. He called for a mission amongst the "abject poor" to be given the highest immediate priority, for charitable not sectarian objectives, and announced the Congregationalists' own commitment to action in three target areas: Ratcliff, Shadwell and Bermondsey.

The campaigning journalist W. T. Stead greatly enlarged the impact of *The Bitter Cry* by publicizing it in his *Pall Mall Gazette*. Cumulatively Besant, Sims and Mearns were at least partly responsible for provoking the foundation of the East End university settlements at Toynbee Hall in Whitechapel and Oxford House in Bethnal Green in 1884, the appointment of a Royal Commission on the Housing of the Working Classes in 1885 and the success of Mrs. Humphry Ward's crisis of faith novel of Christian self-sacrifice, *Robert Elsmere* (1888) in which the hero renounces the theological quibbling of Oxford for the challenges of the East End.

Margaret Harkness, a founding member of the reforming Fabian Society, was also a friend of Marx's daughter, Eleanor, and a lodger with Engels' family. *A City Girl: A Realistic Story* (1887), written by her under the pseudonym John Law, tells the classic tale of a poor girl "ruined" by a heartless bourgeois seducer. *Out of Work* (1888), the story of an immigrant village carpenter, included a description of the 1887 "Bloody Sunday" riots in Trafalgar Square which had convinced William Morris of the utter futility of violent insurrection in Britain. *Captain Lobe: or In Darkest London* (1889) explored Whitechapel through the eyes of a heroic Salvation Army officer and the Salvation Army lassies who lived as "slum saviours" in the hope that their clean lodgings and orderly, godly lives might serve as an example and inspiration before they succumbed to a premature death occasioned by their own self-sacrifice.

Born in Poplar, Arthur Morrison worked as a clerk at the People's Palace before turning to journalism and exploiting his first-hand knowledge of the East End to produce "realist" sketches subsequently published as *Tales of Mean Streets* (1894), which went through five US editions in two years, a German edition and five subsequent British editions between 1913 and 1997. Morrison is best remembered, however, for *A Child of the Jago* (1896), which tells the story of a blighted life in the Shoreditch criminal quarter known as the Old Nichol. The location is barely disguised: Boundary Street became Edge Lane, Chance Street Luck Row and Mean Street Honey Lane. The saintly bruiser Father Sturt is based on Father Arthur Osborne Jay, vicar of Holy Trinity, Shoreditch, who introduced the area to the author after reading *Mean Streets* and informing Morrison that the realities of his parish were even worse than what he had described. Jay was himself the author of *Life in Darkest London* (1891) and *The Social Problem and its Solutions* (1893), and it was his campaigning, reinforced by the success of Morrison's novel, which led to the entire clearance of the Old Nichol and its replacement by the London County Council's model Boundary Street estate, the first publicly-provided working-class housing to be architect-designed.

A wealthy ship-owner, and in his youth a radical, Charles Booth P.C. F.R.S., was determined to disprove the claims made by H. M.

Hyndman of the Social Democratic Federation, that a quarter of London's inhabitants were living in dire poverty. Booth's systematic statistical investigations, eventually published as colour-coded *Maps Descriptive of London Poverty* (1898-9) and in seventeen volumes as *The Life and Labour of the People of London* (1891-1903), actually demonstrated that the immiseration of the metropolitan poor was even worse than had been alleged, blighting the lives of about one-third of Londoners. Beatrice Webb was one of the investigators who paid detailed attention to the East End, and the results of their efforts constitute an invaluable source for the historian. Charles Booth's maps and accompanying notebooks can be consulted on-line at www.booth.lse.ac.uk.

Jack London, whose adventure stories made him briefly one of the world's most highly paid writers (and thus rich enough to drink himself to an early death), had known poverty as a child in California and revisited it again in the East End in 1902 in the guise of an American sailor. Taking up temporary lodgings in Flower and Dean Street, a location notorious from its association with one of the Ripper's victims, he "went down into the under-world of London with an attitude of mind which I may best liken to that of the explorer." The outcome of the author's sojourn in sordidness was a passionate polemic, *People of the Abyss* (1903), twenty-seven chapters ranging over wages and workhouses, drink and dossers, sickness and suicide and the homeless sleeping upright in mid-afternoon because their railed churchyard refuge (Christ Church, Spitalfields) was locked up at night. London stressed constantly the role of chance—of illness, accident, the death of a breadwinner—in condemning the blameless to inescapable degradation in the year of the coronation of portly, jovial, self-indulgent Edward VII.

Omitting the cheery relief associated with the music-hall and the street-market, Jack London's depiction of London is almost unrelievedly negative and almost entirely male—a limitation which was to provoke the complementary but very different investigations of Olive Christian Malvery. Arriving in London as a music student, Malvery successively reinvented herself as a performer, elocution teacher, writer and photojournalist. In 1904, capitalizing on the interest aroused by *People of the Abyss*, Malvery went "undercover" to experience the lives of "London's poorer daughters", dressing to pass herself off as a flower girl, barmaid, shop-girl, tramp or factory worker. Her account of her adventures, liberally illustrated with photographs, appeared in *Pearson's Magazine* as "The Heart of Things".

Unlike other social investigations Malvery's project was largely an exercise in self-promotion in which her own pluck and ingenuity were the key ingredients of an inverted travelogue in which a daughter of Empire exposes the ethnographic underside of its metropolis. As such, it was seriously flawed and haphazard. Much attention was paid to the Italian community while London's far larger Irish and Jewish populations were virtually ignored. Nevertheless the series proved sufficiently popular with readers for her to be commissioned to undertake a second series on "The Alien Question" in 1905. This focused on the male immigrant Jew from Eastern Europe and, published as the contentious Alien Bill was under discussion in Parliament, took a far more hostile tone than the previous series. Thwarted by the angry reaction of the crowd when an attempt was made to photograph applicants outside the Poor Jews' Temporary Shelter in Whitechapel, Malvery resorted to a shot of Jews outside the socialist club in Princelet Street, complemented by an insinuating caption hinting at the arrival of further unknown numbers of potentially criminal, subversive and unassimilable newcomers. When the outbreak of revolution in the Tsarist empire made it impossible for her to visit the regions from which the ghetto Jews were emigrating, she "investigated" their "background" by photographing the poverty of Italy's Mezzogiorno. Whatever her ethical shortcomings as a journalist, Malvery's exercise in self-promotion succeeded in netting her a trophy husband in the form of Scots-born American diplomat Archibald Mackirdy. Their society wedding in fashionable St. Margaret's, Westminster, was graced by an entourage of cockney flower-girls and complemented by a "royal" reception in Hoxton. Financially secure, Malvery turned her attention to the titillating problem of white slavery to produce *The Soul Market*, which went through four editions in less than two years. To be fair, she did use her royalties to finance two shelters for homeless women. In 1911 her husband died, leaving her with three small children; she herself died from an overdose of sedatives in 1914.

Australian by birth, a New Zealander by upbringing and an activist by vocation, Maud Pember Reeves was the wife of the Director of the London School of Economics. In 1909, with the support of the Fabian

Women's Group, she undertook what would later be called a "micro-study" of London poverty by close scrutiny of the lifestyles and budgets of forty-two families in Lambeth. The sample chosen were by no means the poorest of the poor but those whose "work is permanent, as permanency goes in Lambeth". Of the 201 children born to families in the sample 18 had died at birth and a further 39 in childhood and five were mentally deficient. Mrs. Pember Reeves wrote up her findings as a Fabian pamphlet, republished in book form as *Round About a Pound a Week*. Contrary to expectations it was found that drink was not a major problem, as married men on eighteen to twenty-six shillings a week simply could not afford it. She estimated that about eight million Britons were living in families which had to survive on a weekly income of twenty-five shillings or less. Overworked and undernourished, the tragedy of so many mothers was that, even if their meagre education had left them barely literate, unlike Mayhew's poor half a century earlier, they understood that they were overworked and undernourished and that a better way of life for themselves and their children should be possible in the capital of the world's greatest empire. Mrs. Reeves' recommendations for their relief included child benefit, free school meals and free health clinics, suggestions that would be adopted piecemeal by progressive local governments in poor areas such as Finsbury, Poplar and Peckham.

Inter-War Issues
In *The Face of London* topographical writer Harold P. Clunn set out to present "a bird's-eye view of the growth, progress and development of the world's most wonderful city" as it appeared to him in 1931. An unabashed fan of modernization and the motor car, Clunn's breathlessly informative tone was habitually upbeat, as when "a large demolition of courts and alleys" around Petticoat Lane led him to speculate, presciently, if prematurely, "whether in the course of time the East End will develop into some high-class business quarter as important in a different way as even Westminster or the Strand." The East End could, however, still floor him, as in nearby Wentworth Street where "we almost seem to have taken leave of everything English... we might just as well be in some street in Warsaw or Cracow." Clunn's scarcely-veiled anti-Semitism surfaced again around Whitechapel: "during the last ten years the Jewish problem... has become much less acute, since the

inflow has now been stopped." Brick Lane, however, impressed him as "a kind of East End Bond Street... Some of its shop-fronts and window-displays would do credit to a West End thoroughfare." Limehouse, perhaps predictably, roused reactions in Clunn similar to those provoked by Wentworth Street:

> ... *many of the side streets are inhabited almost entirely by Orientals and contain foreign restaurants and drinking shops hardly suitable for unaccompanied tourists... the population consists of Chinese, Lascars, Maltese and a few Japanese... Opium dens and fan-tan saloons still exist, despite the vigilance of the police but it is not wise for the visitor to see these establishments from the inside.*

George Orwell's first published book, *Down and Out in Paris and London*, ostensibly a work of reportage, was based in part on his attempts to pass himself off as a tramp, no easy feat for an Old Etonian ex-copper. Compared with Paris, Orwell described the East End as "much cleaner and quieter and drearier... less drunkenness and less dirt and less quarrelling and more idling." Despite the apparent immediacy he strove for, this was a judgment of hindsight. Orwell's East End "fieldwork" had been undertaken in 1927 and was followed by two years in Paris before he began drafting the book in 1930. More than five years in the making, it was finally published in 1933. Being almost exclusively concerned with the world of lodging-houses, hostels and "spikes" (the worst form of accommodation) and the plight of the totally indigent, Orwell's account throws little light on the condition of the majority of Londoners struggling to cope with the challenge of a prolonged depression.

William Kent, author of a fact-packed, if somewhat lop-sided, *Encyclopaedia of London,* published in 1937, was frequently judgmental beneath a veneer of objectivity. He shared Clunn's acute unease at the "alien" character of parts of the East End, explicitly contrasting Stepney with Poplar. Stepney he summarized as "a borough of innumerable small industries, largely carried on by Jews (their synagogues are everywhere)... The Roman Catholics are strong in Stepney... Limehouse Causeway is the High St. of London's Chinatown—as the names over the shops reveal." In Poplar, by contrast, "the population, unlike that of Stepney, is predominantly British... There is a general breeziness; there is an astonishing number of respectable old houses; there are not a few quiet nooks; and the public houses are small and homely."

The urbane Paul Cohen-Portheim, author of *The Spirit of London* (1935), perhaps caught the often paradoxical London relationship between place and people better than most, judging the East End to be "one of the most mysterious places in the world but of most prosaic aspect." Lacking the "picturesque squalor" of Parisian slums, "it looks mean and drab but this impression is chiefly due to the lack of height in its buildings. Apart from the great main roads it is just a maze of alleys of low little houses of darkened brick." Redemption was to be found in their inhabitants: "it is the people who give interest to the East End streets." Unlike most parts of London, where the residents "vanish into their houses, East Enders 'promenade', as Parisians do," even if the word itself was quite unknown to them. Speculating that the cause might lie just as much in the "lack of comfort and charm" to be found in the home as in any positive zest for street life itself, Cohen-Portheim, a former internee of the Great War who bore no grudges, celebrated the "alien" elements which so unsettled Clunn and Kent:

> *Eastern Jews adore the life and light, bustle and noise of their Whitechapel Road. On Saturday nights, particularly, it is thronged with people parading up and down; there is, in fact, a Corso in progress. I know of nothing quite like it in the more purely English popular parts of London.*

The Chinese exile Chiang Yee was less familiar with the "popular parts of London" than with Bloomsbury and Hampstead but he was equally urbane, if less effusively so. Successively a chemistry teacher, soldier and magistrate, he had fled his homeland as a result of the Japanese aggression against it, leaving behind a wife and four children. In London from 1933 onwards he survived as a language teacher and archivist before establishing himself as a writer of books introducing Western readers to Chinese art and calligraphy. In 1937, after many rejections, he published an account of a visit to the Lake District, illustrated with his own sketches and paintings in the Chinese idiom. It sold out in a month and thus was born "the Silent Traveller". The *Silent Traveller in London* followed in 1938. In part the pseudonym he assumed implies an inhibition imposed on him by his unfamiliarity with English, in part a Confucian regard for silence as an expression of reserve, modesty and wisdom. In fact, although Chiang Yee may have been diffident about his command of spoken English, he wrote it with freedom and elegance, quite unlike the self-consciously cracked "Japlish" which had brought success to the Japanese water-colourist Yoshio Markino twenty years previously. Although constantly punctuating his observations with allusions to and quotations from classical Chinese authors and poets, there was nothing unduly highfaluting in Yee's interests. He met and mixed with academics, with intellectuals like the art critic Herbert Read and the poet Lawrence Binyon and with other exiled Chinese artists and writers but his affectionate account of London is concerned as much with his reflections on gender and generation, food and fog as on high culture as encountered in art galleries or on the stage.

Peripheral Vision
V. S. Pritchett's *London Perceived* (1962) is a rumination. An old Fleet Street hand and master of the short story, Pritchett ponders the qualities of London and Londoners, the way the city has been shaped by Greed and Nature rather than Reason and Planning, its humbug and muddle, its enclaves of exclusiveness, its preference for the square and the street over the *grande place* or the boulevard, its fixations with "property, privacy and order". Petticoat Lane and Speakers' Corner, "the working Thames", Pepys and Defoe, "London talk", Beau Brummel, Dickens and the Gothic Revival are his enthusiasms, representations of what is quintessential London. The book has no index. It would be pointless to index a soliloquy. It does, however, have illustrations, haunting black and white photographs by Evelyn Hofer, a London Cartier-Bresson, the Canaletto of grime. They provide a poignant panorama of the city of my childhood, shabby, battered, encrusted with soot, punctuated with bomb-sites, misty and mysterious. There are one hundred and eighteen photographs in all. The River, the Abbey, parks and markets, the still-Victorian interiors of pubs and houses grand and humble figure prominently. London is not yet bare-headed. A spruce City type at a flower-stall still sports a jaunty bowler. There are helmeted bobbies, bear-skinned Guardsmen, peak-capped ticket-collectors and milkmen, city messengers and commissionaires with cockaded top-hats, Chelsea Pensioners in their undress kepis, Billingsgate fish-porters with

medieval leather hats for balancing baskets on, a Portobello Road spiv in a greasy fedora and watermen, dockers and cabbies in cloth caps. With the sole exception of two little black boys, tersely captioned "Notting Hill", *all* the faces are white.

In direct contrast to Pritchett's panorama stands Edward Platt's *Leadville*, a compelling, claustrophobic micro-study of a blighted stretch of the A40 Western Avenue between White City and the Hanger Lane Gyratory. Written between 1995 and 1998, it chronicles the impact of an ultimately abortive road-widening scheme that succeeds only in wrecking the lives of those whose homes it threatens. Diatribe, elegy and battlefront despatch, *Leadville* details repeated encounters with stranded suburbanites gradually besieged by squatters and druggies as their surroundings rapidly decay and rampant nature repossesses once-trim pathways and gardens. A meditation on what the motor car has done to us rather than for us, the book is Dickensian in its portrayal of tragi-comic characters impaled in a grotesque corridor of polluted subtopia, Orwellian in its prophetic implications.

Iain Sinclair's *London Orbital* (2002) is the outcome of an odyssey around the M25, a pilgrimage through a void, an eccentric project in the course of which the eccentrically erudite author, accompanied by a changing retinue of colourful companions, encounters other assorted eccentrics as he traverses an unregarded toxic wasteland strewn with up-market housing developments, asylums, tunnels, reservoirs, bunkers and golf-courses. Sinclair's archaeologizing embraces both Dracula and the Dome as he combines the fact-grubbing curiosity of a Mayhew with the invective of Cobbett's *Rural Rides* in a prose both dense and shimmering.

OF DIARIES AND LETTERS
A Handwritten Interlude

John Evelyn (1620-1706)

London's most celebrated diarist, Samuel Pepys, observed of John Evelyn: "a most excellent person he is, and must be allowed a little for conceitedness, but he may be so, being a man so much above others." Evelyn was indeed a man whose many talents enabled him to play many parts. A founder member of the Royal Society (he probably suggested its name), he was also a Commissioner of the Privy Seal and Treasurer of Greenwich Hospital. Evelyn managed to perform his public duties and yet keep himself apart from the political turmoil of his day. Whereas Pepys was actually in Whitehall when Charles I was executed

Prince Henry's Room and Pepys' Museum

there, Evelyn purposely stayed away, as he did from the execution of the regicides, which Pepys also watched. Like Pepys, Evelyn lived through both the Great Plague of 1665 and the Great Fire of 1666—but from a more prudent distance. Evelyn has been criticized for not making the most of his talents or his opportunities. He did not have to. Devout, rational, calm, untroubled by anxiety, care or illness, he lived long and well. John Evelyn could have been a leader of his age but was content to be its ornament.

Evelyn wrote much—on sculpture and engraving, on the navy and Jesuits, on how to make a decent salad (just the merest hint of garlic) and, most effectively, on gardens, horticulture and forestry. One of Evelyn's most celebrated pamphlets, *Fumifugium* (1661), denounces the polluting curse of coal smoke and recommends the banishing of fuel-intensive trades like brewing from the city and the planting of groves of sweet-scented trees to the south-west so that the prevailing winds could permanently refresh the atmosphere. (An ingenious academic conjecture suggests, however, that rather than being just a pioneering polemic against pollution *Fumifugium* is also—or really—a covert paean to monarchy in the suitably opaque allegory of a discussion about smoke.) A prolific pamphleteer, Evelyn would have been astounded to learn that he would be known to posterity as a diarist. The journal that he kept for sixty-four years from the age of twenty-one was never intended for publication and was not indeed published until 1818, long after his death. Virginia Woolf admired the artlessness of his art:

> *His writing is opaque rather than transparent; we see no depths through it, nor any very secret movements of his mind or heart... But he writes a diary and he writes it supremely well. Even as we drowse, somehow or other the bygone gentleman sets up, through three centuries, a perceptible tingle of communication, so that without laying stress on anything particular... we are yet taking notice all the time.*

Evelyn's diary is the work of a man who was wealthy, popular, well-placed to observe society and so gifted with charm that he could remain an uncompromised Royalist while having friends in Cromwell's own close circle. Being particularly interested in architecture and gardens, Evelyn is especially informative about new fashions and developments in these fields. He did not like the lay-out of Covent Garden but approved of Bloomsbury Square and admired the splendour of the grounds at Ham House, Sir Henry Capel's orangery at Kew and the profusion of plants available at the Brompton nursery. Evelyn made his London home at Sayes Court, Deptford, and it was near there that he discovered Grinling Gibbons at work in a cottage, spotted his extraordinary talent as a wood-carver and started him on his career as a wonder of his age. Many City churches claim to have carvings by Gibbons; the wonderful altar of St. Mary Abchurch is certainly by his hand.

When in 1698 Tsar Peter the Great of Russia came to study shipbuilding in the Royal Dockyard at Deptford, Evelyn was persuaded to vacate his cherished home in order to accommodate the honoured visitor and his entourage. At their departure the Russians, tersely summarized by Evelyn's steward as "right nasty", left behind a trail of destruction with not a pane of glass in the house unbroken. One of the giant Tsar's particular pleasures had been to be driven at full tilt in a wheelbarrow through Evelyn's prized holly hedge. Evelyn must have wept. The government coughed up £300 in compensation. Sayes Court was demolished in 1729 and a workhouse built on its site. Part of its former grounds became a recreation area in 1878. Otherwise only the names of Evelyn Street, Czar Street and Sayes Court Street perpetuate its memory.

Samuel Pepys (1632-1703)

Samuel Pepys wrote the most famous diary of London life—for his eyes only. And when he thought they were beginning to fail he stopped. His million and a quarter words, deliberately obscured by shorthand symbols, mirror writing and a home-made Esperanto of Euro-speak, cover the years 1660-69, thus embracing the Restoration (Pepys was on the boat bringing Charles II back from exile, attended the coronation and celebrated to the extent of waking up covered in his own vomit), the Great Plague (with typical doggedness he stayed at his post) and the Great Fire (it was Pepys himself who brought news of the catastrophe to the king at Westminster and Pepys who saved his own office and precious papers from destruction by having sailors blow up adjoining houses to create a fire-break). Outstanding naval administrator, courtier, MP, Master of Trinity House, Master of the Worshipful

Company of Clothworkers, President of the Royal Society, flautist, fashion-victim, gourmand, gossip, philanderer, connoisseur and prisoner in the Tower, Pepys was also a dedicated bibliophile who is credited with inventing the glass-fronted book-case and bequeathed his carefully catalogued three thousand volumes to his old Cambridge college, Magdalene.

Plaques record the locations of Pepys' birth (Salisbury Court), retirement (Buckingham Street) and official residence (Seething Lane), near which a modern bust well captures his quizzical alertness. Opposite still stands "our own church", medieval St. Olave's, Hart Street, where Pepys lies beside his wife, and a poignant memorial of that long-suffering spouse gazes down at his accustomed pew. The National Portrait Gallery has John Hyles' £14-portrait of Pepys, in a hired silk gown, gazing over one shoulder at posterity (posing gave him a sore neck) and holding a copy of one of his own musical compositions. In Fleet Street at the entrance of Inner Temple Lane a compact museum of Pepysiana can be found in the picturesquely half-timbered survivor of pre-Fire London which houses the panelled chamber known as "Prince Henry's Room".

Horace Walpole (1717-97)

Horace Walpole was the son of Sir Robert Walpole, recognized in retrospect, though he would have repudiated the title, as Britain's first Prime Minister. Despite his bluff and brutal public *persona*, Sir Robert was a knowledgeable and discriminating art-collector. Horace inherited not only his fortune and title, but also his taste. Born at 17 Arlington Street, he devoted himself, after a brief, unenthusiastic and undistinguished spell in parliament, to his aesthetic and social interests and to writing about them in his letters, over four thousand of which survive. At Twickenham Walpole bought a small villa, Strawberry Hill, which he enlarged and Gothicized to create a battlemented pseudo-castle, embellished outside with stucco and inside with gilded papier-mâché. Even before he had begun the transformation he wrote fondly of his residence as "a little plaything of a house, the prettiest bauble you ever did see." Walpole's other major project was the establishment of a private printing-press, whose products included his own meticulously-kept inventories and building accounts and his pioneering novel *The Castle of Otranto* (1764), which initiated the cult of "Gothick" romances. Walpole also compiled a pioneering essay on the history of English art, *Anecdotes of Painters in England*. But it is for his letters that Walpole was to be valued by literati and historians alike.

Walpole could be woundingly spiteful and had a great gift of phrase. His aesthetic judgments are numerous and often barbed. He admired Inigo Jones' Banqueting House ("the model of the most pure and beautiful taste"), William Kent's stupendous staircase at 44 Berkeley Square, Robert Adam's Admiralty Screen and his make-over of Osterley House ("the palace of palaces"). An early admirer of Adam, Walpole later turned against him, dismissing his Adelphi as "warehouses laced down the seams, like a soldier's trull in a regimental lace coat." A mock-ruin Roman gateway designed by Adam's life-long rival, Sir William Chambers, earned particular scorn: "A solecism may be committed even in architecture. The ruin in Kew Gardens is built with Act of Parliament bricks." (Walpole refers to modern bricks, of the dimensions specified in the Building Act of 1774.)

Walpole judged the young poetaster Thomas Chatterton "a complete genius and a complete rogue". Of Lord Burlington (see p. 218), however, he wrote admiringly that he "had every quality of a genius and artist, except envy... the Apollo of the arts (he) found a proper priest in Mr. Kent." Walpole's epitaph for the boorish Frederick, Prince of Wales, who died in 1751 after being hit by a cricket-ball, crisply dismisses the whole Hanoverian dynasty:

Here lies Fred,
Who was alive and is dead;
Had it been his father,
I had much rather;
Had it been his brother,
Better than another;
Had it been his sister,
No one would have missed her;
Had it been the whole generation,
Better for the nation:
But since 'tis only Fred,
Who was alive and is dead—
There's no more to be said.

Walpole was a party animal, an *habitué* of the Bedford Coffee House in Covent Garden and a member of both gentlemen's clubs, White's and Brooks'. He attended the assemblies at Almack's. He was at the reception to mark the rebuilding of Norfolk House in St. James' Square. He was there in Green Park in 1749 for the firing off of ten thousand rockets to mark the ending of the War of Austrian Succession. (Walpole was unimpressed by the fireworks but liked the music that Handel composed for the occasion.) He was at the opening of the Pantheon and thrilled by it: "Imagine Balbec in all its glory!" This "most beautiful edifice in England" became a gin warehouse before finally being demolished in 1937 to make way for the Oxford Street branch of Marks and Spencer.

Walpole accompanied the Duke of York to investigate the (fraudulent) Cock Lane Ghost, witnessed balloon ascents and heard (and admired) the preaching of charismatic, cross-eyed George Whitefield but deplored "the ridiculous rage of going to Newgate" to see public hangings. Walpole's greatest contempt, however, was reserved for the "masterpiece of absurdity", the statue of King George I mounted above Hawksmoor's new church on Bloomsbury Way. It was balanced precariously on a stepped column allegedly modelled on the Mausoleum of Halicarnassus, one of the Seven Wonders of the Ancient World. Whatever the Mausoleum may have looked like—a best guess is displayed in the British Museum—it certainly did not look like Hawksmoor's version. For once Walpole curbed his customary waspishness in favour of plain ridicule:

> *When Henry VIII left the Pope in the lurch*
> *The Protestants made him head of the church*
> *But George's good subjects, the Bloomsbury People*
> *Instead of the Church, made him head of the steeple.*

Fanny Burney (1752-1840)

The diary of Fanny Burney covers an even longer time-span than John Evelyn's, from when she was sixteen in 1768 until she was eighty-seven. It is doubly important, as being both the first diary written by a woman of social eminence and as the work of a successful writer. The daughter of musicologist Dr.Charles Burney, Fanny stunned her family with the anonymous publication of her first novel, *Evelina*, when she was just twenty-six. Dr. Johnson praised *Evelina* most warmly to her father, not realizing that the author was standing only a few feet away from him. Fanny basked in his approval and the friendship of the most eminent personalities of the day—Reynolds, Burke, Sheridan, Garrick, Captain Cook and, naturally, the blue-stockings (see p. 109). Fanny repeated her literary triumph with a second novel, *Cecilia*, and then, disastrously for her, succumbed to the pressure of family and friends to accept the post of Second Mistress of the Robes to Queen Charlotte, the dull and dutiful consort of an increasingly deranged George III. The five years of ensuing boredom and petticoat politics almost broke Fanny's health before she was allowed to resign her position at Court. At the age of forty-one Fanny then married a penniless French *émigré* officer, fifteen years her senior, the Chevalier d'Arblay, bore him a son and was very happy. None of Fanny's later writings enjoyed the same acclaim as her early efforts, though a novel called *The Wanderer* is said to have netted her seven thousand pounds, an immense sum set against her measly Court pension of a hundred pounds a year. Considering the range of Fanny Burney's experience, her health, leisure, long life and zest for writing, the wonder is that she did not become a rival to Jane Austen. Perhaps the deference she paid to her elders—her father, Dr. Johnson, her husband—made her over-cautious compared with the spirited spinster from Hampshire.

Apart from an insider's description of the stifling routines of "the Royals", as Fanny usually called them, her diary illuminates that life of the upper and more intellectual levels of London society in her day. At the age of eighteen she attended the lavish opening of Carlisle House, Soho Square, where the Viennese adventuress who called herself Mrs. Cornelys launched a subscription assembly offering dancing, cards, concerts and masquerades. The then impressionable Fanny wrote breathlessly that "the magnificence of the rooms, splendour of the illuminations and embellishments and the brilliant appearance of the company exceeded anything I ever before saw." The venture, indeed, proved a triumph, until the shady Mrs. C. went bust and ended up in prison. Nothing that Fanny wrote, however, is more riveting than her calm recollection of her twenty-minute ordeal as her cancerous breast was removed without anaesthetic—a stark reminder that in the past not even the privileged could be protected from pain.

Benjamin Haydon (1786-1846)

The diary produced by Benjamin Haydon was his greatest work of art. Unfortunately what he wanted to produce was great paintings, treating momentous subjects on monumental canvases. An acquaintance warned him against working on a large scale because it simply made his artistic shortcomings even more obvious. Haydon's journal, kept from 1821 until his suicide, reveals a hard-working and intelligent but conceited and disaster-prone egotist. He could, however, be very funny, as when recording the torrent of mishaps attending the christening of William Hazlitt's child or the occasion when the awesome Mrs. Siddons declaimed *Macbeth* to a drawing-room audience too intimidated to relish their tea and toast for fear of making any noise, with the society portrait painter Sir Thomas Lawrence being forced "to bite by degrees and then stop for fear of making too much crackle."

Hazlitt said Haydon was the best talker he ever knew. Haydon's other friends included Wordsworth, Lamb, Leigh Hunt and, especially, John Keats. Haydon was fated to enjoy just enough success to keep him going. In 1820 he hired the Egyptian Hall on Piccadilly to exhibit his *Christ's Entry into Jerusalem* and made a handsome profit from the admission charges. George IV bought his *Mock Election*, a satirical genre piece depicting the debtors in a Southwark gaol amusing themselves by re-enacting the absurdities so often attendant on the selection of a Member of Parliament. But fortune proved fleeting as few of Haydon's gigantic efforts attracted buyers: "My *Judgment of Solomon* is rolled up in a warehouse in the Borough! My *Entry into Jerusalem*... is doubled up in a back room in Holborn. My *Lazarus* is in an upholsterer's shop in Mount Street! and my *Crucifixion* is in a hay-loft in Lisson Grove!" In 1846 Haydon shot himself at 4 (now 12) Burwood Place, off the Edgware Road, leaving a wife and six children. A blue plaque marks his former studio at 116 Lisson Grove.

DULWICH

Many parts of London like to claim a "village" character. In Dulwich the claim feels plausible, thanks to its abundant greenery and Georgian mansions, a half-timbered pub and a village hall, almshouses and weather-boarded cottages and a smattering of shops set back from the road. A fashionable spa in the eighteenth century, Dulwich as late as

Dulwich College

1871 still had only seven hundred houses. Now a comfortable commuter suburb for the comfortably off, it also attracts the visitor thanks to its top-flight picture-gallery, the first one in Britain to be purpose-built. The designer, Sir John Soane (see p. 221), played his usual tricks to combine concealed top-lighting with a forbiddingly blank exterior. The bulk of the gallery's Old Master collection was originally gathered (1790-95) for the king of Poland but the extinction of his country decreed a different destiny. Dickens has Mr. Pickwick retire to Dulwich, where examining the paintings in the picture gallery is part of his regular routine.

A bus-ride away at Forest Hill is the Horniman Museum, the eponymous bequest of a tea tycoon. Housed in a striking Art Nouveau confection by Charles Harrison Townsend, the museum has major collections of musical instruments, natural history and ethnographic artefacts, including Britain's first permanent display of African art.

Dating from 1619, Dulwich College was the creation of Shakespeare's contemporary rival Edward Alleyn (pronounced Allen), arguably the greatest actor of his times, who transcended a socially and financially perilous profession to retire rich and respectable. The main buildings, an eclectic but eye-grabbing exercise in structural polychromy (according to their designer, "North Italian Architecture of the Thirteenth Century") are the work of Charles Barry the Younger, son of the architect of the Houses of Parliament. The main hall, the first in a public school built as a hall rather than a classroom, provided the setting for Reese Witherspoon's graduation from "Harvard Law School" in *Legally Blonde*. Distinguished OAs (Old Alleynians) range from Shackleton to Voysey, P. G. Wodehouse to Bob Monkhouse, C. S. Forester to Raymond Chandler.

Dulwich was originally part of the parish of Camberwell, whose size and antiquity is hinted at in the glorious Gothic of Sir George Gilbert Scott's 1844 rebuilding of the parish church. Camberwell and neighbouring Peckham were once noted for their horticulture. The (now extinct) "Camberwell Beauty" butterfly was discovered here in 1748 and a century later Mendelssohn initially entitled his *Spring Song* as *Camberwell Green*. In 1809 the area was described as "a pleasant retreat of those citizens who have taste for the country whilst their avocations daily call them to town." Rural until the advent of the railway, Camberwell was the childhood idyll of the art critic and sage John Ruskin. The mid-Victorian mansions of Camberwell Grove and Denmark Hill still testify to the area's standing as a redoubt of bourgeois respectability, the birthplace of Robert Browning and Joseph Chamberlain.

Chapter Three
LONDON NAMED

"I cannot think why people should think the names of places in the country more poetical than those in London. Shallow romanticists... stop in places called Hugmy-on-the-Hole or Bumps-on-the-Puddle. And all the time they could, if they liked, go and live at a place with the dim, divine name of St. John's Wood. I have never been to St. John's Wood. I dare not."
G. K. Chesterton, *The Napoleon of Notting Hill*, 1904

The Blackfriat at Blackfriars

Names offer pathways into the past, sometimes straightforward but often deceptive. Corruptions abound. Bunhill Fields, the "Dissenters' Valhalla", where Bunyan, Defoe and Blake lie within yards of each other, was originally Bonehill Fields. Aldgate was the ale gate—perhaps from an adjacent hostelry for travellers. Leather Lane had nothing to do with hides or shoes or cobblers but recalls Leofrun, a woman who once owned land there. Mark Lane commemorates not a Mark but a Martha. Foster Lane is a mangled version of Vedast, an obscure sixth-century French saint to whom the church at its southern end is dedicated. Fetter Lane is a corruption of a medieval word for a vagrant, beggar or layabout (*faitour*). Cannon Street was inhabited by makers of candles, not ordnance. Tooley Street sounds as though it commemorates an Irishman but actually refers to Olaf, the martyred king and patron saint of Norway, who was responsible for pulling down London Bridge in 1014, thus saving the capital from a besieging army of Danes. In the *Heimskringla*, a chronicle of the kings of Norway, compiled ca.1225, by the Icelandic poet Snorri Sturluson, the author quotes the lay of a Norse poet, Ottar Svarte, exultantly hymning this feat: "London Bridge is fallen down, Gold is won and bright renown"—and somehow this resurfaced in the mid-seventeenth century as a children's rhyme.

Some "corruptions" are in fact euphemisms. Cloak Lane, south of Cannon Street, refers to *cloaca*—lavatories. Passing Alley, Clerkenwell, was once a favoured place for urination. Sherborne Lane, near Bank, was once Shitbourn Lane. King Edward Street was renamed for Edward VI, who founded Christ's Hospital School, which originally stood nearby. It was formerly Stinking Lane, presumably because it was next to the "shambles" where butchers slaughtered and gutted livestock bought at Smithfield nearby. Smithfield itself was originally "the smooth field", and being just outside the City walls, served as a convenient location for medieval London's weekly horse fair.

Even apparently obvious names can be misleading. Liverpool Street is named, not for the city, but for the reactionary Lord Liverpool, who was Prime Minster (1812-27) when the street was laid out. In the context of London's history anything called "New" probably isn't, although the London Borough of Newham, a 1965 merger of West and East Ham and Woolwich, is an exception. Newington, as in Stoke Newington, is recorded as Neuton ca. 1200. The New River, which brought fresh water forty miles from Hertfordshire to Islington, was engineered between 1609 and 1613. New Square in Lincoln's Inn was built in 1697. New Bond Street dates from 1732.

Unlike many Continental cities London is not given to naming streets or squares after significant historic dates—which at least means that the names do not have to be changed when they become politically embarrassing. Names do get changed, of course, but often for fairly prosaic reasons. Given that the London region had had no central government for most of its history it is scarcely surprising that much duplication of street names should have arisen, often leading to delay, annoyance and loss of business from misdirection of both people and postal items. In the 1930s the Post Office urged a general drive to eliminate such duplications so that at the least there should be only one Church Street, Queen Street etc. in each postal district. In many instances this was achieved by minor modifications of existing names, the connotations of which were, perhaps, not always considered. Changing Broad Street, Soho, to Broadwick Street mattered little. Prince Street, leading out of Red Lion Square, became Princeton Street, without any connection with the university. North Street, leading out of Smith Square, was elevated to Lord North Street, thus honouring the politician who presided over the loss of the American colonies. And exotically named Puma Court, off Commercial Street, must surely once have been simply Pump Court.

The Lie of the Land
It probably comes as no surprise to learn that Poplar and Plumstead take their names from the particular trees which once grew profusely around those places. Acton (oak) is less obvious, as are Bexley (box) and Purley (pears). Less easy still perhaps to guess that Carshalton takes its name from cress, Banstead from beans, Dulwich from dill, Ruislip from rushes and Croydon from saffron (*croh* in Anglo-Saxon). Bromley, like Brompton, took its name from the broom plant but at Bromley-by-Bow it was brambles that were rampant. Harrow has nothing to do with the agricultural implement but means "a heathen shrine". Limehouse took its name not from the tree (or a house) but from the hursts or kilns which, from at least the fourteenth century, burned lime there to supply the capital's building trade.

Through surviving names London's lost landscape can be conjured—as in the colour of the earth itself (Blackheath, Blackwall, Ratcliff = red cliff), the clearing of the land by fire (Barnet), even the wildlife—cranes at Cranford, kites at Kidbrook. Prominent stones are remembered in Keston and Stanmore. The suffix -ey (from *eg*) may denote high(er) ground as in Bermondsey, Battersea and Hackney or enclosure (*haeg*) as in Haringey. Waterways were important both as channels of communication and boundary markers. Holborn is named after a valley stream (*burna*), and there were other streams at Kilburn and Marylebone. Wells are indicated at Chigwell, Stockwell, Stanwell and Ewell, a spring at Bedfont, a weir at Edgware and ditches at Shoreditch and Thames Ditton. Fords are often differentiated, as in Old Ford, Greenford, Woodford, Deptford (deep), Chingford (shingly) or Romford (roomy). Stratford is deceptive; not straight but "straet", i.e. paved, usually meaning a Roman road. Chislehurst and Chiswell Street both denote gravel, flint or pebbles (*cisel*) but Chiswick derives from cheese (*ciese*). Landing places or *hithes* could also be distinguished by some particular activity: Lambeth for lambs, Rotherhithe for cattle (*hrither*), Chelsea for chalk.

Land use is sometimes implied. Osterley was a grazing ground for sheep (*eowestre*). A grove, meadow or lea—prime grazing—was found at Finchley and Wembley. Covent Garden was the convent garden which grew vegetables for Westminster Abbey. Plaistow—variously pronounced "plastow" and "plarstow"—should by rights, or at least origin, be "playstow", a place for playing or sports. There are streets named for bowling greens in Clerkenwell and Shoreditch. Butts indicates a practice ground for archery. Enfield's importance as a hunting-ground explains the nine local name references to "chase", just as "hatch" refers to a gate which gave access to an enclosed hunting park.

The Arrival of the English

Anglo-Saxons settled around deserted Londinium from the fifth century onwards but were wary of its mournful ruins and established their farmsteads well clear of it. Anglo-Saxon settlement is indicated by the place-name particles -ton (estate, home farm) and -ing (from *ingas*, people or followers of) as in Islington or Ealing. The "ham" usually means village or settlement as in Hampstead, Mitcham, Peckham or Lewisham but may be amended from -hamm, meaning land in a river bend as in Hampton, Fulham, Twickenham, West Ham and, possibly, Balham, Cheam and Epsom. Many such names contain a patronymic element in honour of their founding father, real or supposed, as in Barking (*Berecca*), Dagenham (*Dacca*), Wapping (*Waeppa*), Stepney

(*Stibba*), Havering (*Haefer*) and, less obviously, Brixton (*Brihtsig*) and Beckenham (*Biohha*). Charlton began as a community of free peasants—*ceorls* or churls.

London's long-demolished fortifications are recalled in London Wall, in the name of its first suburb, Southwark (the south *werke* to defend the bridge approach), in the Old Bailey (an outer palisaded courtyard), the Barbican (a small heavily defended gate in a wall) and in many names incorporating the particle -bury (*burh* = stronghold, fortified manor) as in Aldermanbury, Lothbury and Bucklersbury within the circuit of the City walls, Borough Road at Southwark and outlying Highbury, Sudbury and Sunbury.

The World of Work
The commercial life of medieval London centred on Cheapside and Eastcheap, market thoroughfares which derive their names from the Anglo-Saxon word for trading, *ceopen*, which ultimately evolved into "shopping". Specialized centres of dealing are indicated in the names of Milk Street, Bread Street, Wood Street, Poultry, Chick Lane, Ironmonger Lane and Friday Street—where fish was bought for the meat-less days decreed by the church calendar. As a name Vintry, the wine-dealing district where Chaucer, the son of a wine-merchant, was born, has passed out of general use, although Vintner's Place and the hall of the Vintners' Company still stand there. The name of the local parish church, St. Michael Paternoster Royale, refers not to a connection with the monarchy but with La Réole, a wine-shipping location for the trade out of Bordeaux. Lombard Street, Jewry Street, Old Jewry and Petty France mark locations formerly inhabited by economically important minorities.

Craft locations are also recalled, though many take a little linguistic detective work to uncover. Billiters were bell-founders (*belleyeteres*), hence Billiter Lane. Thames Street was once Roper Street, where marine cables were made. Pudding, as in Pudding Lane, is from the French *boudin*, a sausage made of animal guts—otherwise known as "umbles" (as in "eating humble pie" and "shambles" for a butchery). The Ward of Cordwainer is named for workers of the soft leather of Córdoba, making ladies' shoes, as distinguished from down-market leatherworkers, cobbling for common clodhoppers. Fine footwear would be protected from mud and sharp stones by the light clogs or pattens which could be bought around the church of St. Margaret Pattens. Outside the City walls lengths of woven cloth were stretched on tenter frames (hence "on tenterhooks") to dry out after dyeing— hence Tenter Ground in Spitalfields.

The early modern history of Soho as an industrial location is remembered in Brewer Street and Glasshouse Street. Bricks were being made in Brick Lane, Spitalfields, by the fifteenth century and doubtless around a dozen other London locations named for bricks or brickfields. Bermondsey, historic centre of the leather trade, has the expected Tanner Street and Leathermarket Street but also Lamb Walk and Morocco Street. The brewing industry of Southwark has left Porter Street in honour of the strong, dark ale drunk by London's market porters to "put the sweat back in". Thrale Street is in memory of Henry Thrale, long-time friend of Dr. Johnson, whose efforts to join the big league brewers producing 100,000 barrels a year twice drove him to a nervous breakdown.

The Shadow of the Cross

The omnipresence of the church in medieval London is still evident, especially in the City. Bishopsgate commemorates St. Erkenwald, whom tradition credits with rebuilding a gate, known in Domesday as *Portam Episcopi*. Blackfriars was where the learned black-robed Dominicans were once domiciled. Whitefriars Street is for the Carmelites; Austin Friars (since the sixteenth century London's Dutch church) is a contraction of Augustinian Friars. Christchurch, Greyfriars, took its name from the grey habits of the Franciscans. Crutched Friars, now a street near Tower Hill, took its name from the *Fratres Cruciferi* who carried a cross-shaped staff and wore a cross on their robes and followed the rule of St. Augustine. Holywell Lane and Row are self-explanatory (but, ironically, became synonymous with the printing of pornography in the nineteenth century). The name of the Minories recalls nuns, Minoresses, as, more obscurely, does Mincing Lane (*mynecenu* = nuns). Paternoster Row was where the makers of rosaries congregated.

St. Giles was the patron saint of outcasts, so the lazar house dedicated in his name at St. Giles-in-the-Fields was self-evidently placed well clear of the city when it was founded in 1101. The medieval hospital known in abbreviated form as St. Mary Spital is commemorated in the name of Spitalfields. The City street known as St. Mary Axe commemorates a church whose most celebrated relic was the axe which was claimed to have killed St. Ursula. This legendary English saint was supposed to have been murdered in the fourth century by Huns in the Rhineland, along with eleven other virgins, except that some medieval scribal error put the number of collateral victims at eleven thousand.

Religious houses owned about a third of medieval London and themselves mostly occupied an arc sweeping around the city walls, away from the cramped, noisy, dirty riverside so that they could have room for cloisters, gardens and orchards. Almost all of what is now Tower Hamlets belonged at the Conquest to the Bishop of London and became largely sub-let to ecclesiastical tenants. Canonbury was a rural estate granted to the canons of St. Bartholomew the Great in 1253. All the major monastic houses held manorial estates in the countryside around the capital, drawing actual produce from some and contenting themselves with rents and labour services from others. Hence in what are now London suburbs the frequent occurrence of road names incorporating the words "Abbey/Abbot" (seventy plus), "Priory/prior" (sixty plus), "Bishop" (thirty plus) or "Friar/Friary" (twenty plus). Many of the seventy-plus suburban street names incorporating the word "grange" may denote a former outlying farm worked by "lay brothers". The thirty-plus "glebe" references denote lands assigned to a local parish priest for his maintenance. Many of these simply passed into Anglican control at the Reformation, a transition marked by the thirty or more each of "Rectory" or "Vicarage" roads.

The passions and persecution associated with the bloody transition to Protestantism are palely chronicled in the names of the persecuting Bishop of London, Bonner (three) and the "Oxford Martyrs" (who were all Cambridge men), Ridley (eight), Latimer (nine) and Cranmer (fourteen). There is only one road named for William Tyndale, who single-handedly produced the first English translation of the New Testament, but there are five for Miles Coverdale, whose version was the first officially adopted. The Jesuit Edmund Campion (seven) is also remembered but not the Blessed Oliver Plunkett. Of subsequent religious figures Wesley has merited seven references and the Victorian Baptist preacher Charles Hadding Spurgeon three.

Landlords and Builders

The expansion of London beyond its ancient walls is charted in the street-names of landowners and developers. The St. James' area was parcelled out among Charles II's friends, notably Henry Jermyn (hence Jermyn Street), Earl of St. Alban's, and Sir Thomas Bond (Bond Street), a much-favoured financier who funded the development of the Albemarle Street area. This was named for the Duke of Albemarle, who had snapped up the great palace and grounds formerly owned by the king's disgraced minister, Edward Hyde, Earl of Clarendon. Jermyn was also a partner in this enterprise, and Dover Street honours one of his secondary titles, Baron Dover.

Charles II's ebullient love life is indirectly recalled in the name of Fitzroy (i.e. *fils du roi*—"son of the king") Square, Henry Fitzroy being his son by his mistress, Barbara Villiers, Duchess of Cleveland, hence nearby Cleveland Street. Henry was married off (at nine) to the five-year-old daughter of Lord Arlington, who inherited her father's estate at Euston in Suffolk as well as the manor of Tottenham Court, i.e. the area around the present Fitzroy Square. Henry was in due course created Earl of Euston and Duke of Grafton. Their son, Charles, the second Duke, in 1756 built what is now the Euston Road (then the New Road) as London's first by-pass to enable cattle to be driven round to Smithfield without having to pass along Oxford Street to the offence of the residents of the rapidly developing and fashionable districts of Mayfair and Marylebone on either side. The second Duke's grandson commissioned Robert Adam to develop Fitzroy Square in the 1790s.

Bloomsbury is named for the Blemund family who held a farm there for some decades in the thirteenth century. Its development was initiated by the fourth Earl of Southampton (hence Southampton Row) who laid out Southampton (now Bloomsbury) Square, not the first London square as such (that was Covent Garden) but the first to be called a square. The diarist John Evelyn was impressed when he dined at Southampton House, which then filled the north side of the square, in 1665, calling it "a noble square or Piazza—a little Towne". A marriage, an alleged treason and reinstatement into royal favour led to the area passing into the possession of the Russell family, whose name and titles (Duke of Bedford, Marquis of Tavistock) are plentifully recorded hereabouts, as is the name of their Bedfordshire estate (Woburn) and of the family they married with (Gower). In a similar way the Belgravia area, developed by the Dukes of Westminster, is bestrewn with their family name, Grosvenor, title (Belgrave) and given names (Gerald, Lupus), estates (Eccleston) and the name of their rural base, Eaton Hall in Cheshire.

Landholders were also corporate as well as aristocratic. Eton College built a small estate bearing its name in St. John's Wood. The name of Oppidans Road is taken from the school slang for Eton boys who boarded in the town rather than in the school itself ("collegers"). Provost Road recalls the title of what in other less exalted establishments would be called the headmaster. There are also a dozen other roads in the capital named for the school which has produced half of all Britain's prime ministers. Not far away along Maida Vale was land belonging to Harrow School, founded by John Lyon, hence Lyons Place. Other estates were owned by Christ Church and Jesus College, Oxford, and St. John's College, Cambridge.

The ubiquitous, not to say iniquitous, property speculator, Nicholas Barbon (?1640-98), who practised a highly risky (usually to others) form of pyramid financing in the post-Fire period is commemorated only in the name of Barbon Close, a dingy cobbled alley off Great Ormond Street. Ironically Nos. 55-57 in that street, which were probably built by Barbon, for a while served as the headquarters of the Society for the Protection of Ancient Buildings. (If they had all been built to Barbon's usual slapdash standards there would not be any.) Barbon's other developments included Bedford Row, Devonshire Square, Essex Street, Gerrard Street and New Court in Middle Temple. The persuasive Barbon also knew when to humour his clients as well as bamboozle them. Having bought York House off the Strand from George Villiers, Duke of Buckingham, he agreed that the former owner should be remembered in the naming of the streets to be built after its demolition—hence Villiers Street, Buckingham Street, Duke Street and George Street. There was even an Of Alley, later renamed York Place.

Most developers operated on a less megalomaniac scale than Barbon but often had equally bad luck. Richard Frith built Frith Street in Soho and, on the south side of Soho Square, into which it leads, put up a handsome mansion for Charles II's eldest bastard son James, Duke of Monmouth. Monmouth's abortive attempt to seize the throne on his father's death led to his execution—and bankruptcy for the unpaid

Frith. Meard Street, also in Soho, was built by a carpenter of that name but cautiously, in two stages. Baker Street, laid out from 1755 onwards, is one of the few major thoroughfares to take its name from a speculator.

Suburban Sprawl

The massive expansion of London's suburbs following the advent of railways and tramways created the need for literally thousands of new names for streets of often identical houses. The relatively up-market south London suburb of Camberwell, built up from the 1840s, is an example of the sort of marketing "spin" implied in naming practice. Much use was made of the word "Grove" to imply (often truthfully, it must be admitted) lush, leafy, sylvan surroundings. Off long, straight Camberwell Grove run Grovelands Close, Grove Crescent, Grove Park and Champion Grove before it abuts into Grove Hill Road. Parallel Grove Lane, a major traffic thoroughfare, becomes Dog Kennel Lane, but the connotations of the kennel are lifted far above the domestic mutt by naming two side roads Quorn and Pytcherly after two of the most celebrated and exclusive packs of hounds, fox-hunting being in the heyday of its fashion when those roads were being built up. Dog Kennel Hill becomes Grove Vale, from which one can pass through Melbourne Grove, named for Queen Victoria's first Prime Minster, to reach East Dulwich Grove. Figures of local eminence are invoked in De Crespigny (pronounced Crepny) Park, for a French-descended family of knightly status, Lettsom Road, for the eminent Quaker physician and botanist John Coakley Lettsom and Datchelor Place for the founder of a local grammar school.

What one might call the "Grove Syndrome" led to the profuse invocation of road names incorporating words with rural, healthful connotations—garden, glade, green, lake, mead, meadow, mill, wood, etc. Specific national beauty spots, familiar either through the new railway-borne tourist industry or by repute through poetry, were adopted for their lustre, as the index of the *London Street-Finder* reveals: Tintern (eight), Buxton (sixteen), Malvern (twenty-five). The Lake District was especially drawn upon: Thirlmere (six), Penrith (seven) Keswick (ten), Kendal (twelve), Windermere and Grasmere (fifteen each) and Coniston (twenty). Of foreign resorts the spa of Montpellier (twenty) was much favoured. The heritage ploy called on Merlin (ten),

Britannia (eleven), Robin Hood (eleven), Sherwood (twenty-two) and Albion (twenty-nine).

The safest cultural reference was, of course, to royalty; the fifty-three roads named for Albert were exceeded among contemporary royals only by seventy-three for Victoria. The hugely popular Princess Alexandra ran close with fifty and surely accounted for the fact that the capital also has twenty-one streets named for her native Denmark but only two for Norway and one for Sweden. Royal residences were likewise invoked: Osborne (twenty-two), Sandringham (eighteen) and Balmoral (fifteen), as well as the Highland Games patronized by the royal family at Braemar (fourteen). If a royal connection is too unoriginal, why not an aristocratic one? The Cavendish family certainly owned a chunk of what became Marylebone, but that can scarcely account for most of the thirty-five Cavendish location names or the twenty-two taken from their residence at Chatsworth, or the forty-five from their title, Devonshire.

The names of other fashionable places of residence were also shamelessly purloined. Cheyne Walk in Chelsea, home variously to George Eliot, Rossetti, Turner, Whistler, etc., was appropriated for the lead up to the shopping parade and station at Hendon Central, a recreation ground in Croydon and a golf course at the appropriately named World's End, Enfield.

In Memoriam

Naming places after figures of historic or cultural significance is common practice throughout the Western world. Attributions are not necessarily self-evident. Poland Street, Soho, for example, was named, not for the country, but for its heroic king, who led the relief force which raised the Ottoman siege of Vienna in 1683 (one supposes Sobieski Street was thought too difficult to pronounce). Few have now heard of the eighteenth-century Admiral Keppel but he has four streets named for him. Keppel was of Dutch origin. Dagmar, who sounds like a Viking, was in fact a Danish princess, the sister of Queen Alexandra, and has ten streets named for her.

The name of the rambunctious mid-Victorian Prime Minister Palmerston is perpetuated in sixteen streets, only one less than Gladstone. Gladstone's sparring-partner, Disraeli, merits only five—until one remembers that he became Earl of Beaconsfield, which clocks up another two dozen more, plus a further three for his country residence at Hughenden, Bucks.

With the expected exception of Churchill (14 and another 7 Winstons), modern politicians do poorly. There are no roads named for Asquith or Lloyd George. Perhaps the amount of public housing put up by Labour-controlled councils explains why there are three for Attlee, one each for Snowden, Bevin and Gaitskell and five for the much-loved George Lansbury and the same for Aneurin Bevan, creator of the National Health Service. Herbert Morrison never enjoyed much public affection but his virtual dictatorship of inter-war London politics is fittingly marked in the names of three roads. Dagenham and its neighbour Barking, both Labour-controlled for decades, have been particularly punctilious in offsetting the general neglect to which historic left-wing figures have been subjected, naming roads for the leaders of the successful strikes of the dockers and gas-workers which launched the militant "New Unionism" of the 1880s—Ben Tillett, Tom Mann and John Burns. Dagenham is also unusual in similarly honouring Edison and Roosevelt, perhaps an indirect tribute to the massive American-owned Ford factory which was the major employer there for three-quarters of a century. On the Isle of Dogs is a Dockers' Tanner Road to remind posterity of the hourly wage that was at stake, a "tanner" being cockney slang for six pre-decimal pence. For some reason Will Crooks Gardens is in Kidbrooke, south of the river, and not at all near his Poplar stamping-ground. Annie Besant, who organized the match-girls' strike which started the wave of unskilled labour militancy, is appropriately memorialized in the name of a Close just north of the former Bryant and May match factory in Bow. The Close runs off Parnell Road, named for the Irish Nationalist Charles Parnell whose career was destroyed when his extra-marital affair with a Kitty O'Shea became public; Parnell Road now terminates in O'Shea Grove.

Keir Hardie, the first Labour MP, and George Lansbury's wife, Bessie, have also been belatedly remembered, as have pioneer socialist thinker Robert Owen and the "Tolpuddle Martyrs" who were transported for seven years to Australia for attempting to form a union. Although there is an Owenite Street nothing recalls the numerically far greater Chartist movement. Charlotte Despard the (constitutional) suffragist has two streets named for her but there are none for any of the (militant) suffragette Pankhursts.

An emerging contemporary trend, parallel to recognizing the unjustly disregarded figures of the past, is honouring—perhaps in reaction to the perceived shortcomings of the official honours system— local people who have given long and loyal service to their communities but are scarcely known outside them. Bermondsey set the precedent a century ago by naming a street and erecting a statue to Samuel Bevington, first mayor of that borough, colonel of its local Volunteers and a great man in the leather trade. Dedications are nowadays usually attached to short residential streets, often a "Close" or a "Way", rather than a major thoroughfare. The full name is invariably used to avoid any ambiguity about the identity of the person for whom the recognition is intended. Hence John Parker Close in Dagenham acknowledges the MP who served that constituency for decades. Presumably something similar applies to Bill Hamling and Bob Anker, Freda Corbett, Dorothy Evans, Frank Dixon, James Dudson, etc.,

Associated names often occur in clusters. One of the "purest" examples is at Burnt Oak where (cricket) Pavilion Way gives onto a series of Closes named for the legendary batsmen (W. G.) Grace, (Don) Bradman and (Len) Hutton and more recent heroes suave Denis Compton, "fiery" (Fred) Trueman, calculating (Mike) Brearley, the flamboyant "Beefy" (Ian) Botham and battling (Mike) Gatting. On the other side of Burnt Oak Broadway the names of a dozen painters, from Rembrandt to Whistler, are mixed in with nods to aviation history (De Havilland Road, Mollison Way) and some very assorted educational institutions—Eton, Rugby, Sherborne, Winchester, Girton and Sandhurst.

The bloody Battle of Barnet, fought a few miles away to the north-east, in which the Yorkists defeated the Lancastrians in a blinding snow-storm in 1471, is remembered in the sedate streets of the Victorian suburb of New Barnet, some distance from the actual site of the fighting. Here there are roads for King Edward (IV), the youthful victor, the defeated Warwick ("the Kingmaker"), the ambitious Woodville family, the *fainéant* Plantagenet dynasty and the title of the victor (Richmond) and the battle (Bosworth) which would determine the ultimate outcome of the "Wars of the Roses". To confirm the Victorian authenticity of the suburb, however, these references are interwoven with the names of contemporary worthies: the social reformer Lord Shaftesbury, the novelist Bulwer Lytton and the uncrowned king of British-administered Egypt, Lord Cromer.

Echoes of Empire

Imperial pro-consuls like Cromer made much more impact on contemporaries than they have on posterity. Cromer has nine more roads named after him (though they might be for the pleasant and briefly popular Norfolk seaside resort from which he took his title), five further ones in his original name of Baring and perhaps some of the nineteen Evelyns (his first name) as well. Milner of South Africa scores ten and Curzon, Viceroy of India, nine. Outram and Frere, whose weapon-bedecked statues stand uncomprehended side-by-side in Embankment Gardens, rate four and one respectively. Colonial statesmen fare worse. Only one for Cecil Rhodes—a post-imperial embarrassment, perhaps, but the Scholarships might have counted for more. Strangely, considering that both men served in the British Cabinet in both world wars, there are none for either of the outstanding colonial leaders Jan Smuts of South Africa (although there is one for Louis Botha) or Max Beaverbrook of Canada (although there are two for Sir Wilfred Laurier).

The imperial theme is picked up, perhaps a trifle surprisingly, in the names selected for the Canary Wharf complex which was developed as the epicentre of the Docklands revival in the 1980s. Canary Wharf itself is a reference to where bananas were once unloaded from the Canary Islands. The central feature, Canada Tower, takes its name from the adoptive country of the Reichmann brothers, who were the project's main developers. Columbia may be a nod to American banking support. John Cabot was the explorer who claimed Newfoundland for the English throne. Jacques Cartier paved the way for the French settlement of Canada. Frobisher, Chancellor and (William) Adams were also explorers who departed from this stretch of the Thames. Wren and Cubitt were both great builders of London, the latter responsible for Cubittt Town a little to the south. The names of Trafalgar and Churchill add a note of victory against the odds. The Reichmanns still went bust over the project.

Imprint of History

The site of Henry VIII's vainglorious but short-lived Nonsuch Palace, built rapidly and extravagantly at Cheam in a florid Renaissance style so that there should be "none such" like it, is now covered by a park around which are Tudor Avenue, Kingsway Road, Anne Boleyn's Walk, Aragon, Cleves and Seymour Avenues, recalling three more of his wives, and Arundel and Castlemaine Avenues for the courtiers to whom the dilapidated structure subsequently passed. Five of Henry's queens lie similarly disposed around West Ham United "Boleyn" football ground at Upton Park, where the monarch's discarded first wife is doubly complimented in (mis-spelled) Arragon Road and Katherine (locally pronounced Kath-er-ine) Road. Catherine Howard is omitted but the luckless Lady Rochford, who fell to the axe for her alleged role in her adultery, is remembered. Nearby, but on the other side of Barking Road, there are a dozen parallel streets which all appear to have been built rapidly at around the same time and whose names run in clusters. Henry, Navarre and St. Bartholomew constitute an unusual reference to the massacre of French Huguenots in 1572. Ladysmith, Kimberley and Mafeking refer to the three great sieges which dominated the first phase of the Boer War. Compton and Creighton were both bishops of London. Macaulay, Dickens and Thackeray, sandwiched between the battles and the bishops, bring us to the topic of literature.

Literature and Learning

Literary associations, if not constituting an actual cluster, are strong on the ground in Southwark, which has a Leigh Hunt Street and a Kipling estate. The departure point of Chaucer's Canterbury pilgrims yields Tabard Street, Becket Street, Pilgrimage Street and Manciple Street. Dickens as a teenager spent miserable months languishing in lodgings in Lant Street while his father was imprisoned in the Marshalsea prison for debt. Lant Street is still there and so is one long wall of the Marshalsea. The prison provides a major setting for *Little Dorrit*, memorialized locally in Little Dorrit Court. There is also a Quilp Street, a Weller Street and a Pickwick Street. Elsewhere in London there are five others named for Pickwick, plus Barkis, Micawber, Dr. Manette, Dombey, Nickleby, (Miss) Haversham (two), Taplow (two), Dingley (Dell) (three), Copperfield (six) and kindly (Mr.) Brownlow (seven). Other Victorian literary characters named in roads include (Daniel) Deronda and (Sherlock) Holmes (seven).

Overall, literature is better represented than art or science in street names. Perhaps surprisingly Milton (thirty-seven) far outstrips

Shakespeare (fifteen), although, of course, the poet's name does have the advantage of being much shorter to write. And while no one is ever likely to name a road after Milton's protagonists (Satan Street? Beelzebub Broadway ? Moloch Mews?) there are streets named after Shakespeare's creations: Othello, Portia, Prospero, Macbeth, Bardolph (two), Hamlet (six) and even two Elsinores, though nothing for Puck, Titania or Bottom as yet. Of other pre-Romantic writers Chaucer rates fourteen mentions, Marlowe six, Spenser three but Bunyan only one.

Despite the scandals associated with his love life (no barrier now perhaps, but it was when most roads were being named) Byron leads the nineteenth-century poets' pack (23), followed by Tennyson (18), Coleridge (13), Browning (12) and Wordsworth (11). Keats and Shelley tie (9). Private peccadilloes (drugs, flagellation) may have counted against Swinburne (2), as against Wilde (3). Novelists do less well: Dickens (9), Thackeray (6) and the now largely forgotten historical producer of potboilers (Harrison) Ainsworth (4). Mrs. Gaskell and Jane Austen each rate only two and the Brontës one between all of them. The actual name of Trollope (0) clearly counted against him in this context because there are three Barchesters to honour the fictional setting he created. This may also explain the absence of tributes to Poe (who was schooled in London) compared with Emerson (three, plus four for Waldo). On the other hand, potential embarrassment has not precluded the invocation in five instances of the name of the commander of the English fleet against the Armada—Effingham.

Perhaps surprisingly to modern eyes, the most revered nineteenth-century writer appears to have been the art critic and social theorist John Ruskin, with twenty-one roads named after him, plus eight for Brantwood, his retirement home in the Lake District. Thomas Carlyle ranks eleven. His countryman, Sir Walter Scott, is indirectly complimented by references to his novels *Waverley* (28), *Kenilworth* (13) and *Marmion* (4), his characters Ivanhoe (2) and Lochinvar, and his home, Abbotsford (3). Of twentieth-century writers John Galsworthy and John Masefield have each currently been remembered in the names of five roads.

Icons

Francis Chichester Way commemorates the first yachtsman to

circumnavigate the world non-stop and single-handed. Mary Peters *Drive* is well-named—much better than Street or Avenue—for the Ulster housewife pentathlete who won the Olympic gold in 1972 at the age of thirty-three. There is an equally appropriate (Tony) Jacklin *Green* near Woodford Golf Course. Other honoured sports personalities include boxer Henry Cooper, jockey Lester Piggott, cricketers (Alec) Bedser, (Ray) Illingworth (two) and (Tom) Graveney (two), runners Sir Roger Bannister, Derek Ibbotson, Steve Ovett and Gordon Pirie (two).

Changing values change heroes, both present and past. There are seven streets named at the time of writing for Nelson Mandela and others for (Walter) Sisulu, Steve Biko, Martin Luther King and even pioneer black nationalist Marcus Garvey and Haitian revolutionary Toussaint (L'Ouverture). Nurse Mary Seacole, voted Greatest Black Briton in 2004, at last has a Close named for her. And there is surely an expiatory purpose as well as an irony behind naming part of the former Woolwich Arsenal armaments complex Hiroshima Walk.

Puzzles, Jokes and Enigmas

Many other mysteries remain. Why is Richmond's Melancholy Walk so called? Was there a murder there? Or a suicide? Does the explanation lie in the path that intersects it—Cutthroat Alley? Why are there seven streets named for the long-abandoned festival of Lammas (tide) and none for Michaelmas, let alone Christmas or Easter? Is Pierrepoint Road named for Britain's last hangman? Fakruddin was the national hero of the Lebanon but what possible connection can he have had with Shoreditch? Who or what was Ethronvi to have an eponymous road in Bexhill? Why is there an Eighteenth Road and a Nineteenth Road in Mitcham but no Seventeenth or Twentieth? Why does London have fourteen First Avenues but only nine Second Avenues? Are some builders terminally optimistic? (That probably is the answer.) Why are all the roads numbered First through to Eighth always Avenues? Why is there an Effort Street in Tooting and why does it lead into Recovery Street? (Or should it be vice versa?) What were Belle Staines Pleasaunce and Taffy's How Mitch? And who thought up Uneeda Drive—and why?

HOTELS AND HOSPITALITY
An Accommodating Interlude

London was rather late in acquiring hotels. Anyone who was anyone had his own London house or stayed with friends who had one. The rest made do with inns. Dickens described Southwark's inns as "great, rambling, queer old places... with galleries and passages and staircases wide enough and antiquated enough to furnish material for a hundred ghost stories." The galleried George, rebuilt after the great Southwark fire of 1676, survives, though much truncated. Dickens really did drink there and mentions it in *Little Dorrit*. It was from the White Horse Cellars in Piccadilly that a coach service to the West Country was run by Moses Pickwick, whose name Dickens appropriated for the bumbling hero who made him famous.

By the eighteenth century "accommodations" began to appear, usually named after their proprietor and offering "all the retirement and comforts of home with the freedom of access, egress and ingress, which one generally expects". Along Jermyn Street, for example, there were Blake's, Reddish's, Miller's, Topham's and the St. James', where Sir Walter Scott stayed when he came to London to meet his fellow Scot and publisher, John Murray.

Brown's Hotel in Dover Street, established in 1837, is one of the few London establishments to survive from the pre-railway age. The first proprietors, as was often the case, had formerly been in service, in this case with Lord Byron, a testing employer if ever there was one. The hotel had prospered to expand from No. 23 into the adjoining Nos. 21, 22 and 24. Brown's was to be favoured by Cecil Rhodes, Rudyard Kipling and Mark Twain, who wrote jokingly of it as an elephant's graveyard for broken furniture. It was certainly grand enough for Teddy Roosevelt to stay there on the eve of his wedding at St. George's, Hanover Square, in 1886 and for his distant relative Franklin Delano Roosevelt to honeymoon there in 1905. In 1876 Alexander Graham Bell made the first ever telephone-call in Britain from Brown's to the then proprietor, Henry Ford, in the suburb of Ravenscourt Park, five miles away. In 1940 the Dutch government in exile met in Room 36 to declare war on Japan.

Claridge's in Brook Street, Mayfair, was started by a former butler. In 1855 he acquired the neighbouring Mivart's Hotel, which had been

St. Pancras Station Hotel

in business since 1812, letting apartments by the month rather than the night. By 1860 the discriminating *Baedeker* guidebook could describe the expanded establishment as "the first hotel in London", and in that year the Empress Eugenie of France made it her winter quarters. During the inter-war period many aristocratic families found it impossibly expensive to maintain a London house and staff and often took a suite at Claridge's instead for the duration of the London "Season". The American Office of Strategic Services, forerunner of the CIA, established its first headquarters in Claridge's during the Second World War. Visiting royalty and heads of state are normally accommodated at Claridge's when they wish to extend their stay in London beyond the formal period of their entertainment.

London's major railway termini were built by competing companies, each determined to outshine the rest in the splendour of its station and accompanying hotel. At Euston there were two hotels, both designed by Philip Hardwick. The Victoria, on one side of his majestic Ionic archway, was essentially just a dormitory, serving only breakfast, while the Euston offered full hotel service. Hardwick also designed the Great Western Hotel at Paddington. The Great Eastern Hotel at Liverpool Street offered guests the opportunity to bathe in fresh sea-water brought in daily by rail and the choice of two Masonic temples, one Greek in style, the other Egyptian. The fantastical Midland Grand Hotel at St. Pancras was the work of Sir George Gilbert Scott, allegedly recycling a discarded design for a new Foreign Office. The architect observed immodestly in his memoirs that "it is often spoken of to me as the finest building in London; my own belief is that it is possibly too good for its purpose." The *Dictionary of London,* edited by Charles Dickens Jr. in 1879, referred to it as a "gorgeous Gothic pile". The building certainly makes adroit use of an awkwardly-shaped site and the raised elevation required to accommodate the massive cellars under the station needed to store beer brewed in Burton-on-Trent and transported by rail for distribution to London's pubs. The journalist and *bon vivant* George Augustus Sala thought the Midland Grand the best-run hotel in Europe. After years of neglect since its conversion to use as offices in 1935 at the time of writing the St. Pancras station hotel is undergoing a multi-million pound restoration as part of the project to create a new Eurostar depot.

The Langham Hotel, opened in Portland Place in 1864, marked a new scale in hotel construction, having six hundred rooms over seven floors. It was thought to be a risky venture because it was not near any major railway station. The nearby Queen's Hall, however, made it a favourite with musicians like Toscanini and Dvorak. Romantic novelist Ouida (a.k.a. Maria Louise Ramé) lived at the Langham for several years, and two exiled emperors, Napoleon III of France and Haile Selassie of Ethiopia, also stayed there. Devastated in 1940 by a German landmine which smashed its roof-top water-tank, releasing a cascade of 38,000 gallons, the Langham was taken over by the BBC for offices for half a century until the Hilton hotel chain acquired and restored it as a London flagship.

By the 1870s Murray's *Handbook to London As It Is* asserted that the number of hotels in the capital was too great to be listed comprehensively and divided its own selection into distinct categories. Grand Hotels, "5 or 6 stories high, built in the fashion of those in America", could be found at railway termini. Family Hotels were "patronized by the English and foreign nobility and gentry who have no town residences of their own." Private Hotels were similar but quieter and cheaper. There were also hotels "frequented by bachelors and sportsmen", Commercial Hotels for business travellers and "hotels owned and patronized by foreigners". These latter were particularly to be found around Leicester Square. The Hotel de la Sablonnière occupied the former site of Hogarth's house. Manzi's fish restaurant in Lisle Street, just off Leicester Square, was once a German-owned hotel. The elder Johann Strauss stayed there and so did Karl Marx on fleeing from the failed revolution of 1848. Marx was thrown out after a fortnight for failing to pay his bill. He complained bitterly that his children had not even had their breakfast. The *Handbook* especially recommended "the well-conducted house of M. de Keyser" at Blackfriars, where "every guest must be introduced personally or by letter." De Keyser, a Belgian, had worked his way up from waiting on tables to owning a huge establishment spectacularly sited overlooking Blackfriars Bridge. Situated much nearer to the City than other hotels of comparable size, it catered especially for business travellers from the Continent. Residents were assured of Continental newspapers and drinkable coffee. The hotel also undertook the catering for Mayoral banquets at Guildhall. In 1887 the naturalized Polydore de Keyser became the first Roman Catholic since the Reformation to serve as Lord

Mayor of London. De Keyser's was taken over for the use of officers on leave during the Great War and then demolished to make way for the construction of Unilever House.

Bailey's Hotel at Gloucester Road was purpose-built in 1875-6 and prospered thanks to its convenience for visiting the nearby museums of South Kensington. The proprietor, James Bailey lived on the premises with his family and thirty-five live-in staff, thus ensuring by his omnipresence that the enterprise should "in all respects be conducted in the most respectable manner." For many Victorians the very word "hotel" had French connotations of loucheness. Bailey's was an immediate success, extended three times within a decade of its opening. In 1890 electricity was installed, along with an "American elevator". Americans, who generally held no high opinion of English hotels, constituted an important target market and Bailey's hit it. A contemporary guidebook reassured transatlantic travellers that they would find themselves in "rich and substantial surroundings", with the most up-to-date sanitation, stringent fire precautions, an excellent wine cellar and a "cosy, homelike atmosphere"—and all in "the healthiest and most fashionable part of London". Bailey's success made it a nucleus for more than a dozen imitators, along the Cromwell Road and in Harrington Gardens, though these were in converted houses and far smaller that Bailey's three hundred-room establishment.

Many of the capital's current establishments are in converted buildings. The Radisson Edwardian Hampshire on Leicester Square was formerly London's major dental hospital. The Lanesborough on Hyde Park Corner was converted in 1980 from the St. George's Hospital, designed in 1827 by William Wilkins, the architect of the National Gallery and University College. Its name revives that of Lanesborough House, a mansion of 1719, which was rented by the founders of the hospital in 1733.

Perhaps the most extraordinary conversion to hotel use is that of County Hall, the former headquarters of London's metropolitan government. Occupying one of the most prominent sites in the capital, at the southern end of Westminster Bridge and diagonally opposite the Houses of Parliament, it had taken from 1909 until 1933 to build as the home of the London County Council. County Hall was sold off at a knock-down price following Mrs. Thatcher's abolition of the successor Greater London Council in 1986. After a decade of piecemeal and hesitant initiatives it eventually metamorphosed to accommodate a complex of visitor attractions, apartments, eating-places and a Marriott hotel.

Opened in 1889, the Savoy Hotel was intended by impresario Richard D'Oyly Carte to bring to London the standards of excellence—and plumbing—that he had personally encountered in America. The then top-class Northumberland Hotel, opened on Northumberland Avenue a decade previously, had five hundred rooms—and four bathrooms. The Savoy had seventy. Manager Cesar Ritz developed a detailed data-base of individual guests' tastes and idiosyncrasies. Master-chef Auguste Escoffier created Peach Melba in honour of visiting Australian diva Dame Nellie Melba.

The Ritz-Escoffier partnership at the Savoy ended in an unseemly row over kick-backs from kitchen suppliers. Ritz departed to manage the Carlton Hotel at Haymarket, taking Escoffier with him. There he established the Palm Court as a must-have décor feature and pioneered the "theatre supper". Badly damaged in the Blitz, the Carlton was eventually to be demolished to make way for New Zealand House. A blue plaque reminds passers-by that Ho Chi Minh, founder of modern Vietnam, once worked there—in the kitchens. By the time the eponymous Ritz Hotel, built to his personal specifications, was opened in 1906, Ritz himself had suffered an irreversible nervous breakdown, precipitated by Edward VII's appendicitis and the consequent postponement of his coronation, for which Ritz had been commissioned to undertake the catering.

In its heyday the Cavendish Hotel in Jermyn Street was very much a reflection of its idiosyncratic proprietor Rosa Lewis. An East End girl with a gift for gastronomy, she became a celebrity chef and a great favourite of Edward VII, for whom she managed a house of assignation at 55 Eaton Terrace. In 1904 she acquired the century-old Cavendish, which she administered with equal discretion but signal firmness, never afraid to inform guests that they were staying in her house. During the Great War she had the Kaiser's portrait hung upside down in the servants' lavatory and allowed young officers on leave to stay free of charge. Evelyn Waugh caricatured Rosa with merciless accuracy as Lottie Crump in *Vile Bodies*, but even the "little swine" was eventually readmitted to her favour, lunched and kissed. Rosa continued to hold court until her death in 1952.

HAMPSTEAD

Hilltop Hampstead, with its intricate maze of winding streets, stepped lanes and tiny squares, would still be largely recognizable to John Constable, who both lived there and painted it often. Promoted successfully as a spa, Hampstead had already begun sprawling downhill by the time Defoe in the 1720s noted that "the uneven surface, inconvenient for building, uncompact and unpleasant... where there's no walking twenty yards together without tugging up a hill", had still failed to inhibit its hugger-mugger development.

The eight hundred acres of Hampstead Heath are where Mr. Pickwick came to examine pond life and Karl Marx brought his family at weekends to picnic. On Bank Holidays Victorian cockneys made a bee-line for 'Appy 'Ampstead and the Old Bull and Bush, immortalized in a music-hall song of 1903. A section of the Heath behind Terry Gilliam's house provided a backdrop for the filming of *Monty Python and the Holy Grail.*

Architecturally there is much of interest. The relevant volume of Pevsner's *Buildings of England* (*London 4: North*) devotes fifty pages to Hampstead. John Keats, Sigmund Freud and Erno Goldfinger all had homes here. Kenwood, the country seat of Lord Chief Justice Mansfield, superbly remodelled (1766-74) by Robert Adam, houses a fine collection of paintings and provides a majestic backdrop for summer concerts in its grounds. Admiral's House, once the home of that doyen of Gothic architecture, Sir George Gilbert Scott, has an eccentric rooftop quarterdeck which inspired P. L. Travers to make it Admiral Boom's home in *Mary Poppins.* Next door in Grove Lodge, Constable's former home, John Galsworthy, too ill to travel, received the Nobel Prize for Literature in 1932. Architecture enthusiasts will also wish to see Voysey's Annesley Lodge (1896) and Maxwell Fry's Sun House (1935).

Leigh Hunt, residing in the isolated Vale of Health, praised Hampstead as a "village revelling in varieties". One single road, Frognal, has been home to the architects Flitcroft and Blomfield, children's illustrator Kate Greenaway, poet Stephen Spender, soprano Kathleen Ferrier and ballerina Tamara Karsavina, plus Ramsay MacDonald and General Charles de Gaulle. In the churchyard of the parish church of St. John lie John Harrison, inventor of the marine chronometer, architect Richard Norman Shaw, Labour leader Hugh Gaitskell and a

Kenwood House, Hampstead

Set in secluded ground designed by Humphrey Repton, Kenwood is the finest eighteenth-century country house in north London. Originally built ca. 1616 and almost entirely rebuilt in 1694-1704, it was acquired in 1754 by the eminent Scottish jurist William Murray, Lord Chief Justice and first Earl of Mansfield, from a fellow Scot and former Prime Minister, the third Earl of Bute. In 1764 Mansfield commissioned two more Scots, the brothers Robert and James Adam, to carry out improvements, including the addition of a stunning library and a majestic entrance portico. The interior features painted panels by Antonio Zucchi and a picture collection with works by Van Dyck, Rembrandt, Reynolds, Gainsborough, Turner, Lawrence and Landseer. Entrance is free.

galaxy of theatrical talents, from Beerbohm Tree to Kay Kendall.

E. M. Forster aptly epitomized Hampstead as "thoughtful and artistic". In his day the thoughtful element included D. H. Lawrence, Aldous Huxley, J. B. Priestley and George Orwell and the artistic Ben Nicholson, Barbara Hepworth and Piet Mondrian. The Isokon Flats in Lawn Road, built in 1934 as a model of monastically minimalist modernism, were home to Walter Gropius, high priest of the Bauhaus, his disciple Marcel Breuer, who designed the plywood furniture, as well as sculptor Henry Moore and thriller writer Agatha Christie; meals could be ordered from Philip Harben, who became the first TV chef. Contemporary residents of Hampstead include cultural mogul Melvyn Bragg and Dame Judi Dench, while down the hill in Belsize Park live Bob Hoskins, Helena Bonham Carter, Kate Winslet and Sam Mendes.

Chapter Four
LONDON MAPPED

"... a good place for getting lost in, a city no one ever knew."
V. S. Naipaul, *An Area of Darkness*, 1964

Knowledge is Power

Maps are expressions of power—power of ownership, power to command information, power to manipulate its representation. In 1541 Henry VIII tried to suppress unauthorized refuges for wrongdoers and commissioned local authorities to map what they took to be legal sanctuaries. This may account for a surviving schematic sketch of Southwark, a district notorious for the lawlessness associated with its high concentration of taverns and brothels. Depicting Borough High Street and Bankside, the map highlights the pillory, the market facilities, churches, St. Thomas' Hospital and the Marshalsea and King's Bench prisons. The George is shown to gave been already in existence. The Tabard (labelled "the tabete") was already old, for Chaucer's pilgrims had used it as their rendezvous before departing for Canterbury a century and a half before. A plaque now marks its former site.

Continental Connections

The earliest known complete surviving overview of London as a whole was published by G. Braun and the engraver Frans Hogenberg in 1572 in their six-volume *Civitates Orbis Terrarum* (Cities of all the Lands of the World) and was probably based on a survey done about twenty years earlier. The eastern boundary of the city was marked by the foundation of St. Katherine immediately adjacent to the Tower. To the north Spitalfields still consisted of open fields with the exception of a gun-founders' establishment. "Ribbon development" in the form of housing backing onto gardens and meadows straggled out from Aldgate eastwards and from Bishopsgate to the north. Clerkenwell marked the extent of urbanization north of the still clearly defined city walls. Westward the Thames was lined by the town houses of the aristocracy but to their north St. Giles-in-the-Fields was still just that and Covent Garden was a meadow with large trees. The western edge of the map sliced through St. James' Park, where there were deer. There was only a solitary building south of the small river shown flowing into the Thames just opposite Lambeth Palace where the Palace of Westminster now stands. The Archbishop's residence stood in isolation amid Lambeth Marshes. South London consisted of little more than a riverside sprawl from Paris Gardens, a notorious pleasure-ground, opposite Blackfriars, to a "Beere howse" opposite the Tower. Borough High Street and what is now Tooley Street were built up with taverns and brothels, although the rings for baiting bulls and bears were also prominent.

Standing back from the map the overall impression is of a nucleus of tightly-packed streets, beginning to sprawl outwards to the north and west but framed by extensive green fields. The Thames was shown teeming with river-craft; masted galleons below London Bridge, oarsmen and the occasional sailboat upstream and the queen herself in the royal barge. In the foreground was depicted a comfortable bourgeois in a fur-trimmed surcoat, accompanied by his wife, daughter and son. A prominent cartouche in the lower right corner gave details of the Steelyard, the mercantile enclave inhabited by representatives of the Hanseatic League of German and Baltic trading cities.

One of the treasures of the Museum of London is a pair of copperplate maps of the area either side of the streets leading north from London Bridge as far as Shoreditch. Both plates have religious paintings on the back, which explains their chance survival. Engraved ca. 1553-9 as part of a set of perhaps twenty, they show individual buildings and other features with greater clarity and detail than the Braun and Hogenberg map. The top plate depicts washerwomen spreading clothes out to dry in Moorfields, archers practising in the shadow of two windmills at Finsbury and more of them in Spitalfields. The bottom plate shows dense streets of gable-ended houses, many with gardens geometrically sectioned into parterres. A third engraved copper plate was identified in Germany in 1997. Adjoining the lower of the other two plates, it shows St. Paul's before the destruction of its spire in 1561. A cruder, but revised, woodcut version was later published to show this, the building of Sir Thomas Gresham's Royal Exchange and other changes.

The threat of invasion by the Spanish Armada in 1588 caused Robert Adams (1540-95), Architect and Surveyor of the Queen's buildings, to produce a coloured map on vellum showing London's in-depth defences and the route by barge and on horseback taken by Elizabeth I out to Tilbury fort, where the bulk of her hastily-assembled army was mustered. Confusingly this *Thamesis Descriptio* is oriented with Kent at the top rather than the bottom, so London is on the right rather than the left.

The civil war fortifications of the 1640s were fortunately also mapped in detail before their demolition. Captions convey incidental detail such as the existence of pounds for stray animals at Islington and St. Giles and, around St. George's Fields the Dogg and Duck tavern, a windmill and a Lock (venereal disease) hospital.

Bird's-Eye View

Before the copperplate maps came to light detailed knowledge of the topography of Tudor London was derived from the large *Civitas Londinium* bird's-eye view attributed, almost certainly wrongly, to Suffolk surveyor Ralph Agas. Printed from woodcuts, it inevitably lacked the precision of a map produced from metal plates but is still rich in quirky detail—horsemen gallivanting in "Schmyt Fyeld", two men brawling in Lambeth and stags standing stately in St. James' Park. Topographical evidence fixes the date of the map as 1561-71 although surviving copies do not seem to have been published until ca.1633, with amendments to show dramatic changes such as the disappearance of St. Paul's spire, destroyed by storm in 1561. Although the Fleet River and its bridges are depicted, it had already become too fouled by refuse to be passable by boats any longer.

Details of individual estates and buildings can be gleaned from maps prepared for their owners for administrative or legal purposes. A map of the then undeveloped West End, drawn up to settle a dispute over grazing rights in 1585, depicts the area between present-day St. Martin's Lane and Bond Street. Most of Mayfair was grazing-land, dotted with a few cottages, gravel pits, water conduits, windmills and an isolated building for storing gunpowder. Ralph Treswell, whose main living as a "painter-stainer" was derived from painting heraldic banners and coats of arms, also drew plans of London properties belonging to Christ's Hospital school, of which he was a governor, and of other properties belonging to the Clothworkers' Company. The latter show privies protruding from houses to empty straight into the "Fleete Diche". Such maps provide valuable evidence of housing conditions before the Great Fire of 1666, with warrens of courts and passages separating rambling multi-tenanted households.

Around 1600 John Norden produced a highly eccentric bird's-eye view of Westminster, depicting it as though a map of fields had been cut through with scissors and peeled back to reveal the urban development concealed beneath—a reversal of a more familiar cartographic conceit by which streets and squares are shown to follow the pre-existing boundaries of fields and meadows set by hedges and streams. Norden's view also includes, at the top, an enlarged panorama of the north bank of the Thames from Whitehall to "Pawls Wharfe". The main point of interest lies in the succession of palatial residences lining the river south of the Strand and westwards from the Temple: Essex House, Arundel House, Somerset House, Bedford House, Durham House and York House, the last two recalling the despoiled bishops to whom they once belonged. Norden's more conventional map of London, first published in 1593, includes "The Banckes Syde" and was revised in his lifetime to include, uniquely, its newly-built theatres—the Rose (1587)—which he for some reason calls the Star— the Swan (1595) and the Globe (1599), though they are almost lost among a profusion of tall trees. Even so it can be seen that the actual stages were south-facing to throw as much light as possible onto them

Before and After

In 1658 Richard Newcourt and his engraver William Faithorne produced what was fated to be the last large-scale map of old London before the City was devoured by the Great Fire. Although the woodcut depiction of housing is crude and formulaic the northward march of London's suburbs is clearly evident. The Moorfields area, although now walled rather than hedged, was still being used for drying clothes, as it had been a century before, but the gardens are planted with geometrically-patterned orchards. To the west the vast gated garden of Gray's Inn is especially prominent.

It was probably in the same year,1658, that the Bohemian-born artist Wenceslaus (Vaclav) Hollar completed a bird's-eye view of the rapidly developing West End, from Chancery Lane to what is now Charing Cross Road (then Hog Lane). This may have been intended as part of a much more comprehensive project. Hollar had been brought to England in the train of the second Earl of Arundel and appointed drawing-tutor to the future Charles II. As a Royalist he suffered capture, exile and dire poverty during the civil wars and interregnum but nevertheless produced a majestic panorama of London seen from Bankside in 1647. Hollar's perspective on the West End marks Covent Garden's new "Piazza" and provides voyeuristic detail of the elaborate interior layouts and gardens of the aristocratic mansions along the Strand. Although Hollar's fortunes recovered with the Restoration and he was a prolific worker, leaving behind over 2,700 prints, he "died not rich". The exact location of his grave in St. Margaret's, Westminster, is lost but there is a handsome modern memorial to him in Southwark cathedral, from whose tower he sketched his celebrated panorama. The cathedral's hi-tech "Long View of London" exhibition enables the on-line visitor to compare past and present by closed circuit television.

The Great Fire of 1666 was no ill wind for map-makers, at least. In Amsterdam Frederick de Wit hastily adapted an existing map to rush out a delineation of the burned-out area with, in the foreground, a weeping Thames waterman, a family handing over cash for their salvaged goods to be carried away in a cart and an imaginative panorama of the city in flames. In 1667 a survey of the burned-out area was made by John Leake and engraved by Hollar, identifying the eighty-odd churches, fifty-two Livery Company Halls and major commercial premises which had been destroyed. Visionary plans mapping out the reconstruction of the City as a model of metropolitan grandeur were submitted to Charles II within weeks. Christopher Wren proposed a grid, relieved by monumental diagonal boulevards and punctuated by piazzas, the largest of which would concentrate the City's commercial functions—Insurance, Mint, Bank, Goldsmiths, Post and Excise Offices—around a rebuilt Royal Exchange. The rambling wooden wharfs of old would be replaced by a continuous "Key" and "Grand Terras" lined with imposing warehouses. The diarist and dilettante John Evelyn presented a similar but less sophisticated plan along much the same lines, opting for more piazzas, square and elliptical, as well as round. Another proposal envisaged the City enlarged to a huge rectangle, sub-divided into fifty-five identically rectangular parishes, each with a square and a church bang in the middle. Captain Valentine Knight, an army officer, proposed encircling the City with a canal from which the Crown could derive revenue by charging tolls on goods landed from it. The free-spending monarch, normally only too keen to lay his hands on cash, had Knight arrested for even presuming to imagine that he might wish to benefit from "so public a calamity". None of the plans came to anything, except Wren's, which inspired Major L'Enfant's design for Washington D.C. over a century later.

A decade after the Fire the map made by John Ogilby, assisted by his wife's grandson William Morgan, at the scale of 100 feet to the inch, revealed every house and garden of the City with an unprecedented detail and precision not to be bettered until the Ordnance Survey two centuries later. It was the work of a man who had only begun making maps at the age of sixty-nine—not that Ogilby had not had plenty of practice in starting afresh. A Scot by birth, he had been a dancing-master, tutor, secretary, bodyguard, poet, theatre manager and translator. He had just missed being blown up in the civil war, survived a shipwreck, learned Latin and Greek in his fifties, arranged the "poetical part" of Charles II's coronation and managed a lottery before his Whitefriars bookshop went up in flames in 1666 along with £3,000 worth of stock. Indefatigably Ogilby bounced back yet again, not only producing his great map but also being recognized as the "king's cosmographer and geographic printer".

Ogilby and Morgan's map confirms that London's rapid rebuilding, even if almost entirely reproducing the tangled medieval street pattern, did incorporate piecemeal improvements such as the widening and straightening of Thames Street and the dredging of the Fleet to render it navigable once more. In 1682 William Morgan published a map of Westminster which shows that it, too, had been building up rapidly with a "New Chapell" on one side of the Artillery Ground and a New Workhouse on the other and, on a highly topical note, ostriches in St. James' Park, a gift that year from the Moroccan ambassador.

Strype's 1720 edition of Stow (see p.23) included three detailed maps by Richard Blome (d.1705), heraldic painter and con-artist. His map of St. James' of ca.1689 shows that the streets around St. James' Square have been fully built up, although there is a market off the eastern end of German (Jermyn) Street. What were fields to the north of Piccadilly in the 1640s have also been built over, except for the large Pest House Fields and Burying Place between Carnaby Street and Poland Street. The map of London as a whole which served as Strype's frontispiece shows that Mayfair is still Pasture Ground in 1720, as is Bloomsbury. Although development along the riverside is now continuous as far as Ratcliffe, Stepney and Bethnal Green still stand isolated in open ground.

Social Survey

In 1725 John Warburton, Somerset Herald and a Fellow of the Royal Society, published what was, in effect, a map of snobbery and aspiration. Covering Middlesex, Essex and Hertfordshire, it was intended as one of a series of "large, beautiful and most correct maps" which would be the "most usefull and ornamental for libraries, staircases and galleries etc. that were ever published." Although Warburton's map did contain new information, such as indications of the ancient "Roman military wayes", its most striking feature was the inclusion of 724 coats of arms correlated by numbers with the locations of the residences of the armigerous families thus indicated. *Arrivistes* were flattered to pay for their inclusion alongside the most venerable of dynastic lines. Although one rationale for the map was to aid magistrates in the detection of fraudulent use of arms, Warburton had no hesitation in obliging subscribers by including theirs without any test of legal title. The map's cartouche, embellished with cornucopias, a cherub carrying a bundle of merchandise and a Native American proffering a symbolic casket of treasure to a female personification of the City, clearly indicates the mercantile market at which Warburton's production was aimed. The concentration of armigerous households in riverside Richmond is, perhaps, unsurprising but Tottenham and Hackney were also clearly fashionable areas.

Milestone in Mapping

Huguenot immigrant John (properly Jean) Rocque, initially a garden-designer, began his cartographic career with plans and views of gardens, including the royal parks at Richmond, Kensington and Windsor. Working simultaneously as a surveyor of estates, he then branched out into publishing general maps, atlases and town plans and in 1737 began a detailed survey of London (including Westminster and Southwark), which was published in twenty-four sheets between 1744 and 1746. This was the first new map of the capital in more than half a century and its production involved measuring 10,000 acres on foot with surveyor's chains, a theodolite and a "waywiser" and verifying 5,000 place names. Thanks to royal engraver John Pine, Bluemantle Pursuivant at the College of Arms and a friend of Hogarth, London's houses and varieties of land use were distinguished by finely graded shades of grey. Thirteen feet across and half that in height, the completed map was rather unwieldy to consult, so Rocque suggested pasting it onto linen and storing it on a roller to be let down "for Examination at Pleasure". When a fire wiped out Rocque's Whitehall premises in 1750, he started up again in the Strand and survived to style himself cartographer to King George III. Rocque's map of London became a standard source for historians and has been republished by the London Topographical Society as *The A-Z of Georgian London* and can also be accessed online at www.motco.com.

Analytical Approaches

Rocque's achievement was superseded in 1792-9 by Richard Horwood of Mare Street, Hackney. Horwood's 32-sheet *Plan of London, Westminster, the Borough of Southwark and Parts Adjoining Shewing Every House* was, at 94 square feet, the largest map ever printed in Britain to date. There was nothing comparable until the Ordnance Survey's 1st edition at 25 inches to the mile in the 1860s. Produced at a scale of 26 inches to the mile, it delineated every road, alley, garden and field and, as far as possible, the number of every individual house. House-numbering had begun around 1735 but was still not universal at the end of the century. Much detail is also given of commercial enterprises. On the south side of the river, for example, there were no fewer than twenty timber yards between Westminster and Blackfriars Bridges, plus a coal wharf, tan yard, barge builder's, waterworks and factories for making gunshot and vinegar. The area around the former St. George's Fields had been developed by speculators eager to capitalize on the relative cheapness of the land. For the same reason charitable bodies had begun to build almshouses, an Asylum for Female Orphans, the Magdalen Hospital for penitent prostitutes and the Freemasons' school for girls. In 1815 they would be joined by the Bethlehem Hospital, the capital's major insane asylum, whose central administration block now houses the Imperial War Museum.

In 1800 estate surveyor Thomas Milne took advantage of the trigonometrical work undertaken by the Ordnance Survey to produce a map of London and Westminster colour-coded to illustrate nine categories of land use, ranging from enclosed arable to meadows and market gardens, paddocks and parks, osier beds and orchards, drained marshland and woodland. The villas of the affluent were intermixed with commercial horticulture all around the fringes of the metropolis but particularly in Battersea, around Brompton and stretching all the way from Westminster to Hammersmith. Gardens north of Mitcham were devoted to lavender. As the British Library possesses the only surviving copy of Milne's map it evidently failed to imitate Horwood's success.

The Yorkshire brothers Christopher and John Greenwood aimed (but failed) to map the entire country in a manner which combined "superior elegance with the greatest accuracy". Financial difficulties meant that the folding coloured map of London they published in 1827 was taken over by E. Ruff and Co. An enthusiastic reviewer of a fourth updated edition of 1840 praised it as "upon the largest scale adapted for the clubs and public institutions of the metropolis and the only one we have seen deserving a place in the office of a surveyor or civil engineer." Five further editions were issued by 1856. (A searchable version of the 1827 original can be accessed online at: www.bathspa.ac.uk/greenwood/home.htm.)

Going Into Detail

In 1848 the Ordnance Survey began a two-year project to map the capital at the scale of five feet to the mile. To improve the accuracy of their observations the military surveyors established elevated vantage-points including a 92-foot-high platform on top of the cross of St. Paul's. Although the major purpose of the project was to assist the public health authorities in planning drainage arteries as part of their battle against cholera, the completed maps also included invaluable data for the historian, most notably the locations (marked in Gothic script) of demolished buildings. Another version, to the same scale and running to over eight hundred sheets, was produced in the 1870s. This even marked in street furniture such as individual lamp posts, drain-covers and posting-boxes. Statues were not merely marked as they are on current Ordnance Survey maps as "statue" but named in an elegant Italic hand. Even the internal layout of major buildings like the Mansion House was shown, as was the seating capacity (400) of the adjacent church of St. Stephen's, Walbrook.

The Great Exhibition of 1851 inspired the production of over two dozen different souvenir maps, including versions in French and German, another showing the capital as from a balloon hovering over Hampstead and another literally handy version designed to be printed on a glove. Commercial map publisher John Tallis produced a commemorative map framed by forty-nine views enabling the visitor to "possess a faithful memorial of the wonders he has seen". Vignette views and elaborate ornamental framing were characteristic of Tallis products, and his 1851 souvenir map included thirteen named theatres and such now vanished attractions as Vauxhall Gardens, the Colosseum and a Chinese Exhibition. Impressively it also includes impending projects such as the "Proposed Battersea Park", King's Cross station and Lambeth Bridge. Another of the entertainments depicted on the Tallis map was Wyld's Great Globe in Leicester Square, a generous inclusion considering that James Wyld was Tallis' main commercial rival and, by heredity, "Geographer Royal". Wyld's gas-lit Globe, sixty feet high, forty feet in diameter, depicted on its interior the earth's surface at an inch to ten miles on painted plaster casts. Housed in a large circular building, whose walls displayed the finest maps, atlases and globes, this elaborate exploitation of the mid-Victorian hunger for "useful knowledge" long outlasted the Great Exhibition, only closing in 1862 when Leicester Square was given the long-overdue make-over which established its present form.

Cartographic Conservation

While the need for new maps to record a new London was obvious, as a Commissioner for Sewers, Frederick Crace (1799-1859) became increasingly aware of the need to collect old maps recording the London which was being erased by the headlong impetus for metropolitan "improvements". The resulting Crace Collection, dutifully catalogued by its creator's son, is one of the treasures of the British Library. Crace senior had an eye for the aesthetic as well as the pragmatic, having been George IV's interior decorator at Carlton House, Brighton Pavilion and Windsor. His collection of some 1,200 maps not only included many unique items but also successive editions of the classics—Morgan, Rocque, Horwood, etc.—which enable researchers to trace the development of London in detail. When Crace was unable to buy a particular item he often managed to have a copy made, many of these tracings later becoming the only record of subsequently lost originals. (www.collectbritain.co.uk/collections/crace)

Gold Standard

Edward Stanford of Charing Cross was to produce the most commercially successful map of Victorian London. Scaled at six inches to the mile, the first edition of 1862, conceived with public libraries in mind, was followed by twenty more over the following four decades. Stanford became London's premier map publisher. A Fellow of the Royal Geographical Society at 26, he became sales agent for the maps produced by the various branches of government at home and in India. Acquiring the maps prepared for the Society for the Diffusion of Useful Knowledge, he recycled them to create the *Harrow Atlas of Modern Geography* for Harrow School. He went on to become the supplier of maps to the Society for the Promotion of Christian Knowledge, the Metropolitan Board of Works, the School Board of London and the Palestine Exploration Fund. The Stanford range of mountains in British Columbia was named in his honour. Stanford's map and book shop (www.stanfords.co.uk) in Long Acre remains a mecca for geographers, planners, backpackers and hikers.

Crusading Cartography

Dr. John Snow (see p.201) demonstrated forcefully the value of using maps in support of a public health campaign. Other campaigners had other priorities. In 1871 ultra-Protestant paranoiacs put out a map purporting to show "Romish establishments in London and the Public Institutions to which Romish Priests have gained Access". A generation later, in 1899, a similar exercise would plot the distribution of Jews and Gentiles in the East End. Around 1884 the National Temperance League produced a *Map of the Modern Plague of London* to indicate the vast number of drink outlets in the metropolis. The League's Strand headquarters was in the same building as the mapmaker G. W. Bacon, so it was easy to arrange for one of their standard commercial maps to be overprinted with an infestation of virulent red dots, each one representing a public house. This showed that in central London there were a hundred and fifty pubs in Soho alone and thirty, not including hotels, lining the Strand. In Stepney and Whitechapel there were over a thousand. The Duke of Bedford's Bloomsbury estate, by contrast, had only three, earnest of his effort to maintain its *ton*. Charles Booth utilized the same over-printing technique on Stanford's best-selling "Library" map for his colour-coded poverty maps. Their seven-step hierarchy ranged from black for streets inhabited by "the elements of disorder"—occasional labourers, loafers and semi-criminals—through pink for "working class comfort" mixed with the servantless petite-bourgeoisie, to yellow for wealthy families with three or more servants. Booth's basic demographic data were derived from the 1881 census.

In 1983 the Department of the Environment published a *Greater London Urban Deprivation Map* based on the 1981 census. Census enumeration districts, each representing roughly two hundred households, were ranked as "deprived", "severely deprived" and "extremely deprived" according to an index based on mortality, unemployment, overcrowding, proportion of single-parent and ethnic minority households, pensioners living alone and households without basic amenities such as an indoor lavatory or bath. The continuities between Booth's map and its DoE successor were as striking as they were depressing, with major clusters of extreme deprivation concentrated in the northern half of Newham, the western half of Hackney, Spitalfields, North Kensington, south-eastern Brent and Brixton, while affluent Richmond and Barnet were entirely unblighted.

Gentrified Islington, Camden and Battersea replicated the pattern, applicable a century previously in Pimlico and Victoria, of affluence co-existing with pockets of dire poverty.

Cartography and Communication

Changes in London's transport infrastructure were successively reflected on both general maps and those specifically intended for the needs of the traveller and business visitor, providing, for example, details of the postal district boundaries introduced in 1856-7 and of surviving toll-gates and precise calculations of cab fares. The *Circuiteer or Distance Map*, published by Joachim Friederichs of St. Pancras in 1847, superimposed a pattern of circles of half-mile diameter so that the passenger could quickly tot up the distance he had covered to estimate his correct tariff and thus avoid "the monstrous impositions... which have long been the subject of general complaint."

Simpkin Marshall's bi-lingual English-French version, produced for 1851, used equilateral half-mile triangles instead. Railway companies sponsored maps to encourage the use of their facilities. A map issued by the empire-building Metropolitan Railway in 1882 trumpeted the extension of their line to Kingsbury, Neasden and Harrow. In 1887 the District Railway cashed in on Queen Victoria's Golden Jubilee to issue a celebratory railway map of London. A decade later, at the Diamond Jubilee, it followed up with a combined map and guide to the "Victorian era" exhibition mounted at Earl's Court.

The invention of the pneumatic tyre and "safety bicycle" in the 1880s revolutionized both London's labour market and its leisure patterns. For many men possession of a bicycle enlarged the radius of potential employments from a daily walking-distance of, say, five miles to a cycling distance of three times as much, virtually the entire metropolis. Those who had evenings or weekends free and sufficient energy could take advantage of the "magic wheel" to penetrate Epping Forest or the Surrey hills where they could picnic or conduct the stately rituals of late Victorian courtship away from the prying eyes of neighbours. Cycling maps soon appeared, many with cyclist-specific refinements, showing, for example, which hills ought to be ridden down with brakes on and where refreshments were available. The cycling map produced by Edward Grove of Edgware Road covered an ambitious fifty mile radius from central London.

London's underground railways developed as separate and competing lines until 1905 when the American Charles Tyson Yerkes succeeded in uniting the District Line with the three deep Tube railways, the Bakerloo, the Piccadilly and the Hampstead (later Northern). Yerkes summarized his own business philosophy as "buy up old junk, fix it up a little and unload it upon other fellows." Unscrupulous and manipulative, Yerkes nevertheless bequeathed the vision of jointly marketing the erstwhile competing lines as a single system—the Underground. In 1908 a map of the Underground Electric Railway Company of London group appeared and in the same year another map came out showing both the group and the Central, Metropolitan and City and South London lines, although they remained separate entities in terms of ownership and management.

A similar situation applied to London's tramways, many of which had been taken over by the London County Council. In 1906, to publicize the opening of the Kingsway subway, it published a map showing the lines it controlled on both sides of the river. The subway at that time enabled passengers to travel from Bloomsbury along the Embankment to Westminster in just seven minutes, far faster than one could hope to manage a century later. Posters of the 1920s emphasized that although LCC trams did not penetrate the West End, they made it swiftly accessible. The "well-lighted Cars" offered "Reading and Smoking in Comfort" and—a dig at surviving open-top buses—the guarantee to "Travel under Cover all the Way". A 1932 map of the LCC tram network marked interchanges with other providers and carried a summary timetable of All-Night services, thoughtfully juxtaposed next to an exhortation to "Train Mind And Hand" by attending LCC evening classes.

Such was the rivalry between competing bus companies that the first bus route map did not appear until 1911, when the London General Omnibus Company made one available. Issued in the year in which the company completed its three-year transition from horse-drawn buses to motorized vehicles, it was doubtless prompted by increasing competition from the Underground, being prominently emblazoned with the admonition "TRAVEL ABOVE GROUND—WE CARRY YOU ALL THE WAY." A poster map produced in 1961 showed the out-of-town Green Line coach service at its zenith, with pictorial vignettes illustrating desirable destinations from Whipsnade Zoo and Luton Hoo in the north-west to Knole in the south-east.

Mapping the Suburbs

The "Metro-Land" concept, formulated by the publicity department of the Metropolitan Railway in 1915, led during the course of the following decade to the extensive suburbanization of the surplus land lying along the company's routes running north-westwards out of London. Coordinated by a subsidiary Country Estates company established in 1919, development was promoted by an annual "Metro-Land" brochure and map highlighting its five major estates. Priced at a mere twopence, the "brochure" was in fact a substantial publication of more than a hundred pages, subsidized by advertising revenue from building contractors touting their designs and services. Three of the estates were closely clustered at Kingsbury, Chalk Hill and Wembley Park, two more distant—the Grange Estate at Pinner and the five hundred-acre Cedars Estate at Rickmansworth. The map emphasizes both the closeness of each to a railway station and also the abundance of golf courses, ten being marked between Willesden and Chalfont. Golf courses indicated the aspirational tone of such new communities and often came to function as social centres, especially for women, in the absence of tea-rooms and department stores. Moor Park station is marked on the 1925 "Metro-Land" map as Sandy Lodge to underline the presence of the prestigious golf course which had appropriated as its clubhouse a stunning mansion of ca. 1730 (now listed Grade I), designed by Hogarth's father-in-law, Sir James Thornhill.

Design Classics

The Metropolitan was by no means the only Underground line to be extended in the inter-war period. As more stations and longer lines were added to the system the cartographic challenge of depicting it clearly became ever greater. A special map produced for the Empire Exhibition mounted at Wembley in 1924 hit on the device of portraying the central part of the system at a constant scale while outer lines, including the link to Wembley, were shown diagrammatically. Between 1931 and 1933 Henry Beck, an electrical draughtsman, was inspired by wiring diagrams to recast the map of the system to create a design classic of the twentieth century. Exaggerating still further the perspective already adopted by earlier designers, he elongated the central part of the network, reducing the Central Line's meanderings to a couple of kinks to establish it as an east-west axis. The Thames was likewise reduced to a stylised caricature to provide a complementary axial feature. The intervals between stations were determined by the requirements of legibility, ignoring actual distances. Beck's model, first issued by the newly-created London Passenger Transport Board in 1933, was to be widely imitated by other urban transport networks (and airlines) across the world, including New York, Sydney and St. Petersburg. Beck himself received a flat fee of just five guineas for parting with the copyright of the world's first "geoschematic" map—and eventually a posthumous plaque at his home station, Finchley Central.

Another classic and schematic "map" that first appeared in the 1930s was the Monopoly board. Humourist Tim Moore has had the brilliant idea of revisiting every location named on it, accompanied by a best-selling book of the period, Harold P. Clunn's *The Face of London*. Moore's account of his bizarre odyssey, *Do Not Pass Go*, is very funny but also, beneath his serial flippancy, very informative about the extent to which different areas have or have not changed. Whitechapel and the Old Kent Road (which, he reminds us, are both signified by "unequivocal poo brown") were both noted for their lively street markets in the 1930s. Whitechapel still has one, though the Jewish stall-holders have been replaced by Bangladeshis. The Old Kent Road, by contrast, has become a soulless traffic corridor.

Target for Tonight
During the Second World War Luftwaffe pilots used an adapted three inches to the mile version of the 1933 Ordnance Survey map of London, updated from aerial reconnaissance photographs, to highlight major landmark features for pilot recognition and to identify targets omitted from maps on general sale to the public for security reasons. Plumstead Marshes, for example, is shown on the civilian map as a complete blank, whereas the Luftwaffe version has the layout of the Woolwich Arsenal, with magazines, stores and factories for making cartridges, Cordite and Lyddite marked in. The Ministry of Home Security Research Department compiled bomb damage maps to assess the destruction caused by different types of explosives to improve protection for the public. Most London boroughs also did so, usually

coded in seven colours, running from black to indicate total destruction to yellow for minor damage, with the impact of V-1 and V-2 missiles shown by concentric rings. The 1954 Ordnance Survey revealed the state of the northern and central parts of the City from St. Paul's to Finsbury Square and comprising the wards of Bread Street, Cripplegate Within, Farringdon Within and Cripplegate Without as they were in 1951—two-thirds or more simply blank, intersected by the ghosts of streets once close-packed with buildings but now punctuated with the remains of ancient churches and proud Livery Company Halls forlornly labelled "ruin".

New Jerusalem

The London County Council also used its bomb damage maps to identify possible post-war development sites. One outcome was the development of south London's Burgess Park, created out of an involuntary partnership between the LCC and the Luftwaffe. The vast majority of London parks originated from a successful defence of existing space—ancient commons or the grounds of some decayed mansion—against the encroachments of housing, commerce or transport systems. Burgess Park, however, extends over what was once an entirely urbanized area of thirty streets, nine hundred homes and their attendant shops, pubs, schools, churches and factories, plus a goodly stretch of the Grand Surrey Canal. The semi-wilderness created by German bombing by 1943 was reinterpreted by far-sighted LCC planners as an opportunity to open up a recreational area more than two miles from any other one. Most unusually they envisaged a time-scale of half a century for the completion of the project as individual sections and properties were acquired serendipitously to complete the jigsaw puzzle. The core component, inelegantly christened North Camberwell Open Space, was opened in 1950. By 1965 it had been expanded to fifteen acres, by 1974 to over forty. In 1982 an eight-acre boating and fishing lake was added, the first to be created in inner London in the twentieth century, the first ever to be created over formerly built-up land. By 1983 eighty-eight acres, an area equal to St. James' Park, was in use. Writing in that year, Hunter Davies recorded with amazement that "no one, anywhere in the world, has ever bulldozed the urban landscape on such a scale before, just to produce a bit of open space." The "linear park" passing through Mile End and following the line of the Grand Union Canal is another, if much belated, example of the same phenomenon.

MARKETS, SHOPS AND STORES
A Retail Interlude

The morose narrator of the fifteenth-century satire *London Lickpenny* repeatedly declares how "for lack of money" he could not buy any of the delicacies or luxuries thrust on him at every turn. Indeed, such was the vigour of the capital's commerce that he saw his own hood, stolen from him in Westminster in the morning, offered for sale on Cheapside that

Harrods

same afternoon. The retail heart of Roman Londinium had been centred on its vast forum, four times the size of Trafalgar Square, which stood in the east of the city, where the line of Leadenhall Street and Cornhill now bisects Bishopsgate and Gracechurch Street. The main retail artery ran east to west from Eastcheap and Leadenhall markets, which, being nearest to the City's gates and the rural Essex hinterland, dealt chiefly in meat and provisions, through the Stocks market, held on the site now occupied by the Mansion House, to Cheapside, renowned for its mercers, jewellers and goldsmiths.

London was the nation's emporium. Men visiting the capital on legal, parliamentary or other business invariably carried with them instructions to bring back spices, fine cloth, fancy trimmings or other luxuries. The provincial conviction that the very best was only to be had from London made the capital's shopkeepers exporters of luxuries to the rest of England, virtually until the railway age. Many country families employed a regular London agent to make purchases on their behalf. Eighteenth-century requests range from an adjustable wig and a second-hand sedan chair to two gallons of "sallat oyll" and a fringed velvet saddle.

London, like the provinces, also had periodic fairs. Originally these were primarily for retailing, although gradually recreation became more important. The priory and hospital of St. Bartholomew the Great were supported by the profits of Bartholomew Fair, the nation's biggest mart for textiles—hence the street still there called Cloth Fair. The fair was opened by the Mayor himself ceremonially snipping a piece of cloth, whence the common custom of opening buildings or bridges by cutting a ribbon or tape. By the time Ben Jonson wrote his play *Bartholomew Fair* (1614), the event was being taken over by sword-swallowers and mountebanks but it was not finally suppressed until 1855. Southwark Fair crammed the streets and courts of the Borough with temporary stalls and booths to the immense annoyance of permanent local shopkeepers. Hogarth's depiction of it reiterates the triumph of the fairground over the market-place. The May Fair which gave its name to Mayfair was actually first held in the Haymarket and transferred to Mayfair in the 1680s. As Mayfair became residentially respectable the rowdy assemblage was relocated eastwards to Bow, where only the name of Fairfield Road recalls its existence.

Thanks to luxury-loving merchants addicted to lavish hospitality and a spendthrift Court where competitive display was customary, London had enough concentrated purchasing power to keep hundreds of shops permanently in business. The opulence of Tudor London can be appreciated from the contents of the so-called Cheapside Hoard, accidentally discovered in 1912. The hundred-plus items, now on display in the Museum of London, are thought to represent the working stock of an Elizabethan jeweller. They include a finely-wrought timepiece in a hexagonal emerald frame, gold rings set with antique Roman carvings, showy hatpins, hair ornaments, pendants and bracelets and gemstones from as far away as India, Iran and Afghanistan.

The Royal Exchange was established by the Tudor tycoon Sir Thomas Gresham in 1567 primarily as a *bourse* or meeting-place for merchants but its upper storeys were given over to small-scale outlets for armourers, apothecaries, booksellers and milliners. Rebuilt after the

Great Fire, its retail premises proved increasingly difficult to let as the epicentre of fashionable shopping moved westwards along Fleet Street and the Strand towards Covent Garden and the newly-building West End.

The continuing expansion of London's population and area was reflected in the establishment of new markets. Covent Garden began informally when stall-holders set up in business against the back wall of Bedford House, the Strand residence of the then Earls of Bedford. Spitalfields was chartered in 1682. Others included Clare Market, where the London School of Economics now stands, and Newport Market at the end of Gerrard Street, where there are still a few stalls catering to the local Chinese community.

Displays of goods were difficult to see clearly until very large panes of glass could be made cheaply, an innovation of the early nineteenth century. Fixed prices were pioneered at Mr. Palmer's London Bridge establishment in 1750 and initially proved a startling novelty, but the habits of haggling and buying on extended credit—in the case of the aristocracy very extended—were slow to die.

The concentration of stylish shops in what became, by virtue of that concentration, stylish thoroughfares meant that their upper floors could be profitably rented out as short-term lodgings to the *beau monde* while the proprietor, his family and assistants crammed into the back or the basement. Eighteenth-century Bond Street's temporary residents included Swift, Gibbon, Pitt the Elder, Sterne, Boswell, Nelson and Sir Thomas Lawrence. Pall Mall residents included Gainsborough, the miniaturist Richard Cosway, William Cobbett and George IV's "secret" wife, Mrs. Fitzherbert. St. James' Street was home to Wren, Pope, Fox, Byron and the caricaturist James Gillray.

Several of today's specialist outlets can trace a history stretching back up to three centuries. Twining's Strand tea-shop, established in 1706, claims to be London's oldest retail establishment trading in the same business on the same site and associated with the same family. Fortnum and Mason, grocers to the posh, also dates back to the reign of Queen Anne. The nearby Jermyn Street cheese-mongers Paxton and Whitfield began around 1740 in Clare Market. Floris, their near neighbours in Jermyn Street, was established there in 1730 by Juan Floris of Minorca who began as a barber but soon abandoned the trade for the more lucrative business of selling fragrances and imported carved combs to his courtly clientele. Hamley's world-famous toy-shop began in Holborn in 1760 as "Noah's Ark". Asprey's, the Bond Street jeweller's, grew out of a Mitcham family of silk printers.

As the centre of the printing trade London also became renowned for shops specializing in the sale of prints and books. Rudolph Ackermann's Strand premises were used for the sale of artist's materials, prints and books, including the part-works he himself commissioned to illustrate the *Microcosm of London*. Ackermann also opened England's first specialized art library in his shop, publicizing it by means of vogueish Wednesday *soirées*. James Lackington's bookshop outgrew its first home in Chiswell Street and reopened in premises with 140 feet of frontage on the corner of Finsbury Square, where it became known as "The Temple of the Muses".

Street-sellers remained a key component of retailing well into Victoria's reign, both in newly-building suburbs before an adequate range of shops established themselves and, more permanently, in poorer parts of the metropolis. Often vendors would move from the one sort of district to the other in the course of their working day, especially when selling products like fish or shellfish, whose appeal depended on their freshness, offering them at a premium in the morning and at the end of the day selling off what was left over for what it would fetch. Many street-sellers dealt in provisions or other items of daily consumption, such as firewood, candles or "small coals". Others sold the little luxuries of the employed poor like chapbooks, combs, toys or ballads.

Women, the elderly, the disabled and children were common among the ranks of street-sellers. The often picturesque (i.e. ragged) appearance of street vendors inspired the publication of popular print series by Marcellus Laroon, Paul Sandby, Francis Wheatley and Thomas Rowlandson which are to be found on table-mats to this day.

The Victorian provision trade was revolutionized by London-based crusades against food adulteration, backed by the twin forces of journalism and science. The Soho Square firm of Crosse and Blackwell, manufacturers of pickles, jams and sauces, was among the first publicly to renounce the addition of harmful colorants and flavourings. Frederick J. Horniman made enough money to found the south London ethnographic museum named after him by the simple device of selling tea in sealed packets of guaranteed weight and quality which could not be tampered with by the retailer without detection. Sainsbury's began in Drury Lane, offering customers competitive prices and reliable quality on a limited range of perishable daily foodstuffs such as eggs, cheese and "the best butter in the world". Lipton's, originally a Glasgow firm which relocated to the Old Street area, likewise concentrated on a few major lines, buying in bulk to sell cheap. Both companies recognized the value of well-lit premises, with hygienic surfaces of marble and tile, staffed by assistants in freshly-laundered uniforms.

The co-operative movement in retailing was essentially a creation of the industrial towns of the north of England from the 1840s onwards. In the London area societies were founded a generation later, in Stratford (1862), which became the London Co-operative Society, Brixton (1864), which became the South Suburban, Woolwich (1868), known as the Royal Arsenal, and Enfield (1872). London's co-operative societies laid special emphasis on running their own dairies, perhaps because milk was so universally watered (and carelessly infected with tubercular matter) by the backyard cow-keepers who supplied the bulk of London homes and fed their livestock on brewery waste. The "co-ops" also became the capital's largest funeral directors.

An ingenious variation on the co-operative form of organization was Trotter's Bazaar at 4-6 Soho Square. Opened in 1816 by army contractor John Trotter, it represented a modest philanthropic pay-back for the fortune he had made out of the Napoleonic Wars. The Bazaar was a showcase where the wives, widows and daughters of disabled or dead service officers could offer for sale their own handiwork in the form of embroidery, gloves, lace, millinery, potted plants etc. Stalls were hired out at threepence per foot per day and there were facilities where the lady stall-holders could change out of their travelling clothes. This supervised and vetted environment protected the genteel vendors from the coarseness of the common market-place. Patrons, invariably from the same social background as the stall-holders, could be assured that by purchasing their products they were helping to support those worthy of support. This "very extensive, novel and curious establishment" survived until 1885.

London's earliest shopping mall, the Royal Opera Arcade, was built by John Nash in 1816-18 and still survives, tucked away behind Her Majesty's Theatre, with bijou outlets selling fishing-tackle, country clothing and New Zealand specialities. The much better known Burlington Arcade on Piccadilly dates from 1819. Nothing, however, remains of the Lowther Arcade at the western end of the Strand, demolished in 1904. Opened in 1830, its small shops catered for the gift market and by the 1860s nearly all were toyshops, a child's garden of delights.

The first purpose-built department store in England, Bon Marché, was located, not in the West End at all, but in the then solidly bourgeois south London suburb of Brixton. Its French name betrayed its Parisian inspiration. Bon Marché was opened in 1877 by James Smith, a Tooting printer who had won a fortune from horse-racing at Newmarket. Although Smith was soon bankrupt, the store itself survived into the 1970s.

The establishment which once boasted the telegraphic address "Everything, London" began modestly when Henry Charles Harrod, an Eastcheap tea merchant, took over the grocery business of a troubled client, trading in a converted Georgian house at what was then known as Middle Queen's Buildings. Charles Digby Harrod bought out his father in stages and diversified into non-perishables such as stationery, perfumes and patent medicines. Disaster, in the shape of a horrendous fire, struck in 1883, but Harrod turned it to brilliant advantage with a bravura display of customer care, writing to all account-holders to assure them that all outstanding orders would be faithfully filled. Reversing his previously strict "cash only" policy, in 1885 Harrod introduced credit accounts for approved customers such as Oscar Wilde and royal mistress Lillie Langtry. Harrod's was then virtually re-launched by Richard Burbidge under whose direction the profits increased ten-fold and the store was rebuilt to the exuberant designs of C. W. Stephen, the architect of Claridge's Hotel. It incorporated London's first "moving staircase", a proto-escalator installed in 1898.

Sir Arthur Lasenby Liberty began his working career with Farmer and Roger's "Great Cloak and Shawl Emporium", which specialized in imported shawls from India. Impressed by the goods he saw at the International Exhibition of 1862, he persuaded them to open an Oriental Warehouse. In 1875 Liberty opened his own "East India House" on Regent Street and was soon able to capitalize on the craze for *japonoiserie* stimulated by the immense success of Gilbert and

Sullivan's *Mikado*, for which he had himself supplied the costumes and props. Liberty's soon became the store of preference for the aesthetic elite, numbering among its clients William Morris, Leighton, Rossetti, Whistler, Ruskin, Alma-Tadema and Burne-Jones. The present Liberty buildings bear a visual reminder of the founder's Orientalist tastes in a frieze depicting camels, elephants and Buddhas. The timber façade on Great Marlborough Street is made from the remnants of two of the navy's last wooden warships, HMS *Impregnable* and, very appropriately, HMS *Hindustan*.

It took William Whiteley ten years to save the seven hundred pounds he needed to open his first shop on Westbourne Grove in 1863. By 1867 he had premises on both sides of the street. By 1876 he had fifteen shops and 2,000 staff. The "Universal Provider" diversified from drapery into dry goods, dry cleaning, estate agency and whatever else might endear him to the Bayswater bourgeoisie. The relentless expansion of Whiteley's establishment provoked local traders into burning him in effigy in 1876. Various of his premises were destroyed by fire, quite possibly arson, on at least six separate occasions. Whiteley simply bounced back to become an expert in fire sales. His personal demise was as sudden as it was unexpected. In 1907 Horace George Rayner, claiming to be Whiteley's illegitimate son, shot him dead in his office when he refused to help him out of debt and then shot himself in the head but recovered to stand trial. Rayner's case aroused wide public sympathy and interest and he was spared the hangman's rope. Whiteley's business moved into its imposing Queensway premises in 1911 but was taken over by Harry Gordon Selfridge in 1927.

Wisconsin-born Selfridge was already a millionaire when he moved to London to show the British what a real state-of-the-art department store should look like. His monster premises, designed by Daniel Burnham of Chicago, opened in 1909 at what he had been told was the wrong end of Oxford Street. Selfridge believed that in getting customers to part with their cash price was less important than ambience. Considering that the department store should offer the lady in town for the day the same level of amenity that her husband could find at his club, Selfridge ensured that as well as shopping she could meet her friends for coffee, lunch or tea, have her hair dressed and even write and post letters. Hence the slogan "Spend the day at Selfridge's". Customers had the use of a library, rest-rooms and a roof-garden. A press room with telephones and typewriters was made available to journalists. Selfridge's private life proved less successful than his professional one, being fleeced of virtually his entire fortune by two cabaret dancers, the Hungarian Dolly sisters—a state of affairs obliquely referred to by the *Dictionary of National Biography* as "various personal follies".

THE ISLE OF DOGS

With Cesar Pelli's 850-foot stainless steel Canada Tower as its phallic focal point, Canary Wharf became both the physical and the symbolic epicentre of the breakneck redevelopment of the Isle of Dogs from

Canary Wharf, Isle of Dogs

1981 onwards. Retaining many of the redundant docks, wharves, chimneys and cranes of its previous incarnation as the heart of London's docklands, the peninsular "Island" was brashly promoted to prospective investors and incomers under the self-congratulatory slogan: "Looks Like Venice, Works Like New York." Early converts would find the area singularly lacking in the charms of the one, the efficiency of the other and the amenities of either.

Most of the fourteen thousand "Islanders", many of them third- or fourth-generation locals, lacked the skills required for the new jobs in the high-wage, hi-tech, high-rise towers conjured up by the fiscal magic wand of the London Docklands Development Corporation. Openings in construction, catering, transport and security offered limited consolation and the result was a decade of low-intensity class-warfare between the marginalized locals and the Porsche-driving *arrivistes*. Skills-training programmes, a diversification of employment and funding for heritage and environmental projects have helped to reconcile the former while a proliferation of facilities has enriched the off-duty hours of the latter. At Canary Wharf alone the workforce rose from 7,000 in 1993 to 55,000 by 2002. The number of shops and eating-places rose from two dozen to over two hundred, plus Britain's biggest sports club.

The Isle of Dogs is now in its fourth incarnation. Cultivated throughout the Middle Ages, with its own chapel, manor house and ferry, the peninsula was severely flooded in 1448-9 and largely depopulated. Known as Stepney Marsh for centuries, the area was then used for re-fattening livestock rendered tough and stringy by the long trek overland to the London markets. The name of Millwall recalls a cluster of windmills which pumped out local drainage dykes. At Blackwall sturdy armed freighters were built for the East India Company.

All this changed rapidly after the opening of the West India Dock in 1802 as a tight-packed necklace of wharves, yards, mills, factories and foundries ringed the waterside and eponymous developer William Cubitt (1791-1863) established a complete industrial suburb to the south of the docks. Local products ranged from Duckham's motor oil to Maconochie's army rations, from jam to paints, from lifeboats to Brunel's *Great Eastern*, at its launch the biggest ship ever built. The container revolution, which forced dock closures between 1967 and 1980, brought industrial implosion in its wake and an uneasy decade of drift before the Thatcher government kick-started the Island's history in a fresh direction. The state-of-the-art Museum in Docklands now provides a perceptive panorama of the peninsula's parlous passage from marsh to millennium.

Chapter Five
INTELLECTUAL CAPITAL

"... there is more learning and science within the circumference of ten miles from where we now sit than in all the rest of the world."

Dr. Samuel Johnson

Dr. Samuel Johnson, outside St. Clement Dane's, where he worshipped

Type "London + Intellectual" into an Internet search-engine and the result is a list of lawyers specializing in intellectual property rights. Type "London + intelligentsia" and up comes "Hampstead". There is no entry for "intellectual" in *The Oxford Companion to British History*, nor in the *Hutchinson Encyclopaedia of Britain* nor in Brewer's classic *Dictionary of Phrase and Fable*. The specialized "Brewer" devoted to Politics is more helpful, defining intellectuals as "a respected political vanguard in continental Europe, a key constituent of the revolutionary Communist movement (as in 'workers, peasants and intellectuals') and a term of abuse in England".

London as the historic focus of political power, the training-ground for the learned professions and the dominant centre of printing and publishing has, for at least half a millennium, accommodated the most extensive network of the nation's intellectual resources. Dr. Johnson's famous dictum that "a man who is tired of London is tired of life" was preceded by the assertion that "you find no man, at all intellectual, who is willing to leave London." For the intellectual the metropolis is the field of opportunity but also of temptation and of danger.

The Perils of Power

The meteoric and ultimately tragic career of Thomas à Becket, who called himself Thomas of London, illustrates all too clearly the perils awaiting an intellectual in politics. A trained lawyer, *en route* to the top he served as Constable of the Tower and in 1155 became the first Englishman since the Conquest to attain the highest secular office, Chancellor. Becket's translation to the see of Canterbury, however, pitted his personal loyalty to Henry II against his commitment to the privileges of church and clergy. The price was martyrdom.

Becket's tragic trajectory was paralleled by Thomas More, another born Londoner who also rose through the law to achieve the post of Lord Chancellor. Once again loyalty to the sovereign was outweighed by religious conviction and once again the price was death, although this time execution rather than murder. Unlike Becket, however, we know much more about More, both the man and his mind. As a young man he had tested his vocation for the priesthood by spending four years in the Charterhouse. Founded in 1370 by Sir Walter de Manny, a veteran of the Hundred Years War, this Carthusian community at Smithfield offered an enclave of contemplative quiet on the very edge of the city. Inmates lived as hermits in separate accommodations during the week, meeting together on Sundays for worship, a meal and a communal walk outside their walls. Charterhouse claimed that it was "never reformed because never deformed" and unlike other, laxer, houses it enjoyed immunity during outbursts of anti-clerical feeling. The fact that it could attract the austere and high-minded More speaks for its integrity; the fact that he ultimately abjured holy orders speaks for his. More chose a secular career and family life and enjoyed both. His Chelsea household was full of music and disputation and attracted as house-guests cultural superstars like the Dutch polymath Erasmus and the German artist Hans Holbein. More even believed in educating his womenfolk. In his sketch of an ideal community he indirectly offers us a critique of the mendaciousness of early Tudor London and the obsession of the powerful with wealth and display. In his imagined world gold is used for making chamber-pots and gemstones are given to toddlers to play with. The title of this famous work is both ironic and wistful; *Utopia* is Greek for "nowhere".

Other intellectuals at the Tudor Court had the good fortune to die before Henry VIII's divorce and break with Rome faced his servants with the unavoidable test of loyalty which sealed More's fate. Like Becket John Colet was the son of an immensely wealthy London merchant, whose country retreat, modestly known as "the Great Place" then stood just opposite the still surviving medieval church of St. Dunstan, Stepney, where Colet became vicar. As Dean of St. Paul's Colet used the huge wealth inherited from his father to found St. Paul's School, the largest in the kingdom, with 153 places—one for each caught in "the miraculous draught of fishes" described in the Gospel.

Monarchs and aristocrats kept in-house intellectuals as status symbols. The architect Inigo Jones, designer of the Queen's Chapel at St. James' Palace, the Banqueting House in Whitehall and the Queen's House at Greenwich, was successively a client of Queen Anne of Denmark, the Earl of Salisbury, Henry, Prince of Wales, the Earl of Bedford and two sovereigns. The philosopher Thomas Hobbes had a lifelong attachment to the Cavendish family and Dukes of Devonshire and was also a tutor to Charles II. John Locke had rooms in Exeter House off the Strand, home of the Earl of Shaftesbury, to whom he acted as both political adviser and family physician.

Arenas of Ideas

In the sixteenth and early seventeenth centuries the Inns of Court, which had evolved to train and accommodate legal professionals, gave intellectual polish to generations of young men, from Sidney, Drake and Raleigh to Donne and Cromwell, who had no intention of becoming professional lawyers. With the demolition of the power and privileges of the Catholic Church, Oxford and Cambridge were no longer valued as the recruiting-grounds for a safe ecclesiastical career. Both cities were, moreover, two days ride from booming London with its theatres and taverns, the best tailors and fencing-masters, the place to see and be seen and make connections with the Court rather than the courts. Given the choice, which would most young men of spirit opt for? As the attraction of the Inns of Court waned they were overtaken by the proliferation of coffee-houses. Charles II once attempted, briefly and vainly, to close them down as centres of sedition but foreign visitors hailed their vigorous debates as the very essence of English freedom. Others recognized them as "Penny universities", to which entrance could be gained with a small coin and where wit, not rank, commanded admiration. Over succeeding centuries many would metamorphose into exclusive gentlemen's clubs, such as White's, Brooks's and Boodle's.

The Royal Society, the world's oldest continuously existing scientific society, originated in an informal series of meetings at Wadham College, Oxford, which, at the Restoration, transferred to London, initially to Gresham College. Formally constituted in 1660, it was granted a Royal Charter in 1662, its early members including men of affairs such as Pepys and Evelyn as well as intellectual heavyweights like Newton, Wren and Hooke. Charles II, a keen amateur experimenter, took an active interest in the Society's activities although he was wryly sceptical of such projects as attempting to weigh air. In 1710 the Society found a permanent home in Crane Court off Fleet Street, then in 1780 moved to Somerset House, where its affairs were dominated for forty years by the naturalist Sir Joseph Banks. Later based in Burlington House (1857-1967), it is now at Carlton House Terrace. Apart from programmes of lectures, demonstrations and experiments and the publication of its *Philosophical Transactions*, the Royal Society was also responsible for changing the calendar in 1751 and organizing Captain Cook's momentous voyage of 1768-71 to observe the transit of Venus and Sir John Franklin's disastrous expedition of 1845 to find a North-West Passage through Arctic waters.

The Society of Dilettanti certainly sounds gentlemanly. It was formed in 1734 by "some gentlemen who had travelled in Italy, desirous of encouraging at home a taste for those objects which had contributed so much to their entertainment abroad." Horace Walpole observed with characteristic waspishness that "the nominal qualification is having been to Italy, the real one being drunk." The Society's funds were augmented by a system of fines imposed on members every time they were enriched by inheritance, marriage or an official appointment or promotion. The Dilettanti did usefully sponsor scholarly expeditions to sketch and measure classical remains and published the results. The Society also played the leading role in founding the Royal Academy in 1768 and funded travelling scholarships to enable young men of promise to study in Italy and Greece. The Club, also known as the Literary Club, was founded in the winter of 1763-4 by Dr. Johnson at the suggestion of Sir Joshua Reynolds and initially met at the Turk's Head in Gerrard Street, Soho. (The building still stands and is now a Chinese supermarket.) The nine original members included the witty, wealthy, splendidly named Topham Beauclerk, who had a library of thirty thousand volumes, and two distinguished Irishmen, Edmund Burke, who had lodgings in Gerrard Street, and Oliver Goldsmith. Later membership expanded to over thirty and included Garrick, Boswell, Fox, Banks and Adam Smith.

Originating in the 1750s, the ladies' circle known as the blue-stockings flourished for half a century, organizing evening assemblies for "rational conversation" without card-playing. Their name was acquired from the work-wear habitually worn by the *littérateur* and amateur botanist Benjamin Stillingfleet, whose poverty denied him the black silk stockings conventionally worn for fashionable gatherings. Mrs. Elizabeth Vesey, credited with being the pioneer of the movement, favoured breaking her parties into small ever-changing groups, whereas Mrs. Elizabeth Montagu arranged her guests in a formal semi-circle, assuring Garrick that, regardless of their birth, wealth or rank, "I never invite idiots." Mrs. Elizabeth Carter taught herself eight languages and was revered by Johnson as a Greek scholar. Hannah More carried the blue-stocking tradition into the next century, describing its charms in a poem "Bas Bleu". Initially famed as a tragedian, she became concerned about the condition of the poor, writing a series of pamphlets which sold two million copies in four years and led to the formation of the Religious Tract Society in 1799. The last of the line was Mary Monckton, who became Countess of Cork. Short, fat, rouged and flamboyantly dressed, an intimate of the tragedienne Sarah Siddons, in her youth she numbered Reynolds, Burke and Horace Walpole among her guests, then the Prince Regent, Byron and Scott, and in old age Peel and the youthful Disraeli. Advancing years exaggerated her eccentricities, which included kleptomania, so that thoughtful friends left out an item of cutlery in the hall for her to conceal in her muff on the way out. "Blue-stocking" was recorded as a synonym for a woman of literary tastes or learning as early as 1804 but was subsequently devalued to mean an unattractive, humourless, female pedant—in other words very much the opposite of the original.

Some gentlemen's clubs had an intellectual or cultural tone. The Athenaeum was founded in 1824 "for the Association of individuals known for their literary or scientific attainments, artists of eminence in any class of the Fine Arts and noblemen and gentlemen distinguished as liberal patrons of Science, Literature and the Arts." It included among its founding members the portraitist Sir Thomas Lawrence, sculptor Sir Francis Chantrey, Sir Walter Scott and the scientists Davy and Faraday. The nearby Reform Club had a more overtly political orientation. The Garrick, founded in 1831, so that "actors and men of education and refinement might meet on equal terms", was much favoured by Thackeray. The literary Savage Club, named for Johnson's rakish friend, Richard Savage, was founded in 1857 by the journalist and *bon vivant* George Augustus Sala and numbered among its members Gilbert and Sullivan, popular authors G. A. Henty, Edgar Wallace and Somerset Maugham and the composer Edward Elgar.

Critics and Critiques

The working-class radicalism that emerged in the capital in response to the American and French Revolutions spawned a plethora of debating and political groups. The more intellectual end of the spectrum was represented by William Godwin (1756-1836), a Dissenting minister turned atheist and anarchist, who married Mary Wollstonecraft, author of the pioneering feminist tract, *A Vindication of the Rights of Woman.* Mary would die giving birth to their daughter, Mary. Mary would marry Shelley and write *Frankenstein.*

William Cobbett, ex-soldier and ex many other things before he found his *métier* as a polemicist, once had a farm where Boots the Chemist now stands in High Street, Kensington, but loathed London with a passion, denouncing "The Great Wen" in his *Twopenny Trash* as the home of stock-jobbers, paper money, Jews and every other malign influence corroding the rural England he loved and idealized. Clerkenwell, an area densely populated by the sort of literate, skilled craftsmen who read Cobbett's vituperations, became strongly associated with the radical tradition. Fittingly it is now home to the Marx Memorial Library, housed in a building which was once a school for the children of Welsh cattle-drovers and where later Lenin would produce the subversive newspaper, *Iskra* (Spark), which was smuggled into Tsarist Russia to ignite a revolution.

Reporting on the revolutionary violence in Paris during the *coup d'état* of Louis-Napoleon Bonaparte in 1851, Walter Bagehot assured his London readers that such scenes could never occur in their city because no Englishman would ever dream of killing another merely for the sake of an idea. (He must have forgotten about Cromwell's New Model Army.) The French, he concluded, were simply too clever ever to be free, because stupidity was the main precondition for stability and that could only be achieved through the obedience of the masses, which was secured by the fact that they could not imagine being anything else but obedient. Bagehot, a graduate of University College, London and later editor of *The Economist*, was himself a heavyweight intellectual. Although he passed much of his time in Somerset, Bagehot had a London home in Belgravia and, like Trollope, well understood the role of the capital as the national arena of political and financial power. In *The English Constitution* he confronted the republican movement that looked to America for a model of constitutional modernity. Bagehot explained teasingly that Britain already was a republic. It was just dressed up like a monarchy to keep the ignorant in their proper place, as the state opening of Parliament so clearly illustrated. The mob cheered the crowned monarch in a glittering coach, surrounded by swaggering soldiers. Those who appreciated the realities of politics—readers of *The Economist*—understood that real power lay with the dull men in dull suits who waited to greet the constitutional peacock.

Perhaps alleged English indifference to the power of abstract ideas explains London's attraction for free-thinking radicals like the Swedish mystic Emanuel Swedenborg, whose writings could not be published in his native land. Swedenborg numbered among his disciples both Blake and Coleridge. Marx and Engels likewise agreed that the country they most vilified as the exemplar of capitalist exploitation also afforded them the largest possible practical measure of freedom to promote its downfall.

Learning for All

The very word "university" implies in its derivation that it should be for the benefit of all. But Oxford and Cambridge came to represent by the eighteenth century both social exclusiveness and intellectual torpor. It was in London that the challenge of educating the masses for an emerging democracy was met with positive response.

The provision of higher education in London was traditionally oriented towards preparation for professional practice. The Inns of Court and, until their extinction, the preparatory Inns of Chancery functioned as training schools for aspiring lawyers, organizing lectures and mock trials known as "moots". St. Thomas' and "Bart's" in effect served as medical schools long before establishing departments actually named and organized as such. Trinity House supervised the training of pilots. Regulatory bodies like the Society of Apothecaries, the company of Scriveners and the Royal Colleges of Physicians and Surgeons augmented the activities of the larger bodies. There were intellectually demanding colleges for the training of Dissenting ministers on the eastern fringes of the City at Hoxton, Wellclose Square and Stepney Green. At Bromley-by-Bow there were specialist schools for youths intending a commercial career with the East India Company. Gresham College lectured liberally, if desultorily, to those who cared to come along. Inaugurated in 1596, the College originally had professors of Astronomy, Divinity, Geometry, Law, Music, Physic and Rhetoric, the "new learning" of Gresham's age. Revived after periods of desuetude, the College has since 1991 been based in Barnard's Inn, Holborn, where its programme of free lectures continues (www.gresham.ac.uk).

The Royal Institution in Albemarle Street was founded in 1799 by Benjamin Thompson, Count von Rumford, to spread knowledge of science and technology for the enrichment of everyday life. Thompson's supporters in this venture included the tyrannical President of the Royal Society, Sir Joseph Banks, and the pathologically reclusive millionaire scientist, Henry Cavendish. The first presiding genius of the Royal Institution was, however, Sir Humphrey Davy, the inventor of the miner's safety lamp. The foremost experimenter of the age, the self-educated Londoner Michael Faraday, was initially employed as Davy's lab assistant. In 1826 it was Faraday who inaugurated the celebrated Christmas Lectures which continue still and which represent the most successful aspect of the founder's original popularizing intentions.

Thanks to the initiative of physician George Birkbeck, London had from 1824 the country's first Mechanics' Institute, where evening classes offered working men the opportunity to learn something of the theoretical principles in which their practical skills were grounded. Widely imitated in provincial cities, Birkbeck's initiative has, as Birkbeck College, a constituent college of the University of London, retained its commitment to the education of mature students through evening provision (hence its motto "Consilium in Nocte"). Annie Besant, Ramsay MacDonald and Sir Arthur Pinero are numbered among Birkbeck's alumni. Another similar initiative was The Working Men's College in Queen Square, founded in 1854. Frederick Denison Maurice, its first principal, had resigned as professor of theology at King's College rather than teach the cruel doctrine of eternal punishment and declared himself a "Christian Socialist". Both William Morris and John Ruskin supported Maurice by serving as lecturers. Ford Madox Brown's symbolic painting *Work* is dominated by muscular labourers mending a road; observing and, in a sense offsetting their efforts, stand two thoughtful figures—Thomas Carlyle (see p.222) and F. D. Maurice.

In the East End alumni of Toynbee Hall included the bookbinder J. M. Dent, who became the publisher of the encyclopaedic *Everyman* series of cheap classics, and Thomas Okey, a basket-weaver who became Cambridge University's first professor of Italian. Further east, at Mile End, the People's Palace was opened by Queen Victoria in the year of her Golden Jubilee 1887. Directly inspired by Sir Walter Besant's recent and visionary novel *All Sorts and Conditions of Men*, it was intended to combine the functions of a cultural centre and an institute of further education. The latter purpose soon overwhelmed the former and in 1934 it became part of the University of London as Queen Mary College.

The Regent Street Polytechnic, first established in 1839, was in effect re-founded in 1882 by Old Etonian sugar tycoon and philanthropist Quintin Hogg, who put in £100,000 of his own money to provide targeted provision for the 16-22 age group. Hogg saw that very little technical or vocational education was available in a London that was increasingly in competition with Europe and the US. Young people, many newcomers to the metropolis or living alone, were, moreover, especially open to the temptations of the public house and the billiard hall, or worse, unless they could find more fruitful alternatives. The "Poly" therefore did far more than provide courses in crafts and commerce and offered sports facilities, including a first-rank fencing club, as well as running a debating society, a magazine, a savings bank and a low-cost travel programme. Hogg's enterprise proved so successful that within a decade the newly-established London County Council took it as the model for a dozen more publicly funded "polys". Hogg's original foundation later merged to become a constituent of the University of Westminster. Hogg himself died when he left his old-fashioned house in Cavendish Square to use the new bathroom facilities around the corner in the Poly and was asphyxiated by a faulty geyser.

A University for London

Until the 1820s London had no university dedicated to the provision of undergraduate education across a range of liberal arts and intellectual disciplines or to the advancement of knowledge through systematic research. Oxford and Cambridge were largely irrelevant both to the education and to the careers of the most powerful and influential intellects of the nineteenth century. Bentham went to Oxford at twelve and had quit by fifteen. Darwin dropped out of Cambridge. Ruskin, treated as a semi-invalid, was granted a "special" degree by Oxford. Other leading intellectual figures were, in effect, funded by fortunes made through London's trade and finance. John Stuart Mill, educated by his formidable father, an East India Company bureaucrat, could translate Latin to Greek and vice versa by six. Self-educated David Ricardo made a City fortune before devoting his leisure to the foundation of classical economics. Banker George Grote retired to write the standard multi-volume history of ancient Greece. As a woman George Eliot was, of course, denied a university education. Herbert Spencer was self-educated. J. R. Green was, it is true, very much an Oxford man, but it was as a slum priest in the East End that he honed the style which made his *Short History of the English People* an instant success. J. A. Froude, a casualty of Oxford's religious politicking, supported himself by journalism in London while pioneering modern British historical writing based on archival research. Many of these intellectuals exerted their influence and supplemented their incomes through their contributions to a vigorous London-based periodical press consisting of titles such as *The Athenaeum*, *The Nineteenth Century* and *The Quarterly Review*.

Macaulay died while perusing Thackeray's contribution to the first issue of the *Cornhill Magazine*.

The foundation of the University of London was inspired by the example of "free", i.e. non-religious, universities in Germany. The moving spirits behind the establishment of University College, London in 1826 were the philosopher Jeremy Bentham and James Mill, father of John Stuart Mill. Unlike Oxford and Cambridge, their institution required neither religious tests nor residency. Outraged by the advent of the "godless college on Gower Street", the Anglican Establishment swiftly riposted by founding King's College on the Strand. In 1836, by a judgment of Solomon, the government decided that neither institution should style itself the University of London but that an over-arching body should be established to supervise the work of what grew into a federal conglomerate of dozens of colleges, schools and institutes. UCL itself would proliferate internally to spawn a teaching hospital, the Slade School of Fine Art, the Galton Laboratory, established by the pioneer of eugenics, Sir Francis Galton, the Flinders Petrie Egyptology Museum and the Museum of the Jewish Historical Society. Alexander Graham Bell, inventor of the telephone, was once a lecturer at UCL, specializing in problems of teaching the deaf to speak. The London School of Economics and Political Science was created largely through the efforts of Fabian intellectuals, most notably Sidney and Beatrice Webb and George Bernard Shaw. Realizing that its intended purposes—research in support of reform—were unlikely to gain it enthusiastic support from the Establishment, it eschewed the pursuit of a royal charter and was simply founded as a limited company. LSE's Directors include William Beveridge, who devised Britain's first National Insurance Scheme and inspired the post-war Welfare State. Imperial College was created in 1907 out of an amalgamation of the Royal College of Science (1845), the Royal School of Mines (1851) and the City and Guilds College (1884).

"Bloomsbury"

The origins of the Bloomsbury Group—"a circle of couples who lived in squares and loved in triangles"—lie not in London but in the University of Cambridge, among a semi-secret, co-optative club of aesthetes and critics who called themselves "the Apostles" and met late into the night to read and discuss papers on abstruse topics. If they subscribed to any unifying set of beliefs it was the prescriptions of the Cambridge philosopher G. E. Moore that the only things in life that mattered were personal relationships and the appreciation of beauty in all its forms. "Bloomsbury" emerged from the desire of some former Apostles, notably Thoby, the son of Sir Leslie Stephen, to replicate their former Cambridge network in London, to which they gravitated after graduation. Thoby's sudden death added a poignancy to their gatherings but meant that it was his sister, (Adeline) Virginia Stephen, the future Virginia Woolf, who became the pivotal figure.

The Bloomsbury area proved a convenient residential location for them. By the first decade of the twentieth century it had become rather run-down, despite the best efforts of the estate managers of the Dukes of Bedford to prevent the conversion of formerly opulent residences into small, slightly seedy hotels. Given its relative centrality, it was quite affordable and it was noted for its bookshops, publishers' offices and the Reading Room of the British Museum. Those who retained active personal or academic links with Cambridge were within a few minutes' walk of King's Cross station, from which the Athens of the Fens could be reached in little more than an hour.

Virginia Woolf, who had not been to Cambridge, Lytton Strachey, who had, and John Maynard Keynes, who as a Fellow and influential administrator of King's College, *was* Cambridge, all came to live in houses on the east side of Gordon Square. Virginia's home became the regular rendezvous for gatherings on Thursday evenings. This was the servants' night off, hence the cue for uninhibited discussion of topics inappropriate within the hearing of the lower orders—the penalty of their absence being the restriction of refreshments to whisky, coffee and buns.

The "Bloomsberries" may well be, in relation to their number, the most written about social group in the history of London. Certainly they wrote a great deal about each other and about themselves. There is no general agreement, however, as to just how many of them there were or just what they constituted—a group, a network, a movement, a *tendance*, a conspiracy or an infection in the body cultural. The biographical *Dictionary of Bloomsbury*, compiled by Alan and Veronica Palmer, contains over a hundred and forty entries. Personal relationships were more important than talent in determining membership of the inner core. The Bloomsbury stance is reflected in the ironic title and clinically destructive content of Lytton Strachey's *Eminent Victorians*. Unlike the conventional Victorian biography, a three-decker in which failure was only mentioned to be overcome triumphantly and from which all hint of impropriety or scandal was completely banished, Strachey's terse essays portrayed the imperialist "martyr" General Gordon as a periodic dipsomaniac with an alarming interest in small boys and Florence Nightingale as a manipulative exploiter of a self-induced state of semi-invalidism.

Bloomsbury overlapped with "Bohemia" but was distinguishable from it. Bohemian artists and writers in Fitzrovia sometimes did live quite literally on the edge of starvation. Most of the Bloomsbury *eminenti* were well-cushioned from penury either by a private income or by being paid relatively well for doing relatively little. Virginia Woolf, who certainly never thought of herself as a materialist, could earn as much for an essay that took her a couple of days—£50—as she paid one of her own servants in a year. Despite the attractions of Bloomsbury itself, many of its residents would have agreed with Lord Burghley (even if they probably agreed with him on nothing else) that London was a wonderful place to live in providing you could get out of it. Hence the value they attached to having a country place, however dilapidated— more scope for self-expressive home decoration—or for a sojourn in the remoteness of rural France.

"Bloomsbury" is now hailed not so much for literary or artistic achievements as for being an experiment in life-styles, an experiment which declared that the quality of a dinner-party was unrelated to the number of courses served or of servants in attendance and that it was quite acceptable to paint your living-room walls with murals of your own devising. Bloomsbury continued to exist after the Great War but somehow it was no longer "Bloomsbury"—perhaps because the growing acceptance of customs and opinions that had once seemed outrageous no longer did so. In addition, the rise of fascism in Continental Europe suddenly flooded London with refugee intellectuals—Sigmund Freud, Ernst (*The Story of Art*) Gombrich, publishers George Weidenfeld and Andre Deutsch, historians Geoffrey Elton and Eric Hobsbawm, philosophers Karl Popper, Friedrich von Hayek and Arthur Koestler, film-maker Emeric Pressburger and Stefan Lorant, pioneer of photojournalism. Beside these dazzling talents Bloomsbury's Bohemianism would look less faded or tepid than simply irrelevant.

Creative Industries

The post-war expansion of higher education means that the University of London has been joined by a dozen more universities scattered across the metropolis from Barking to Uxbridge and twice that number of other degree-granting institutions. Among these the London School of Economics has, if anything, attained an even greater cultural prominence, even if University College outranks it across the disciplinary board and the School of Oriental and African Studies rivals it as a centre of specialist expertise. Commentators on Britain's post-war decolonization often joked that it had become a Darwinian struggle between graduates of Sandhurst and alumni of the LSE. Truth to tell, LSE graduates *have* included Prime Ministers of Barbados, Dominica, St. Lucia, Jamaica (2) and Mauritius and Presidents of Ghana (2), Kenya (2), Fiji, Kiribati and India. More to the point, the writers of *Yes, Minister* made their creation, Jim Hacker, an LSE graduate and the creator of the *West Wing* conferred the same distinction on President Bartlet.

London graduates not re-recruited back into academia have found employment in the greatly expanded bureaucracy of central government, in a plethora of think tanks, institutes and foundations and in the BBC and other media.

There are still clearly Intellectuals with a capital I, now most prominently seen as presenters of improving series of television programmes. Often global in scope, these are still usually master-minded from London. Pioneering work was done by Sir David Attenborough's nature programmes and Jacob Bronowski's *Ascent of Man*, a history of scientific endeavour. Opera director Jonathan Miller has dealt with the human body and atheism. Novelist, broadcaster and cultural commissar Melvyn Bragg has explored the *Adventure of English*. Simon Schama, a Jewish scholarship boy in the mould of Bronowski, became a small screen superstar with his soft-spoken *History of Britain*. The combative David Starkey, formerly of LSE, has taken several tours around the Tudors and outlined the whole history of Britain's monarchy. Sir Roy Strong, former director of the National Portrait Gallery and the V & A, has, by contrast, confined himself to big books and branched off into gardening. Lesser lights have, since 1980, found their house journal in the *London Review of Books*, to which Alan Bennett, Frank Kermode, Hilary Mantel, Tom Paulin and Michael Wood are regular contributors,

More remarkable than the reinvention of the individual Intellectual as a talking head with a populist mission is the sheer volume of London talent employed in what have become known as the "creative industries". With a fifth of the UK's designated collections concentrated in its two hundred museums and galleries, with forty thousand listed buildings and structures, two thousand libraries and three hundred plus archives, London has inevitably required appropriately qualified staff to work in them. London also has seventy per cent of all the UK's recording studios with some twenty thousand people employed in the music industry. Its hundred theatres turn over a billion pounds a year and employ twice as many people as the music business. Almost two thousand book publishers employ some ninety thousand staff. Seven thousand magazines and journals are also published from London. Total employment in "the creative industries" surpasses the half million mark. This has at least benefited the educated, if not necessarily the intellectual.

NOVEL ENCOUNTERS
A Fictional Interlude

"Nothing can happen nowhere." Elizabeth Bowen

As a literary canvas, London has been patchily painted. Soho and the East End provide recurrent settings for the examination of the human condition. Muswell Hill has yet to find its Balzac. The early nineteenth century, the 1880s, the Blitz and the immediate post-war years seem to share a similar appeal in terms of period. At the micro-level the boarding-house and the pub, with their contrasting potentialities for claustrophobia and introspection, expansiveness and performance, have repeatedly proved attractive to writers. *Hangover Square: A Story of Darkest Earl's Court* (1941) by Patrick Hamilton exploits the counterpoise between pub drinkers and boarding-house boredom to set up a (literally) skull-shattering *dénouement*. In Lynne Reid Banks' first and best-known novel *The L-Shaped Room* (1960) her five-storey Fulham abode accommodates convenient ethnic stereotypes in the form of a Jewish writer and a black jazz-player. In Maureen Duffy's

Senate House, University of London

Londoners: An Elegy (1983) the androgynous narrator escapes a bedsitter in search of the human warmth of the nearby pub. Muriel Spark's boarding house in *A Far Cry from Kensington* (1988) is shabby-genteel rather than seedy but still populated by life's casualties. In Barbara Vine's *King Solomon's Carpet* (1992) the misfit occupants of a crumbling former school overlooking the Jubilee Line are drawn together by their various but common connections with the Tube. Dennis Clegg, the deranged central character in Patrick McGrath's *Spider* (1990) lives in a dilapidated East End boarding-house and pursues his delusional fantasies in the "clotted web of dark compartments and narrow passageways" which hem it in and which, he believes, contain the key to his mother's murder.

George Gissing claimed that the writer of integrity "will oftener find his inspiration in a London garret than amid the banality of the plutocrat's drawing-room." In his autobiographical novel *The Private Papers of Henry Ryecroft* (1903), Gissing looked back on his own impoverished but studious and productive early years in an Islington garret as a time of "pleasure, zeal, hope", snuggled up with a fire and a book, oblivious to the dark and damp outside his window. In a freezing room in Notting Hill Arthur Machen, by contrast, envied a nightwatchman outside with the comfort of his brazier. Machen's boarding-house contained just the sort of real-life assortment of strangers—Greek, Irish and Armenian—that would seem to beg for fictionalization but instead he found himself drawn to that "detested habitation of the dead", Kensal Green Cemetery, where he was bewitched by "shattered pillars and granite urns and every sort of horrid heathenry". This led Machen into an exploration of London as a "goblin city" of the menacing and the macabre. Labyrinthine and maze-like, London offered the writer the materials of the alchemist—"all the wonders lie within a stone's throw of King's Cross station." A forerunner of the "psycho-geography" school of writing, Machen found success in the 1890s ploughing the adjacent fields of paganism, occultism and horror in the *Great God Pan* (1894) and *The Three Imposters* (1895). Turning actor then journalist, he was subsequently responsible for the war-time "Angel of Mons" myth.

The contrasts of which London consists are frequently presented in terms of a journey, be it a leisurely walk, as in Mrs. Dalloway's dilatory odyssey from Pimlico to Bond Street, or a determined trudge, as in Reardon's six-mile trek from Islington to attempt a reconciliation with his estranged wife in Westbourne Park in Gissing's *New Grub Street* (1891). In the same novel the destitute Biffen passes through Kensington Gardens to Fulham and across the river to Putney where he kills himself. In Richard Marsh's extraordinary *The Beetle* (1897), which anticipates Kafka's insect reincarnation and combines it with a dollop of the Isis cult, there is a frantic chase from Limehouse to St. Pancras to save the heroine from the horrors of white slavery. An Underground trip from Sloane Square to Lancaster Gate provides a minutely detailed setting for the initial encounter between Kate Croy and Morton Densher in Henry James' *The Wings of the Dove* (1902). John Somerfield's agitprop *May Day* (1936) follows its characters across the capital from early morning to late night, in Ken Worple's memorable phrase "*Mrs. Dalloway...* written by a Communist party bus driver."

Even among writers with what at first sight appears to be an obsessive topographical awareness acts of literary displacement frequently occur. The London Conan Doyle used for his Sherlock Holmes stories combines the very precisely real with the imagined. On coming to settle in London Holmes first takes lodgings in Montague Street, next to the British Museum, so that he can use the Reading Room. Holmes' permanent home was famously established at 221B Baker Street but there is no such address and the descriptions given of it imply that it would, in any case, have been at the other end of that lengthy thoroughfare, i.e. 21B. Holmes' favourite Italian restaurant in Soho is likewise a fiction, though an entirely plausible one. Virginia Woolf's Mrs. Dalloway stands at one of the gates to St. James' Park and watches the double-decker buses on Piccadilly—although there is nowhere you can do this. In Margery Allingham's *The Tiger in the Smoke* (1952) urbane detective Albert Campion threatens to lose his cool as escaped convict Jack Havoc ("Tiger") eludes him for three days during London's last great "pea-souper" (smog) in a chase from the East End to exclusive but imaginary "St. Petersgate Square". In Peter Ackroyd's *The House of Dr. Dee* (1993) the protagonist inherits the house in Clerkenwell which once belonged to Elizabeth I's magus. Dr. Dee in fact lived reclusively in Putney; it is Ackroyd himself who dwells in Clerkenwell. Martin Amis' *London Fields* (1989) is less about Highbury than Notting Hill, "Dogshit Park" being a contemptuous veiled reference to railed-off, exclusive Ladbroke Square.

Chronological displacement, into an imagined future or a re-imagined past, is equally common. In *The Napoleon of Notting Hill* (1904) G. K. Chesterton's London of 1984 has been split into autonomous boroughs fiercely assertive of their independence against the homogenizing forces the author so deplored, bureaucracy and big business in particular. The Provost of Notting Hill dares to oppose an assault on his neighbourhood by "modern improvers with their boards and inspectors and surveyors". In Richard Jeffries' cataclysmic *After London* (1885) the capital has entirely reverted to become a poisonous swamp inhabited by malicious dwarves. In Will Self's *Great Apes* (1997) the Londoners have all become chimpanzees. In *Come Before Christ and Murder Love* (1997) Stewart Home conjures an occult sexual current linking Elizabeth I in Greenwich with John Dee up-river at Putney. Once energized this will spawn the entire British empire, but only when the vital spark has been supplied by a human sacrifice.

Another tactic is to commandeer actual historical Londoners and confront them with a literary invention. The grisly murders in Ackroyd's *Dan Leno and the Limehouse Golem* (1994), set in the East End in 1880, draw in not only the eponymous clog-dancing comedian but also George Gissing and the inventor of the proto-computer known as the Difference Engine, Charles Babbage—who had actually died in 1871. Paul West's *The Women of Whitechapel* (1991) reworks the Ripper story with a cast of real historical personalities: the half-witted, bi-sexual Prince Eddy (a.k.a. Prince Albert Victor Christian Edward, heir to the heir to the throne), the royal surgeon Sir William Gull, the Impressionist painter Walter Sickert and his model, a shop-girl, Annie Crooke, who is (fatally for her) a Roman Catholic and therefore doubly unsuitable, by rank and by religion, to bear an accidental heir to the heir to the throne. When the luckless Annie does indeed become pregnant by the hapless Eddy, the Ripper murders are organized to cover up a potential royal scandal. As West himself confessed, he based his account on facts but "few enough of them".

Iain Sinclair's *Downriver* (1991), an aqueous parallel to Joyce's *Ulysses*, excoriates Mrs. Thatcher's London by means of twelve tenuously linked stories with a mixed cast of real and imagined characters ranging from the (for Sinclair) reasonably predictable (Jack the Ripper) to the (for Sinclair) predictably unexpected—aboriginal cricketers, the driver of a train carrying nuclear waste through Hackney and Lewis Carroll's "Alice". A formless novel to match an increasingly formless and dislocated city, Sinclair's saga mixes the horrors of the 1878 *Princess Alice* pleasure-boat disaster, when over six hundred Londoners drowned in sewage, with the whimsical notion of the colonization of the Isle of Dogs by the Vatican, which re-brands it as the Isle of Doges.

If the Thames is a corridor to Iain Sinclair, to Angela Carter it was a frontier. Her last novel *Wise Children* (1991) begins with the observation "Why is London like Budapest? Because it is two cities divided by a river." Tracing the history of London's popular culture from music-hall to TV game-shows, the novel symbolically reunites a Brixton family from "the left-hand side, the side the tourist rarely sees, the bastard side of Old Father Thames" with up-market relatives in north London.

Christopher Marlowe's death in an alleged tavern brawl in Deptford has inspired several fictional attempts to provide plausible explanations for his (presumed) murder. In *Albert Angelo* (1964) B. S. Johnson offered his own very peculiar take on the mystery, page 149 having a hole in it, made, it was claimed, by the fatal knife-thrust which despatched Marlowe and through which, it was further claimed, the future could be read. Australian author Peter Carey's *Jack Maggs* (1997) skilfully appropriates the storyline and characters of *Great Expectations* to produce a fiction in which the eponymous hero returns secretly from Australia after twenty years' transportation to pass himself off as a footman and to attach himself to a thinly-disguised Dickens, a cocky young novelist with a penchant for hypnotism and a literally fatal infatuation with his sister-in-law. *The Quincunx: The Inheritance of John Huffam* (1995), by Charles Palliser, similarly pastiches the Dickens genre (Huffam being one of Dickens' middle names) with a plot of Byzantine complexity and a cast of hundreds, revolving around the supposed search for a missing will. Sarah Waters' *Fingersmith* (2003) likewise expertly evokes the stifling sordidness of a thieves' kitchen in the Southwark of the same early Victorian decades. Mathew Kneale's *Sweet Thames* (1992), set against the 1849 cholera epidemic, plunges its high-minded sanitary reformer into a threatening world of slums, sewers and scavengers.

G. K. Chesterton's whimsical fantasy was written when Notting Hill was the epitome of bourgeois respectability. By the time Percy Wyndham Lewis penned his dyspeptic *Rotting Hill* (1951) it had become incredibly run down, its fine stuccoed mansions crammed with stateless refugees and bewildered immigrants from the Caribbean. Trinidadian Samuel Selvon (1923-94) gave the latter a voice— literally—with *The Lonely Londoners* (1956), one of the first novels to be written entirely in a Caribbean *patois*. This was the author's own confection, a fusion of the differing speech-rhythms and vocabularies of Barbados, Jamaica, Antigua, Dominica and so on, which in the West Indies existed as separate and distinct but in London rubbed up against each other in drinking-clubs and labour exchanges. Selvon's evocation of the migrant experience is as much reflective as descriptive, including, for instance, a ten-page discourse on the nature of love in the city, written without a single colon or even a comma. As episodic and plotless as the city itself, *The Lonely Londoners* reflects life along the

Bayswater Road, where hopeful newcomers in search of prosperity and personal liberation all too often endured the gloom and isolation of confinement in a damp and dreary basement. *City of Spades* (1957) by Colin MacInnes, a Notting Hill resident, was an outsider's exploration of the same phenomenon. Its sequel, *Absolute Beginners* (1959), chronicles the early days of sex and drugs and rock 'n' roll, culminating in the 1958 "riots" which made the neighbourhood nationally notorious. Guyanese-born crime writer Mike Phillips drew on his own intimate knowledge of the very different, gentrified Notting Hill of the 1980s in *Blood Rights* (1989). Notting Hill and Ladbroke Grove also feature prominently in Michael Moorcock's monumental *Mother London* (1988), a tragi-comic chronicle of London since the Blitz, structured around three characters variously damaged by wartime bombing; to many critics it is the definitive post-war London novel.

With characteristic bathos Colin MacInnes described the Grand Junction Canal, which serves to define north Kensington's northern boundary, as a body of water "that nothing floats on except cats and contraceptives". Margaret Drabble's *The Radiant Way* (1987) features a psychopath who cuts the heads off people venturing to stroll along the canal towpath. In *Mother London* the Scaramanga sisters live in (fictitious) Bank Cottage on the south side of the canal, opposite Kensal Green cemetery. Erno Goldfinger's gigantic 1973 Trellick Tower, which overlooks the canal, has inspired similarly dystopian visions. In J. G. Ballard's *High Rise* (1975) technological breakdown is followed by social breakdown as the occupants of the tower's different floors wage war on each other. In Amis' *London Fields* the tower is the home of Keith Talent, "a very bad guy". In Nick Barclay's *Crumple Zone* (2000) part-time teacher Cee Harper comes home to find her flat trashed—presumably by a neighbour, as it is thirty floors up and there is a mysterious new hole under her floorboards...

The Senate House of the University of London, a Stalinist-style stone tower lowering over Russell Square, was nearing completion when the Second World War broke out and it was taken over to house the newly-established Ministry of Information. A piece of statement architecture if ever there was one, hailed as London's first skyscraper and at the time only overtopped by St. Paul's, the building was soon to be immortalized in fiction. Graham Greene made it *The Ministry of Fear* (1943), from which a shadowy group of agents pursue paranoid former mental patient Arthur Rowe through the blitzed-out capital after he innocently implicates himself in the mercy killing of his wife. George Orwell, who as a working journalist had had to cope with the edicts issued by Senate House censors, made Senate House the model for the Ministry of Truth in *1984* (1948), where Winston Smith works, daily falsifying past and present news to make it conform to the dictates of The Party. In Evelyn Waugh's *Sword of Honour* trilogy (1952-61) a lunatic prowls the building's endless corridors with a bomb ticking away in his briefcase as one bureaucrat after another redirects him to someone else.

The Blitz itself is the destructive force that precipitates *The End of the Affair* in Graham Greene's novel of that title (1951). In *The Heat of the Day* (1945) by Elizabeth Bowen the chaotic impact of the Blitz on London mirrors the uncertainties of an affair in which a suitor reveals that his rival is actually a spy. Rose Macaulay's *The World My Wilderness* (1950) explores the bombed-out post-war cityscape through the eyes of a young French girl fascinated by "streets, caves and cellars, the foundations of a wrecked merchant city, grown over by green and gold fennel and ragwort."

Five minutes' walk and a million miles away from Senate House in Bloomsbury lies Soho. In relation to its size few areas of London can match this compact patch for literary prominence. In Conrad's *The Secret Agent* Soho is the setting for the pornographic book shop which serves as a cover for agent Verloc's subversive activities. *Casanova's Chinese Restaurant* gives a title to one of the novels in Anthony Powell's saga, *A Dance to the Music of Time*. Razor-scarred Frank Norman's memoir of 1950s Soho, *Stand on Me* (1960), revolves around the "86" café on Frith Street, epicentre of a universe populated by oddballs with bizarre nicknames and outlandish lifestyles. Tanked up on a preferred cocktail of benzedrine and cider, the author progresses with all the inevitability of a Hogarthian print series from purloining books from Foyles to passing dud cheques and a spell in prison. Norman's circle of acquaintance overlapped with that of the multi-talented but self-destructive Daniel Farson, whose *Soho in the Fifties* (1987) achieved a canonic status. Farson's self-conscious use of the "Day in Soho" framework underlines the contempt with which his coterie regarded conventional time-budgeting as they lurched from pub to club to restaurant to street-corner to pub... Colin Wilson's *Adrift in Soho*

(1964) makes the same point in its title. In *Sour Sweet* (1983), Timothy Mo's second novel, Hong Kong migrant Chen stoically slaves long hours in a Soho Chinese restaurant in pursuit of the good life for his wife and damaged but beloved infant until wider family obligations drag him to destruction at the hands of Triad clans. The bar-side spleneticisms of the last Soho "character", Jeffrey Bernard of the Coach and Horses, intermittently published in his irregular newspaper column and aptly encapsulated as "a suicide note in instalments", were transferred to the stage in 1989 with characteristic deftness by Keith Waterhouse as *Jeffrey Bernard Is Unwell.* The formidable landlord of the Coach and Horses composed his own memoir of his reign with the appropriately uncompromising title of *You're Barred, You Bastard.* Boozy dandy Julian Maclaren-Ross, the model for X. Trapnel, in Anthony Powell's *Dance to the Music of Time,* in his own *Memoirs of the Forties* (1964), gives a vivid depiction of "Fitzrovia", the down-at-heel western periphery of Bloomsbury where you could still get a room for ten shillings a week. The *genius loci* was the prolific, promiscuous portraitist Augustus John, his chief acolyte the drunken, dishevelled Dylan Thomas, their favoured venues the Fitzroy Tavern in Charlotte Street, the Wheatsheaf in Rathbone Place and, sandwiched between them, the Eiffel Tower restaurant at the corner of Percy Street.

Clerkenwell is the setting for George Gissing's best-known novel *The Nether World* (1889), where the characters are immured, not for once in a sordid boarding-house, but in the barrack-like Farringdon Road Buildings, supposedly "model dwellings", representing "the economy prevailing in today's architecture" and omitting "no depressing circumstance". In an effort to escape these surroundings Sidney and Clara Kirkwood flee to Crouch End which could

> *still remind one that it was country a very short time ago. The streets have a smell of newness, of dampness; the bricks retain their complexion, the stucco has not rotted more than one expects in a year or two; poverty tries to hide itself with Venetian blinds.*

Clerkenwell also exerts its depressive powers in Arnold Bennett's *Riceyman Steps* (1923). Although Bennett's name is reflexively associated with the Potteries where he grew up, he lived most of his adult life in London. *The Grand Babylon Hotel* (1902) much resembles the Savoy, whose chef returned the compliment by devising the recipe for Omelette Arnold Bennett, a sybaritic supper compote of eggs, black pepper, flaked haddock, parmesan cheese and double cream. No such indulgences are ever likely to be seen in *Riceyman Steps*, where a run-down second-hand bookshop is inherited by miserly, middle-aged Henry Earlforward whose late marriage to a widow is doomed with all the certainty that the gloom of their environment implies.

Early novelists of the East End wrote from first-hand experience. W. W. Jacobs was born in Wapping, the son of a dockworker. His often humorous tales featured dockers and sailors, as the titles of his collections imply: *Many Cargoes* (1896*), Light Freights* (1901) and *Night Watches* (1914). Jacobs' gentle touch appealed to a genteel readership whose desire for an insight into low life was tempered by a concern that it should not be too low. Simon Blumenfeld's *Jew Boy* (1936) highlighted the emergence of a new East End identity among young Stepney Jews generationally distanced from the religious and familial claustrophobia of their grandparents' ghetto experiences of Eastern Europe. The same author's *Phineas Kahn* (1937) traced the odyssey of Jewish migrants from a Russian *shtetl* to the East End of the 1930s where renewed persecution reappears in the shape of the bully-boys of the British Union of Fascists.

Whereas these authors and others, like Arthur Morrison, were noted for the realism of their treatment of the East End, many post-war writers have tended to treat the area as a locus for the fantastical. Iain Sinclair's *Lud Heat* (1975) chronicled the author's time as a parks gardener and brewery worker to produce a melange of poems, diary entries and reflections on books, myths and drinking-partners and the psychic symbolism of Hawksmoor's churches. In *The Chimney Sweeper's Boy* (1999) Barbara Vine forsook her familiar territory in affluent W11 to produce a surprisingly well-informed evocation of the steamier goings-on in the steam-room of the now closed Mile End baths. London's potential for making normally separate cultural worlds collide is taken to its extreme in Stewart Home's *Red London* (1994) when Fellatio Jones invades the Hampstead Everyman cinema at the head of the Stratford Skinhead Squad to slaughter the audience of archetypal intellectuals as they are engrossed in a Fellini masterpiece.

North London, more particularly Holloway, is the setting for George and Weedon Grossmith's satire on suburban pretensions, *Diary of a Nobody* (1892). Bank clerk Charles Pooter of newly-built Brickfield Terrace battles valiantly to maintain a petit-bourgeois gentility against the contrary efforts of uppity servants, deceitful tradesmen, nosy neighbours and a layabout son with a dangerous penchant for amateur dramatics. A century later, north London's middle-class ghettoes provide the setting for Nick Hornby's best-selling sequence based on contemporary fetishes—*Fever Pitch* (1992) (male obsessive and soccer), *High Fidelity* (1995) (male obsessive and music), and *About a Boy* (1998) (male obsessive and emotions).

In south London Lambeth probably comes off best, or worst, fictionally speaking, as an epitome of misery and squalor. Gissing's *Thyrza* (1887) was set there. In the spring following its publication, the author came back to a boarding-house in Lucretia Street to view the emaciated corpse of his estranged wife. *Mord Em'ly* by W. Pett Ridge chronicles the struggles of the feisty daughter of a drunken mother from Pandora Buildings, Walworth; like the box of classical legend, her life proves full of the unexpected. Girl gangs, reform school, domestic service, the Salvation Army, socialism, waitressing and the world of boxing all figure in the central character's search for a better life. *Mord Em'ly* was translated to the silent screen in 1922 and reprinted as recently as 1992. Pett Ridge's usual output, however, drew heavily on his years as a railway employee and appealed largely to railway buffs.

The Elephant and Castle (1949) by R. C. Hutchinson was an early exploration of inter-ethnic tension as imagined through a marriage between a West End girl and the son of Italian immigrants living in Southwark. In *The Magic Toyshop* (1967) Angela Carter sends spoiled country girl Melanie to live in Brixton with poor relations—brutish cousins, a repressed aunt and a mad uncle. Muriel Spark's dark comedy of (bad) manners, *The Ballad of Peckham Rye* (1960), depicts late 1950s Peckham as a curiously enclosed community, more like a village than an adjunct to a former imperial metropolis. Nell Dunn established her career with two accounts of working-class life in south London—*Up the Junction* (1963) which dealt with the realities of sex as experienced by women and *Poor Cow* (1967), which tackled abusive men.

South London's contemporary chroniclers have sought to mine (or undermine) the area to comic effect. In *The Buddha of Suburbia* (1990) the Bromley in which the author, Hanif Kureishi, grew up is a prison of conformity to be escaped by fleeing to near but oh-so-distant central London. Nigel Williams' Wimbledon is a land of Muslim fantasists and permanently frustrated poisoners. In Scottish writer Martin Millar's surreal first novel *Milk, Sulphate and Alby Starvation* (1987) the Milk Marketing Board takes out a contract on a south London comic-collector and drug-dealer who is also on the run from a Kung-fu mafia gang. In the same author's frenetic *Lux the Poet* (1988) the amiable but impossibly vain aspirant teenage bard is pursued through a Brixton riot by the police and the vengeful Jane Austen Mercenaries.

ISLINGTON

Islington is north London's Notting Hill and followed a similar trajectory of sliding from respectability to seediness and then recovering through gentrification to become a bastion of café culture, fringe theatre and, as Ed Glinert observes, "spiritual homeland of New Labour".

Medieval Islington was an agricultural settlement, much of it owned by the church. The oldest surviving building, Canonbury Tower, dates from around 1509, when it was rebuilt by William Bolton, the last prior of St. Bartholomew the Great. Later occupants were to include Francis Bacon, Oliver Goldsmith and Washington Irving. In the seventeenth century Islington acquired a new significance as the terminal point of Sir Hugh Myddelton's New River project, which brought fresh water to London from forty miles away. His statue now appropriately dominates Islington Green, where the area's two major thoroughfares, Upper Street and Essex Road, converge. The name of the nearby Underground station, Angel, recalls the most famous of many local coaching-inns, where Tom Paine is claimed to have penned his *Rights of Man*. By the eighteenth century Islington was known for its taverns and tea-gardens, nurseries and academies, cricket, cream and cheese-cakes. Sadler's Wells evolved from a medicinal spa to a musical theatre. Today's Almeida Theatre began its life as a Literary Institute.

Pentonville was developed from 1773 onwards as one of London's earliest planned suburbs. Dickens made it the home of kindly Mr. Brownlow, saviour and unknowing grandfather of Oliver Twist, making his gracious residence a symbolic counterpoint to Fagin's squalid

Sadler's Wells

thieves' kitchen on Saffron Hill, little more than a mile away. Residential development began in earnest in the 1820s with the building up of Barnsbury, Canonbury and Highbury. Charles Lamb, who had chosen Islington for his retirement, moved on to still rural Enfield after a few years. Half a century later Islington had acquired a distinctly artisan atmosphere, signified by the popularity of Collins' Music Hall (1862-1958) overlooking the Green. Sadler's Wells became a pickle factory. Once gracious squares declined to become "shabby genteel", attractive only to contrary types like Walter Sickert and George Orwell, who based Winston Smith's seedy "Victory Mansions" in *1984* on his own place in Canonbury Square. Basil Spence, architect of Knightsbridge barracks and Kensington Town Hall, was something of a lone pioneer when he moved to Islington in the 1950s. In 1967 a survey revealed that sixty per cent of Islington houses were in multiple occupation, more than anywhere else in London.

A decade and a half later the first edition of *The London Enyclopaedia* observed that "although rediscovery by the professional classes since the 1960s has revived social amenities—like Camden Passage antiques market and small theatres—the borough as a whole has remained depressed with a serious unemployment and housing problem." Another decade later still the *Virgin Insider's Guide to London* could, however, refer to Islington as "a highly sought-after and expensive place to live"—and that was the year *before* Tony Blair famously lunched with Gordon Brown at the since defunct Granita restaurant to determine which of them would lead the Labour Party into the new dawn.

Chapter Six
THE BLASTS OF WAR

"The greatest target in the world, a kind of tremendous, fat, vulnerable cow tied up to attract the beast of prey... The flying peril is not a peril from which one can fly. We cannot possibly retreat. We cannot move London."
Winston S. Churchill, House of Commons, 1934

St. Paul's under fire, based on a photograph by Herbert Mason

London did not even have walls until about a hundred and fifty years after its foundation but everywhere bears evidence of the imprint of war. The name of the Borough of Tower Hamlets recalls that its settlements were the original recruiting-ground for the garrison of the fortress which straddled the City's eastern boundary. Time, however, erases memory. Few now know that the Almeida Theatre and up-market Maida Vale both take their names from victories of the Napoleonic Wars. The visitor from France, the French visitor especially, arrives at Waterloo, a station triumphantly named for Britain's last great victory over the French. To rub the point home, apart from Waterloo Bridge, there are a dozen other locations bearing the same name and forty-eight named for the victorious commander, Wellington. Trafalgar Square commemorates Nelson's great naval victory and is remembered in the names of a dozen thoroughfares; Nelson himself in a further thirty. The Duke of Marlborough's victory over the French at Blenheim in 1704 is commemorated in thirty-two street names and Marlborough himself in thirty-seven more. Many of these Blenheims and Marlboroughs are in suburbs built well over a century after Marlborough's death. The battles of the Crimean War would have been in current memory during the Victorian era of suburbanization, so there are sixteen locations named for the Alma, three for the Redan, two for Balaclava, and one each for Inkerman and Sebastopol. The British commander, one-armed Lord Raglan (1788-1855), has eleven roads named after him, compared with twenty-four Nightingales and twenty-one Florences. The Great War was too traumatic for anyone to want to live in a road named for Gallipoli, Loos, Passchendaele or the Somme, although there are three streets named for the Marne and one for Mons, as well as half a dozen for Kitchener and a couple for Haig. Wars, battles and heroes figure even more prominently as the names of public houses than they do in the topography of London's streets. The Bull and Mouth is a corruption of Boulogne Mouth, a 1544 naval victory of Henry VIII. Portobello refers to the seizure of the Spanish base at Puerto Bello in Panama in 1739 by Admiral Vernon with just six ships.

Legionary London

Roman Londinium was an administrative and commercial centre, rather than a military stronghold, although it was the hub of a road system whose purpose was primarily strategic. The city also had military origins in the sense that Roman sappers built the first bridge across the Thames and laid out the grid plan on which settlement developed. The fort which stood at the north-west corner of the city's walls, more or less where the Museum of London now stands, was less a citadel than a barracks to accommodate a modest-sized garrison to guard the governor, regulate traffic in and out of the city and guarantee public order. It probably also served as a stores depot, issuing kit, especially warmer clothing, to legionaries newly arrived from warmer climates and preparing to move up-country to safeguard the chilly borders with Scotland and Wales. The amphitheatre at Guildhall would have been used as a military drill-ground. One of the city's bath-houses was probably intended for separate use by the military. The Temple of Mithras, found during the digging of the foundations of Bucklersbury House in 1954, would certainly have numbered soldiers among its worshippers. A relief of the god ritually slaying a bull, found along the former course of the Walbrook in 1889, had been dedicated by Ulpius Silvanus, a veteran of the II Legio Augusta. (That particular legion, usually committed to frontier duties, has inspired an historical re-enactment group accessible on www. legiiavg.org.uk.) Mithraism, unusually among the "mystery religions" widely practised throughout the Roman Empire, offered the promise of an afterlife and was therefore particularly attractive to those whose lives more than usually exposed to the risk of sudden death. The cult, confined to males, was based on an elaborate hierarchy of adherence, involving tests of endurance, and functioned as a sort of freemasonry for men without families or fixed ties. The traders of Londinium also doubtless benefited from the city's function as a centre for "rest and recreation". One of the more intriguing acquisitions made by the British Museum was a set of graphically illustrated tokens used by patrons of brothels to request specific services; they are not on display to the general public.

The declining security situation of late Roman Londinium is tellingly illustrated by the fate of the tomb of Classicianus. Appointed Procurator by Nero in AD 62, Gaius Julius Alpinus Classicianus was a high-born Romanized Gaul. He died in office and his interment was marked by a hefty tomb (now in the British Museum) erected by his grieving widow, Julia Pacata Indiana. As Londinium came under increasing threat from the raids of Germanic pirates in the mid-fourth century it was decided to strengthen the eastern wall of the city with protruding bastions on which weaponry could be mounted. Classicianus' tomb was accordingly one among many monuments apparently smashed up to make builders' rubble. One major fragment was found in 1852, a second, confirming his identity in 1935.

Castles and Crusaders

Whereas the Romans relied on a professional army the Anglo-Saxons considered every able-bodied man a potential fighter. London's ancient division into wards, headed by aldermen, probably originated as the organizational framework of its militia. The fortress William the Conqueror ordered to be built at the eastern extremity of London evolved into the Tower of London. The Tower was ringed by a circuit of other castles, each a day's march from each other, to offer mutual support in case of insurrection. Of these Windsor remains as Europe's largest and oldest occupied castle.

English involvement in the Crusading movement was initially limited but the military orders it spawned in the early twelfth century, the Templars and the Hospitallers, soon established monastic settlements in London, the first in the area subsequently known as the Temple, the second in Clerkenwell where the great gateway to their former properties still stands. Properly called the Knights of the Hospital of St. John of Jerusalem, they gave their name to the St. John's Wood area which they owned. The story of the order and its modern reincarnation is displayed in their museum at St. John's Gateway, Clerkenwell. The round Temple church was consecrated in 1185 by Honorius, Patriarch of Jerusalem, who had made the immense journey from Palestine in the (abortive) hope of persuading Henry II to take up the cross. Richard I "Coeur de Lion" is famously supposed to have said that he would sell London itself if he could find a buyer in order to finance the Third Crusade. Apart from his coronation Richard had little to do with the city apart from raise money from it, spending only six months of his ten-year reign in England. He is nevertheless commemorated by a stupendous statue in Old Palace Yard. But the king's needs and perhaps his prolonged absence, too, allowed for the emergence of a major new figure in London's history, its first known mayor, Henry FitzAylwin.

Apart from the large-scale expeditions organized by monarchs there was always a trickle of knights going out on crusade as individuals or in small groups. By tradition they are said to have left London from the church of the Holy Sepulchre in Newgate Street. Just to the west there was for centuries an inn appropriately named the Saracen's Head. A few hundred yards from there, on the wall of St. Bartholomew's Hospital is a plaque marking the execution site and honouring the memory of Scottish patriot William Wallace, the foremost victim of Edward I's wars which aimed, and failed, to unite Britain as a single imperium.

The Hundred Years War (1337-1453), by which English kings intermittently pursued their claim to the French throne, may have enriched London with booty but also caused two major popular uprisings. The Peasants' Revolt of 1381 was a reaction to the imposition of a third successive poll tax which pressed far more cruelly on the poor than on the rich. Cade's rebellion of 1450 was at least in part a reaction to the bloody end-game which saw the English finally ejected from their conquered territories. Shakespeare features the event in *Henry VI Part II* and a plaque in an alleyway off Borough High Street marks the former site of the White Hart Inn, which was Cade's temporary headquarters.

Manufacture and Militia

Henry VIII boosted London's role as a centre of armaments production, importing German armourers to Greenwich and establishing the first arsenal at Woolwich. Another community of sword makers developed at Hounslow Heath. There were already regulated, chartered City companies of Armourers and Brasiers, Bowyers and Fletchers. In 1637 a Gunmakers' Company was added to their number and is still actively involved in the gun-making trade. Royal warships were fitted out at Wapping and Blackwall from the fourteenth century. Under Henry VIII royal dockyards were established at Deptford. The medieval militia was recast by the Tudors as "Trained Bands". Organized by City Companies, they mustered periodically on open spaces like Mile End Waste to practise basic drills and have their arms and equipment checked. Although most wore their ordinary clothes rather than uniforms, in terms of organization, training and fighting effectiveness these London units were markedly superior to their county equivalents but, as "townies", much less inured to rough living and harsh weather when it came to actual campaigning.

The superiority of the trained bands reflected the provision of their officer corps by the Honourable Artillery Company. Chartered in 1537 by Henry VIII as the "Overseers of the Fraternity or Guild of St. George", this unit was originally intended for "The better increase of the Defence of this our Realm and maintenance of the Science and Feat of shooting Long Bows, Crossbows and Hand Guns". With its practice ground in Spitalfields, where there is still an Artillery Row, it became known as "The Artillery Company", artillery being understood to comprise any projectile weapon. Ranked as the oldest regiment in the British army, the HAC still exists and provides guards of honour on ceremonial City occasions (www.hac.uk.com). There is an equivalent body in Boston, Massachusetts, founded in 1638 by members of the HAC, which is the oldest military body in North America.

Repeated reorganizations of London's military resources suggest that efficiency and enthusiasm waned periodically. The threat of a full-scale Spanish invasion at the time of the Armada in 1588 certainly jolted government and citizens into frantic preparations to protect the capital from seizure. The focal point of the defence was a boom downriver blocking the Thames between Tilbury and Gravesend. Decayed artillery blockhouses established on either bank there by Henry VIII in 1539-40 were hastily repaired. In the event, the Armada had already been scattered by the time Elizabeth came to encourage her troops at Tilbury, so her famously defiant speech was really an exercise in spin: "I know I have the body of a weak and feeble woman but I have the heart and stomach of a king and of a king of England, too." Stirring stuff, but how she would have been heard by twenty thousand men and who recorded her words is not at all clear. What is known is that the "speech" was not published until half a century later. The author of the relevant volume of the *Victoria County History of Essex* denies that it was ever made. The Tudor fort at Tilbury was erased in 1670 when the Dutch engineer Sir Bernard de Gomme replaced it with a state-of-the-art Continental-style pentangle bastioned fort, now in the care of English Heritage and the finest example in London's immediate environs of the military architecture of that period.

Parliament's Powerhouse

London's strength as a source of manpower, weaponry and cash was decisive during the civil wars of the 1640s. The king, having fled the capital, spent the rest of the war, in effect, trying to get London back. Officers of the HAC fought on both sides but were mostly Parliamentarian, and the unit's tough professional commander, Captain

Philip Skippon, trained up Cromwell's infantry. When Charles I advanced from the west, hoping to seize the capital and thus end the war at a single stroke, it was the trained bands who out-faced him at Turnham Green, outnumbering his force by two to one. Backing off to Kingston-upon-Thames, the king forfeited what proved to be his best chance of taking London. The trained bands also marched to break the siege of Gloucester and fought with disciplined determination at the first battle of Newbury, confounding critics who derided them as Sunday soldiers, although they did earn a reputation for grumbling ceaselessly when the day's marching or fighting no longer ended with a short stroll home to a hot meal, a pot of ale and a warm bed.

London meanwhile transformed itself (temporarily, as it proved) into Europe's largest fortified city by means of a *levée en masse* of citizens to construct an *enceinte* of shot-absorbing earthworks and timber palisades. Up to a hundred thousand Londoners, from Puritans to fishwives, played their part, though the skilled work of constructing strong-points was done by paid professional carpenters and masons under the direction of Dutch military advisers. Mounted with 212 cannon and punctuated by twenty-three star-shaped forts and batteries, the line of fortifications stretched from Whitechapel in the east to Hyde Park in the west and from Islington in the north to Vauxhall in the south. The rather inappropriately named Royal Fort, which stood in St. George's Fields on the site now occupied by the Imperial War Museum, could house a garrison of three thousand. Whether even London could have raised sufficient armed men to hold its defences against a determined enemy is doubtful. In the event the circuit was never even probed, let alone tested. In 1647, at the close of the first civil war, Parliament ordered the demolition of the defences.

In the same year as its defences were being torn down representatives of the victorious Parliamentary army met with civilian radicals in the parish church of St. Mary the Virgin at Putney to debate the future shape of England's government. Cromwell sent them packing but not before their discussions had been recorded, most memorably Colonel Rainborough's declaration that "really I think that the poorest he that is in England hath a life to live, as the greatest he; and therefore truly, Sir, I think it's clear that every man that is to live under a government ought first by his own consent to put himself under that government." A handsome plaque bears witness to the "Putney Debates" inside St. Mary's today. Cromwell is commemorated by a statue—sword in one hand, Bible in the other—fittingly located outside the Parliament he ruled without. Wax impressions of his death-mask can be seen in the British Museum and the Museum of London.

The Second Hundred Years War

As the Parliamentary victory in the civil wars underlined, there are three things necessary for a successful war: money, money and more money. The Bank of England was founded in 1694 to fund the titanic struggle of King William III against Louis XIV's France. The development of a market in government securities marked a major milestone in the emergence of London as a global financial centre, although not until 1844 was its role as the central bank and manager of the nation's currency system formally acknowledged by statute. William III is commemorated by a suitably martial equestrian statue, dressed as a Roman general, in St. James' Square, and also by a rather more effete one in front of Kensington Palace. William and his consort Mary were responsible for founding the Naval Hospital at Greenwich as a maritime counterpart to the Royal Hospital, Chelsea, founded by Charles II to accommodate army veterans.

The many wars of the eighteenth century affected London powerfully but indirectly. Britain was enriched rather than impoverished by overseas conflicts that extended both her trade and her territories and enlarged the incomes and assets of prize-wealthy admirals and profit-laden military contractors. As wars absorbed both manpower and cash London building was constrained but when they ended funds became more freely available and discharged ex-servicemen could be recruited as labourers. In 1715 the main government foundry was moved from Moorfields to Woolwich. Methodists would eventually establish their first church in the abandoned foundry while Woolwich became the home of British artillery and also home to a museum which tells its story. On Whitehall the Horse Guards building was erected in 1750-58 to the designs of William Kent and John Vardy as an administrative headquarters for the army, while Robert Adam designed a handsome neoclassical screen for the Admiralty. The army was one of George II's few serious interests. He not only made uniforms more uniform but regularized the drill-book so that regiments no longer felt free to dispose themselves on the battlefield as their individual colonels thought fit. George II also introduced the ceremonies of the Changing of the Guard and of Trooping the Colour on the sovereign's birthday.

There were only two occasions in the eighteenth century when the capital's military capabilities were put to the test. In 1745 Bonnie Prince Charlie's Scottish supporters got as far south as Derby before turning back northwards. Even so, there was real panic in the capital. Hogarth's satirical painting *The March to Finchley* depicts a scruffy, shambling contingent of Guards sallying forth along Tottenham Court Road turnpike amid a rag-tag entourage of wives, lovers, tarts, gin-sellers, thieves, beggars etc., *en route* to confront the Jacobite army. Produced in 1749-50, after all the fuss had died down, it was a sardonic comment on George II's attempts to tighten up military efficiency—the king failed to see the joke. The artist disposed of the painting through a lottery of 2,000 tickets. It was won by the Foundling Hospital, which just happened to be Hogarth's favourite charity, and became part of the core collection of what was in practice London's first public picture gallery and out of which the Royal Academy evolved.

The second occasion was the Gordon Riots of 1780 when an anti-Catholic mob ran amok in the un-policed metropolis, releasing criminals from prisons and plundering breweries and distilleries. Order was eventually restored with bullet and bayonet by the army, supported by the HAC, which was given its first cannon by the City Corporation as a token of its gratitude.

Revolution and Counter-Revolution

The American colonies' war for independence was also a civil war that deeply divided both colonial societies and the mother country. The City of London, in particular, was hostile to the conflict as hugely damaging to trade. The City's own MP, Barlow Trescothick, was himself an American by birth. Cartwright Gardens in Bloomsbury is named for, and has a statue of, Major John Cartwright, who resigned his commission rather than fight the colonials and raised a fund to relieve the widows and children of Americans killed at Lexington and Concord. The American emissary Henry Laurens, intercepted at sea on his way to raise a loan for the rebel cause in the Netherlands, was imprisoned in the Tower for his pains and treated, he thought, unduly harshly. American visitors to London will doubtless be bemused to find that the Gloucester Place home of Benedict Arnold (1741-1801), a name for them synonymous with treachery, bears a plaque proclaiming him an "American Patriot". They may at least take some comfort from the fact that he died in poverty. Not so another American traitor, Edward Bancroft, who received a handsome pension for his work in passing on to the British government all the secret correspondence that he was conducting with the French on behalf of the rebels. Bancroft died unsuspected, his treachery unrevealed until 1890. The site of his house at the junction of Percy Street and Rathbone Place bears no commemorative plaque. Nor is there any formal remembrance of the thousands of Loyalists and ex-slaves who passed through London following the achievement of American independence. The former slaves, promised emancipation in return for fighting for Britain, were evacuated and shipped out to Sierra Leone where almost all of them succumbed to sickness.

The money, more money etc. principle was vindicated again during the wars against revolutionary France and the Napoleonic empire as London funded a succession of allied coalitions. The house of Rothschild consolidated its position on London's Exchange by bankrolling Wellington's troops through the Peninsular campaigns. The Dartford iron-founders Donkin and Hall produced Britain's first canned foodstuffs as emergency rations for the Royal Navy. The Ordnance Survey was established in 1790 to produce a systematic cartography of the British Isles so that the armed forces could have some idea of what they were supposed to defend. The Royal Veterinary College, established at Camden Town in 1791 to help farmers care for livestock, was diverted to turning out veterinarians for a rapidly expanding army. When Napoleon really did seem likely to invade in 1802 many Londoners joined Volunteer rifle and yeomanry companies, which inspired much ridicule. Ezekiel Baker of Whitechapel showed that the British had learned something from the American debacle by designing the Baker rifle so that the snipers of the 95th Foot could pick off French officers. A flintlock factory was established in 1804 at Enfield, a name which was later to become synonymous with British army rifles.

The Admiralty on Whitehall, linked by a new-fangled signalling system to the main naval base at Portsmouth, master-minded a global strategy that augmented the empire by the acquisition of a foothold in the future South Africa and control of Sri Lanka. "The City of London... exists by victories at sea," wrote Nelson in 1802. The City certainly agreed and presented him with a sword, richly enamelled and encrusted with diamonds, which is now one of the treasures of the Museum of London. Overseas expeditions, however successful, often had unexpected side-effects. Moorfields, the world's oldest and largest specialist eye hospital, was opened in 1805 as the London Dispensary for Curing Diseases of the Eye and Ear in response to an epidemic of trachoma, brought back by British troops from fighting the French in Egypt. The art market was boosted by the flight of treasures which accompanied *émigrés* fleeing the guillotine. London became awash with refugee Roman Catholic priests. Would-be rebels against Spanish rule in South America came to London looking for diplomatic support, money, guns and volunteers. Bolívar, San Martín and Miranda are all honoured with statues. Nelson received a splendid lying-in-state at Greenwich Naval Hospital and was buried right under the dome of St. Paul's in a sarcophagus made for Cardinal Wolsey. Wellington was eventually honoured with London's first nude statue. Cast from captured cannon by Sir Richard Westmacott in 1822, it stands behind his London residence, Apsley House, and supposedly represents Achilles.

Pax Britannica

Throughout the century of domestic peace following Waterloo Britain continued to fight its wars well off the premises. London, however, remained a significant centre of military production. Many Savile Row tailors specialized in making splendid uniforms. In the 1850s Col. Colt opened a factory on Millbank to make revolvers. The Royal Navy's first iron-clad, HMS *Warrior*, was built on the Isle of Dogs. Yarrow's yard at Cubitt Town specialized in making torpedo-boats and then built the Royal Navy' first destroyers. The workshops at Woolwich grew into a gigantic armaments complex and in 1886 gave birth to what would become in due course one of London's premier football clubs, Arsenal, a.k.a. The Gunners.

The second Boer War (1899-1901) in South Africa was the first imperial conflict to involve large numbers of volunteers from the civilian population. Even London's bus companies were plundered for horses to be used for army transport. A memorial in Guildhall honours

City workers who died on the *veldt*. In the Mall are monuments to the Royal Marines and the artillery and another to the cavalry is at Chelsea Bridge. Streets named for Pretoria (11), Mafeking (6) and Bloemfontein (2) also recall the conflict. Fulfilling military contracts brought a welcome injection of cash to the manufacturers of uniforms, tents and ropes in the East End. Maconochies of the Isle of Dogs prospered from the mass-production of a meat-and-vegetable sludge, which, its tin proclaimed, "may be eaten cold" (but was highly advisable not to). Spratt's factory in Poplar switched from making biscuits for dogs to making them for their owners. The war did nothing for Britain's international popularity but it did make a national hero out of Robert Baden-Powell who capitalized on his celebrity as the successful defender of besieged Mafeking to found the scouting movement in 1907. His statue stands outside the Scout headquarters and museum in Prince's Gate.

Great War

The outbreak of war with Germany in 1914 was greeted with cheering crowds and a rush to the recruiting offices. The Camberwell office alone signed on a hundred thousand volunteers from south London in the two years before conscription came in. Three hundred London double-decker Type B buses were also hastily recruited to shuttle the professionals of the British Expeditionary Force to the front. One of them, "Ole Bill", named for cartoonist Bruce Bairnsfather's stoic, moustachioed foot-slogger, can be seen in the Large Exhibits Hall of the Imperial War Museum. Mrs. Pankhurst suspended her militant suffragette campaign for women's votes and demanded for women "the right to serve". Sixty thousand women moved into London factories as "munitionettes". The entertainment industries benefited from free-spending servicemen on leave. *Chu Chin Chow*, a musical based on the traditional pantomime of *Ali Baba and the Forty Thieves*, opened at His Majesty's Theatre in August 1916 and ran for 2,238 performances, beating a thirty-year record set by *The Mikado*. Pubs, however, were forced to close in the afternoons to ensure that well-paid workers returned to finish their shift, a practice maintained after the war to effect a profound change in Britain's drinking culture. Casualties arrived daily from France at Waterloo and Victoria stations, usually by night to minimize the impact on public morale. The London Chest Hospital switched from trying to cure tuberculosis among the city's older inhabitants to trying to salvage their sons from the ravages of poison gas.

German bombing brought death to Londoners themselves, with thirty-one raids by Gotha bombers by day and, even more terrifying, silent Zeppelin airships by night. Bomb-scars can still be seen on Stone Buildings in Lincoln's Inn and on the Smithfield facade of St. Bartholomew's Hospital. The most searing single incident was probably the "Poplar Outrage" of June 1917, when in the course of the first daylight raid 97 people were killed and 439 injured as seventeen Gotha bombers attacked a swathe of the city from East Ham to Aldgate, inflicting twice as many casualties as any other raid of the war. At Upper North Street School, Poplar, a fifty-kilogram bomb penetrated to the ground floor, used by five year olds. Fifteen were killed outright, three more fatally injured and twenty-seven maimed for life. In January 1917 the East End was stunned for the second time in less than six months when an accidental explosion of some fifty tons of TNT at a chemical works in Silvertown killed seventy-three people, injured over four hundred more and damaged over seventy thousand properties. The noise was heard a hundred miles away in Norwich and Southampton. Had the explosion not occurred at 6.52 p.m., when most employees had left the works and most locals were inside their homes at supper, the fatalities might have been much higher.

Memorialization dominated the decade after the Armistice. The unveiling of Lutyens' austere Cenotaph in Whitehall by George V on Remembrance Day 1920 was accompanied by the burial of the Unknown Warrior in Westminster Abbey, escorted by an honour guard of a hundred Victoria Cross holders. Mick Jagger's grandfather, Charles Sargent Jagger, established his reputation with the muscular bronze mourners of his Royal Artillery memorial at Hyde Park Corner. Nearby stands a lithe, naked David with two-handed sword, representing the Machine Gun Corps. At Grosvenor Gardens a Tommy of the Rifle Brigade complements a regimental comrade from the Napoleonic era. At Chancery Lane a brooding infantryman represents the 22,000 dead of the Royal Fusiliers. In the courtyard of the Prudential Insurance headquarters nearby angels bear a fallen soldier heavenwards from a plinth bearing over a thousand names of company employees. Along the Embankment can be seen a statue of Lord Trenchard, creator of the

RAF as the world's first independent air force and memorials to the Camel Corps, to Belgian Refugees and to Submariners. Hatless, the Commander in Chief, Earl Haig, surveys Whitehall astride a strangely stylized steed. Marshal Foch, commander of the largest conquering army the world had ever seen, greets arrivals at Victoria looking for the fast coach service to Oxford. Kitchener, a secretive and inveterate intriguer, is appropriately side-lined at Horse Guards Parade. Beattie and Jellicoe, commanders of Britain's main fleet at the inconclusive battle of Jutland rank only modest bronze busts in the shadow of Nelson's column.

People's War

No one was on the streets cheering when the Second World War broke out. This time Londoners knew what they were in for—or thought they did. Lord Privy Seal Sir John Anderson, whose name was given to the corrugated steel shelters that would adorn the gardens of Londoners fortunate enough to have one, warned gloomily of "an invasion by air— sudden, swift and continuous". Preparations had been accelerated since the Air Raid Precautions Act of 1937, but scarcely adequate ones and often the wrong ones. When the Borough of Finsbury wanted to build deep shelters for the residents of its close-packed streets it was refused permission by the Treasury on grounds of exceeding its budget. Wealthy Westminster went ahead on its own initiative, even installing beds in its shelters and setting up the nation's first training centre for air raid wardens. The Committee for Imperial Defence secretly estimated that 175,000 Londoners might be killed by enemy action in the first twenty-four hours. Considering the near-chaos caused by a death-toll less than one per cent of this as a result of the first serious raid, if the estimate had been accurate the city would have totally overwhelmed. Military planners thought in terms of poison gas and secondarily of high explosives and gave little thought to the effect of incendiaries. The large number of wounded, dazed and homeless in relation to numbers killed outright was not foreseen. Plans were made for mass-graves and even funeral pyres on an industrial scale but the Heavy Rescue Squads who dug ten thousand Londoners out of the wreckage of homes and shelters were an improvisation, as was the recruitment of market porters, used to shifting heavy dead weights, to convey corpses to mortuaries. It was expected that bombing attacks would be intense but brief; shelters were built without amenities for sanitation, sleeping or eating. Many shelterers would find more comfort in church crypts or, as at Chislehurst, even in caves.

Thanks to lessons learned from a realistic rehearsal at the time of the Munich crisis, evacuation proceeded relatively smoothly, emptying London of five-sixths of its school-age children plus infants and their mothers and the chronically sick, disabled and blind. This not only relieved many families of anxieties but freed medical resources for emergency treatment and released school premises for use by air raid wardens, auxiliary firemen and Women's Voluntary Service personnel. The evacuation of many of the capital's treasures had received even greater foresight, being despatched to destinations as distant and various as the National Library of Wales, Belvoir Castle and Shepton Mallet prison. The Elgin Marbles were stored in the Kingsway tram tunnel and porcelain dinner services from Buckingham Palace stowed beneath Aldwych Underground station. (Mrs. Roosevelt was bemused to find herself at the Palace eating rationed Spam off plates of solid gold.)

With invasion anticipated hourly, a call for Local Defence Volunteers was issued. Men older and younger than the regular military cohort of 19-41 were recruited with a view to their using local knowledge and improvised weaponry to delay invaders pending the intervention of regular troops. Sceptics translated the LDV of their hastily-improvised brassards as meaning "Look, Duck and Vanish". Happily re-named the Home Guard, the organization expanded rapidly to take over many routine security duties, releasing the professionals for more pressing matters. The Post Office alone raised eight battalions, London Transport seven, and others were raised by public institutions including the BBC, the University of London and the Palace of Westminster. The first member of the Home Guard to be mentioned in despatches was sixteen-year-old Peter Derrick Willeringhaus who was blown off his motor-bike during a night raid but, despite being wounded and covered with debris, picked himself up and ran three-quarters of a mile to deliver his message before collapsing. The author George Orwell, having had recent combat experience in Spain, was appointed a sergeant instructor in St. John's Wood where he nearly killed his audience fumbling a live grenade during a demonstration of how to use one safely. Just as Senate House became the Ministry of Information, many other buildings were turned to new uses. School meals were cooked in the Bethnal Green Museum. The former Fascist Party headquarters on Charing Cross Road (now a branch library) became a club for New Zealand service officers. Old uses, rather than new ones, were revived for some buildings. When Rudolph Hess landed in 1941 as a self-appointed peace emissary on Hitler's behalf he was initially confined in the Tower of London.

When the Luftwaffe launched its bid for air superiority as a precursor to a German invasion in the summer of 1940 the defence was co-ordinated from Fighter Command headquarters at Bentley Priory near Harrow. Sector control over London and the South East was exercised from 11 Group HQ at Uxbridge. The capital itself was closely ringed with airfields that took a leading role in the "Battle of Britain", notably Hornchurch (10 squadrons), Biggin Hill (9), Northolt (7), Croydon (7) and Hendon (2). Aerial combats took place over the heart of the capital itself, one downed plane famously crashing behind Victoria Station. The crucial contribution of "The Few" is acknowledged in glowing stained-glass windows in the Henry VII chapel in Westminster Abbey.

The Battle of Britain reached its climax on 15 September, overlapping with the Blitz, which was intended to close down the port of London, hinder the operations of government and industry and terrify the civilian population.

The first Luftwaffe raid on London on 24 August 1940 took place contrary to orders and resulted in nine being killed, fifty-eight injured and a hundred people in Bethnal Green rendered homeless. Instant retaliation on Berlin led to continuous bombing beginning on the afternoon of 7 September 1940 when the East End, and in particular Poplar, was attacked and then attacked again by night. On 29 December, when the City of London was even more than usually deserted on account of Christmas, raiders dropped 100,000 incendiaries, setting fire to 160 acres around St. Paul's Cathedral, which remained miraculously unscathed. Low water in the Thames and a direct hit on a water-main severely hindered fire-fighting efforts in an area then much devoted to publishing. Six million books, eight Wren churches and ancient Guildhall went up in flames, despite the presence of 1,500 fire appliances.

The king and queen responded to the assault on their capital by undertaking well-publicized and, by the standards of the day, studiously informal visits to bomb-damaged areas. The queen, skilfully swathed by the royal dressmaker in pastel shades that would not show the dust in press photographs, became among the war generation a national icon until her death. More immediate comfort was given by local heroes like the archetypal left-wing slum-priest, Australian-born Father St. John Groser and the "Angel of Cable Street", Dr. Hannah Billig, who won the George Medal for her devotion.

The George Medal and George Cross had been established to recognize the dangers faced by non-combatants. Two of the first three were awarded to Lt. R. Davies and Sapper G. C. Wylie for defusing a delayed-action land mine, which, had it exploded, would have wrecked St. Paul's Cathedral beyond hope of repair.

The final raid of the first phase of the Blitz, on 10 May 1941, destroyed the chamber of the House of Commons and many other historic buildings and key installations. Spasmodic raids continued, but the worst single incident of the mid-war years occurred as a result of an accident in March 1943. The sudden and unannounced test firing of a new rocket battery in Victoria Park was mistaken for enemy bombardment and a panic-stricken rush for shelter ensued. As a result, 173 people were suffocated and crushed to death on the steps of Bethnal Green Underground station.

Great importance was attached to the maintenance of civilian morale from the outset of the war. The BBC's skilful news management and even more deft distribution of coded information to resistance groups in occupied countries made the name of London synonymous with liberty and the hope of liberation. Columbia Broadcasting System administrator Edward R. Murrow (1908-65) became a media superhero to the British. His eyewitness accounts of the Blitz were held to be invaluable in winning over American opinion. At a New York dinner in Murrow's honour the poet Archibald MacLeish paid tribute to the measured vividness of his reportage: "You laid the dead of London at our doors and we knew the dead were our dead." At the end of the war Murrow made his own typically gracious and eloquent testimony to his London years: "I have been privileged to see an entire people give the reply to tyranny that their history demanded of them."

Listening to the main BBC nine o'clock news bulletin each

evening became a national ritual. The BBC's domestic output also included the inspired (but now virtually incomprehensible) catch-phrase lunacies of Tommy Handley's ITMA (It's That Man Again) show and the cheery banter of cockney comediennes "Gert and Daisy", who were ingeniously recruited by Food Controller Lord Woolton to cajole housewives into making pies without most of the essential ingredients.

Rationing, especially of food, was one of the bureaucracy's successes. Nutritionist Professor Jack Drummond (1891-1952) of University College, London set the management of the nation's diet on a sound scientific basis to effect what the American Public Health Association hailed as "one of the greatest demonstrations in public health administration that the world has ever seen." Communal Feeding Centres, felicitously re-branded by Churchill as "British Restaurants", played an especially valuable role in feeding Londoners working long shifts or unsocial hours. The royal parks set an example in the "Dig for Victory" campaign. Chickens reappeared in suburban back gardens. Police and fire stations recycled their kitchen waste to fatten pigs. Boroughs competed in salvage drives to assemble mountains of waste paper. Soap firms sponsored mobile laundries and baths. Civilian living standards nevertheless fell by fifty per cent. To be shabby was patriotic.

Yet despite frequent disruptions of transport and power, London continued to function as an arsenal of democracy. The postal and telephone services were maintained with remarkable efficiency. Ford's giant Dagenham plant switched from family cars to army trucks. Bryant and May at Bow switched from matches to detonators. Former furniture workshops made parts for the all-wooden Mosquito fighter-bomber. Aeroplanes were assembled in an uncompleted extension to the Central Line.

Official war artists like Henry Moore, John Piper, Feliks Topolski, Eric Ravilious, Graham Sutherland and Edward Ardizzone famously sketched, etched or painted the privations of Londoners in shelters, firemen braving the Blitz and housewives stoically queuing. Eric Kennington produced a series of striking portrait sketches of fighter aces. Meredith Frampton's meticulous, near-photographic rendering of the London Regional Civil Defence Control Room, a treasure of the Imperial War Museum collection, conveyed both tension and authority in its rendering of Sir Ernest Gowers (he of the *Plain Words*) and his colleagues. Photographers, ranging from society portraitist Cecil Beaton to German-born social commentator Bill Brandt, added another dimension to the contemporary record. The British film industry, almost entirely centred in and around London, enjoyed its finest hour, infusing feature films with the spirit and techniques of the indigenous documentary tradition, often mixing established stars with ordinary people playing themselves in films such as Humphrey Jennings' *Fires Were Started*, filmed at a Wapping fire station, and Noel Coward's *In Which We Serve*, which employed dozens of real-life sailors on shore-leave after being torpedoed.

A week after the D-Day landings seemed to mark the beginning of the end, the first V-1 missile landed at Grove Road, Mile End, scoring a direct hit on a bridge carrying the main railway line into Liverpool Street. The bridge was back in use within thirty-six hours but the adjacent streets, demolished by the flying-bomb, have never been rebuilt. Five days later the Guards' Chapel at Wellington Barracks was destroyed by a direct hit during the Sunday morning service. The less thickly-populated middle-class suburbs of south-east London suffered worst from the V-weapons, thanks to false data fed back to Germany by double agents who claimed that the rockets were overshooting their targets. But the last V-2 to fall on the capital hit the East End on 27 March 1945, totally demolishing Hughes Mansions in Vallance Road, Whitechapel, killing 134 people, almost all of them Jewish, including several servicemen home on leave.

In 1947 William Kent published *The Lost Treasures of London*, mourning the loss of thirty-one City Livery Company halls, the gutting of sixteen Wren churches and the devastation of Gray's Inn but thankfully recording that Westminster Abbey had escaped relatively unscathed as had the bridges over the Thames. Thousands of individual tragedies and dislocations went unchronicled. Leonard and Virginia Woolf's Hogarth Press in Tavistock Square was bombed out, as was sculptor Sir Jacob Epstein's Chelsea workshop. By the end of the war just under twenty per cent of the East End had been destroyed, compared with five per cent "up west". Of Stepney's 34,000 homes some 32,000 had been damaged. Of Poplar's 25,000 dwellings just *one* escaped unscathed.

The Savage Wars of Peace

London bore the visible scars of its ordeal for more than a decade. But the city felt safe, so safe that few gave safety a second thought. There was, of course, the Cold War and the threat of nuclear annihilation, a threat of which Londoners were constantly reminded by the marches, rallies and demonstrations of the Campaign for Nuclear Disarmament. But that was *out there*, not in London as such, even if a number of London boroughs did see fit to ring their boundaries with road signs proclaiming to motorists that they were about to enter "A Nuclear-Free Zone" (sometimes without the hyphen, which rather changes the meaning).

In 1970-71 an anti-capitalist group calling itself the Angry Brigade conducted a campaign of minor bombings, largely but not exclusively aimed at symbolic targets, like banks, the Ford Motor Company and the homes of Tory politicians. These were accompanied by incoherent pronouncements that gave only the vaguest indications of their supposed objectives but implied an admiration for the far more deadly activities of their assumed counterparts in Germany, Italy and Spain. As it turned out the "group", scarcely an organization, consisted of a loose network of activist-squatters, with sidelines in fraud, theft and drugs. A dedicated police unit was established to deal with this novel threat and a house raid in Stoke Newington produced a damning cache of weapons and explosives, leading to arrests and ten-year prison sentences. Neither *The Oxford Companion to British History* nor *Cassell's Companion to Twentieth Century Britain* rates the Angry Brigade worth even a mention, let alone an entry. A revaluation may, in retrospect, be merited. The "members" of the Angry Brigade were too casual to be competent, but their sense of self-appointed mission and undiscriminating nihilism pointed the way to far worse than they actually accomplished. They did succeed in setting ablaze both a West End cinema and a fashionable store and the devices they planted at an airline office and at Paddington Station simply failed to go off. That no fatalities resulted from their operations may have been sheer luck.

There was nothing casual or disorganized about the bombing campaign begun by the Provisional IRA in March 1973 when two of its devices exploded, one outside the Central Criminal Court in the Old Bailey, killing one person and injuring almost two hundred. Thereafter the target and the pattern varied: in June 1974 Westminster Hall, in

September 1975 the Hilton Hotel. In November 1975 two died and twenty-three were hurt in a restaurant blast. In January 1977 seven bombs were detonated across the West End. In March 1979 Mrs. Thatcher's close aide, war hero Airey Neave, a hard-line Tory spokesman on Ulster, was assassinated by a bomb in his car in the House of Commons underground car-park. In July 1982 Royal Horse Guards and military bandsmen were targeted as bombs exploded in Hyde Park and Regent's Park, killing eleven and wounding fifty. At Christmas 1983 a bomb outside Harrods killed six, including three police. Targets like the Tower of London were subsequently eschewed as the Harrods experience suggested that to endanger American tourists was to endanger an invaluable source of emotional and financial support.

This time the enemy was neither novel nor unknown. In the 1860s London had suffered what were then called "outrages" at the hands of bombers of the Fenian Brotherhood, ancestral forerunner of the IRA. In front of the Central Criminal Court at the Old Bailey a railed-off island in the roadway marks where London's last public hanging took place in 1868. The condemned man, Michael Barrett, had attempted to rescue some comrades-in-arms from a Clerkenwell prison by means of explosives but mainly succeeded in blowing up nearby houses, killing half a dozen innocent people and maiming fifty more. The Metropolitan Police "Special Branch" was subsequently formed out of its detective department to keep tabs on later generations of American-financed Fenians. The IRA even tried a London bombing campaign in 1939-40, acting on the maxim that "England's peril is Ireland's opportunity."

The on-going IRA terrorist campaign in Northern Ireland accustomed Londoners to a constant trickle of horrors on their nightly news-bulletins, a beating, a bombing, the murder of a policeman or a British soldier, retaliatory assassinations between members of Republican and Loyalist paramilitaries. Though few would have admitted it, these tragedies were to an extent reassuring—it was happening *over there*. Interventions in the capital, however, if discontinuous, became far more spectacular than the constant drip-drip of death and injury in Ulster. In 1991 the IRA mortar-bombed Downing Street itself during a Cabinet meeting, which continued to its normal conclusion. In 1992 the City came under fire with the destruction of the Baltic Exchange in St. Mary Axe and the injury of ninety-one people. In April 1993 a massive truck-bomb was exploded on nearby Bishopsgate. A coded warning enabled police to begin clearing the City, normally deserted on a Saturday, but there was still a death and over forty injuries, plus £350,000,000 worth of damage. The financial markets opened as usual the following Monday morning. In February 1996 a recent and youthful IRA recruit was killed at Aldwych when his device exploded prematurely, demolishing the bus he was travelling on. The last IRA "spectacular", at Canary Wharf in 1996, killed two and caused £85,000,000 worth of damage. Since then the Provos have been "on cease-fire". They do not, however, have a monopoly on violence and minor explosions have continued—three in 2001 alone, including one outside the BBC.

Throughout all this there has never been concerted hostility against Irish people themselves. They account for five per cent of London's population and long constituted its largest single ethnic minority. Doubtless many have found it prudent to be prudent but, if there may have been wariness of the police and the courts ("Innocent until proved Irish"), they had little reason to fear their neighbours.

The quadruple suicide bombings of 7 July 2005 moved London's experience of terrorism into a new era. Irish bombers may have been prepared to risk their lives but had never opted for certain self-sacrifice. The supposed "cause" was neither national nor in any conventional sense political. The perpetrators were British-born. Their victims were a random cross-section of commuters and tourists. The emergency services implemented plans long prepared. Spontaneous heroes showed humanity at its best. The security services thwarted a repeat operation a fortnight later. Over the following weeks London re-normalized but at the cost of increasing still further its reliance on scanners and surveillance and the patience, vigilance and co-operation of its citizens—the new daily tariff for maintaining "the Mansion House of Liberty".

OF QUACKS AND CURES
A Medical Interlude

The history of medicine in London progresses from piety to professionalism, along a path well populated with quacks and mountebanks. The first major step towards creating the modern medical profession was made in 1518 when royal doctor Thomas Linacre persuaded Henry VIII to grant a charter to the Royal College of Physicians, which became the first institution to confer a recognized professional status on practitioners as a result of competent

Edward Jenner, Italian Garden, Kensington Gardens

performance in examinations. In 1540 this body was joined by the Royal College of Barber-Surgeons, a less prestigious company, who dealt with the messy business of wounds, amputations and fractures and whose trade is today remembered in the colourful barber shop pole, representing bloody bandages. In 1617 the Society of Apothecaries also received a charter. Apothecaries functioned as pharmacists and general practitioners, dealing with everyday ailments. These three bodies were mainly concerned to defend their privileges and to drive out the "unqualified"—especially women—rather than to develop medical services for wider public benefit. Special professional venom was therefore reserved for those, like the Spitalfields herbalist and astrologer Nicholas Culpeper, who treated the poor for free and, even worse, translated the Royal College of Physicians' own *Pharmacopeia* from Latin into English, so that any literate lay person might read it. The physicians accused him of drunkenness, lechery, atheism and, of course, producing a rotten translation. Despite this campaign of revilement Culpeper's offending book went through three editions in three years and was followed up with *The English Physician Enlarged, with 369 Medicines made from English Herbs that were not in any impression until this*. That went through thirty-five editions before the end of the century and was still being reissued a century after that.

The presence in London of three major hospitals—St. Thomas', St. Bartholomew the Great ("Bart's") and the Bethlehem (Bedlam)—maintained a permanent pool of patients from whose ailments systematic conclusions might be drawn. In 1628 William Harvey of Bart's published his account of the circulation of the blood, hailed by modern scholarship as "probably the most important physiological discovery ever made". An early convert to the therapeutic properties of coffee, Harvey bequeathed his favourite pot and a store of beans to his professional colleagues so that they could drink a cup to his memory after their monthly meetings.

The other outstanding London practitioner of the seventeenth century was Thomas Sydenham, "the English Hippocrates", who stressed the importance of observing the actual course of a disease as opposed to theorizing about the internal workings of the body. Sydenham distinguished the symptoms of venereal infection, wrote a treatise on gout and recognized hysteria as a distinct affliction—three ailments which could all be readily encountered in London. Sydenham also gave his name to the mild convulsions suffered by children ("Sydenham's chorea") and to a form of liquid opium widely used in medical treatment ("Sydenham's laudanum"). Sydenham had little use for science, never joined the Royal Society and when asked by a student what books he would recommend replied *Don Quixote*—because medicine could not be learned out of books.

Leading London practitioners could become very rich; few, after all, took any interest in treating the poor. Sydenham lived on Pall Mall. John Radcliffe was more famed for his witty bedside manner than for his professional competence. He still made over seven thousand pounds just out of William III in eleven years' attendance, once saving his life during an asthma attack. Radcliffe's fortune went to found the Radcliffe. Library, Observatory and Infirmary at Oxford. Radcliffe's protégé was Richard Mead, who began his practice in the Stepney house in which he had been born and ended up in a fine mansion in Great Ormond Street with a library of ten thousand books and a collection of antiquities worth ten thousand pounds. Its site is now appropriately occupied by the Hospital for Sick Children. Mead's patients included Pope, Newton, Walpole and George II, and it was at the suggestion of the last, when Prince of Wales, that in 1721 Mead conducted an experiment to test out the Turkish practice of inoculation against smallpox by deliberately giving a person a mild dose of infective matter. The infected persons were seven condemned criminals—all of whom recovered. The royal family thereupon took up inoculation and authorities up and down the land paid to have the procedure inflicted on soldiers, workhouse inmates, children at boarding schools and anyone else unable to object

Sir Hans Sloane, a pupil of Sydenham, like his rival Mead also used his fortune to indulge a passion for collecting. Sloane's far larger hoard of books, manuscripts and natural history specimens was eventually bequeathed for sale to the government at a knock-down price. It became the core collection of the British Museum. Sloane had also become wealthy enough to become Lord of the Manor of Chelsea (hence Sloane Square) and to buy its Physick Garden for the use of the Society of Apothecaries.

While even leading physicians like Radcliffe habitually gave consultations in coffee-houses, in the eighteenth century wealthy subscribers began to support new hospitals where they, their families, servants and nominees could receive treatment. The Westminster (1719), Guy's (1725), St. George's (1733), the London (1740) and the Middlesex (1745) were complemented by more specialized institutions for "lying-in" and the treatment of venereal diseases, skin diseases, chest complaints etc. Medical instruction was greatly advanced by the efforts of the Scottish Hunter brothers. William Hunter, as physician extraordinary to the fecund Queen Charlotte, concentrated on obstetrics, which he helped to establish as a distinct medical specialism. Hunter was also appointed as the first professor of anatomy at the Royal Academy. John Hunter initially acted as his elder brother's assistant at dissections, then honed his skills in the army as a battlefield surgeon. As surgeon at St. George's Hospital the younger Hunter made systematic investigations into gunshot wounds, inflammation and embryology and wrote a *Natural History of Human Teeth,* which was a landmark in the history of dentistry. Whereas fashionable physicians like Mead and Sloane collected antiquities and curios, Hunter collected bodies and bones to pioneer the discipline of comparative anatomy. Hunter's vast teaching collection of 13,000 specimens was eventually bought by the Royal College of Surgeons.

The Quaker physician John Coakley Lettsom never published a major contribution to medical knowledge, but churned out pamphlets on subjects ranging from temperance and prison reform to the cultivation of the mangel-wurzel (a variety of the beet). As a workaholic practitioner with a large family and generous impulses he claimed that for nineteen years he had never taken a single day's holiday. Earning up to twelve thousand pounds a year, Lettsom used his income to amass a huge botanic collection at his residence, Grove Hill in Camberwell. Lettsom was the first to persuade his professional colleagues to treat the London poor free at out-patient clinics like the General Dispensary he founded in Aldersgate Street. In 1773 he founded the Medical Society of London at whose gatherings physicians, surgeons and apothecaries could meet together as equals to discuss topics of common interest. Unlike many professional coteries, the Society survived the death of its founder to become permanent. Another of Lettsom's achievements, as a founder of the Royal Humane Society, was to popularize the artificial respiration of drowning victims. With a fine flair for publicity he held an annual dinner at which the current year's crop of revived near-dead were paraded around the room in triumph.

The epoch-making discovery of vaccination against smallpox was made by Edward Jenner in a remote rural practice in Berkeley, Gloucestershire, but, as a former pupil of John Hunter, Jenner had remained in close touch with the London medical establishment and returned to the capital to open the world's first immunological clinic at Streatham Street, Bloomsbury, with the charitable backing of the ground landlord, the Duke of Bedford. Declining the prospect of a metropolitan fortune, Jenner soon returned to Gloucestershire, having also refused to profit from his discovery by patenting it. Although vaccination was being used to combat a smallpox epidemic on the Kentucky frontier within five years of the publication of the pamphlet in which Jenner described the procedure, the significance of his achievement was only very belatedly (1858) recognized by the erection of a statue in Trafalgar Square and even then most of the cost was subscribed from abroad. Jenner's statue was removed from its prominent site within five years and now presides over the fine fountains and flower-beds of the Italian Garden in Kensington Gardens. Apart from the usual blue plaque on his home in Danvers Street, Chelsea, and another on St. Mary's Hospital in Praed Street, Paddington, where he discovered penicillin in 1928, there is no major public memorial in London to Sir Alexander Fleming. The discovery, as he himself admitted, came about more or less by chance. Too limited as a bio-chemist to develop his discovery and too indifferent as a lecturer to communicate its potential, he left it to others to transform it into the first antibiotic—just in time to save the lives of an estimated three thousand men on D-Day alone.

During the early nineteenth century the foundation of new general hospitals enlarged access to treatment for the less affluent. Charing Cross Hospital (1818) was founded by Benjamin Golding who opened up his own house "to such poor persons as desired gratuitous advice." The Royal Free Hospital (1828) was founded by William Marsden after finding a young woman dying on the steps of St. Andrew's, Holborn and being unable to get her admitted to any existing hospital. Marsden himself is commemorated in the south London hospital for the treatment of addictions. University College Hospital (1828) was founded as the first institution in England, outside Oxford and Cambridge, where students could study for a full medical degree. Joseph Lister became a student in 1844, being unable, as a Quaker, to enter either of the ancient universities. Lister's development of antiseptic procedures would immediately cut surgical fatalities by at least a third. In 1846 the first major operation under anaesthetic was performed at UCH premises in Gower Street when Robert Liston amputated a leg, having learned of the successful use of ether in Boston only a few weeks previously. The first professor of surgery at UCH had but recently been dismissed for performing operations on hypnotized patients with only variable success, so Liston turned triumphantly to his admiring audience of medical students to proclaim "This Yankee dodge, gentlemen, beats Mesmerism hollow."

The Hospital for Diseases of Women was established in 1843 to deal exclusively with "those maladies which neither rank, wealth nor character can avert from the female sex." Unfortunately the hospital's very name seemed to imply that its exclusive concern was sexually transmitted infections and the name was hastily changed in 1845 to the Hospital for Women. When the Hospital for Sick Children was founded in 1851, 21,000 of London's annual toll of 50,000 deaths were of children under ten but there was no specialist hospital provision for children anywhere in the metropolis. The hospital found an energetic and effective fund-raiser in Charles Dickens, who on one occasion raised three thousand pounds with an after-dinner speech. It later benefited to the tune of tens of millions of pounds when the dramatist Sir James Barrie bequeathed it the copyright income from *Peter Pan*.

Standards of medical ethics were raised from 1825 onwards by the publication of *The Lancet* by Thomas Wakley. A weekly campaigning journal, it was intended to expose and denounce abuse, fraud, quackery and incompetence in the medical profession—hence its title. *The Lancet* later widened its scope to embrace public health issues and was largely responsible for the passage of the world's first Adulteration of Food and Drink Act in 1860.

Victorian Londoners were, in the mass, far more affected by improvements in public health than by advances in medical treatment. Cholera and tuberculosis, threatening all social classes alike, startled a penny-pinching public into sanitary self-defence. The efforts of dour, obsessive, tactless Edwin Chadwick, author of the ground-breaking *Inquiry into the Sanitary Condition of the Labouring Population* (1842) and the *Report on the Supply of Water to the Metropolis* (1850), were only recognized by the bestowal of a knighthood just before his death. It was truly observed that if, as a general, he had been responsible for killing as many people as he had in fact saved from death, the nation would have been dotted with statues in his honour. "The Lady of the Lamp", Florence Nightingale, by contrast, was honoured by the erection of a statue (with the wrong sort of lamp) in Waterloo Place in recognition of her life-saving efforts during the Crimean War, though her greater achievements were to organize modern nursing training, update army health regulations and vitalize public health programmes in India (without ever actually going there).

The first English woman doctor, London-born Elizabeth Garrett Anderson (1836-1917), qualified for practice by passing the Apothecaries' examinations and opened a dispensary (now the Elizabeth Garrett Anderson Hospital on Euston Road) where she also instituted medical training for women. In 1870 she belatedly achieved the degree of MD—from the University of Paris. By the time Sophia Jex-Blake became a maths tutor at Queen's College for Women in Harley Street, that particular thoroughfare had already become synonymous with the nation's leading consultants. She had to go to New York to begin her medical training before proceeding to Edinburgh where the University, having allowed her to enter, study and qualify, disgracefully reversed its decision in retrospect. Her response was to open a London School of Medicine for Women (1874) and to campaign successfully for a change in the law which finally permitted medical examiners to examine women students. As a result, Jex-Blake, having already gained the degree of MD in Berne, finally obtained a British qualification from the Irish College of Physicians.

Dozens of London doctors are best known for having become something else. Oliver Goldsmith renounced treating the poor of Southwark for a more rewarding literary career. Tobias Smollett is better remembered for his vivid description of his hero Roderick Random's epic pub crawl through Covent Garden and Humphrey Clinker's sojourn in a London gaol than for his professional practice as a surgeon in Downing Street. Poet John Keats trained at Guy's and qualified as an apothecary. Dr. John Barnardo built a philanthropic empire of orphanages and training programmes which rescued at least 55,000 destitute children from the streets of London. David Livingstone, who studied medicine at UCH, became the first white man to cross tropical Africa from coast to coast. T. H. Huxley, inventor of the word "agnostic", was another UCH alumnus and worked as a naval surgeon before appointing himself to be "Darwin's bulldog" in the ferocious public debates over evolution. The medical career of Poet Laureate Robert Bridges was cut short after just five years by pneumonia but was certainly taxing while it lasted. As a casualty physician at Bart's he recorded in 1878 that he had treated in the course of one year 30,940 patients, giving an average of 88 seconds to each case. Sir Arthur Conan Doyle turned to writing about Sherlock Holmes when adequate numbers of patients failed to materialize at his Marylebone consulting rooms near Baker Street. Somerset Maugham trained at St. Thomas' in the 1890s. Specializing in obstetrics, he was required to attend at least twenty confinements in the slum areas around the hospital. What he saw provided the raw material for the novel that launched his literary career, *Liza of Lambeth* (1897). Jamaican-born Harold Moody, a graduate of King's College Hospital and a life-long General Practitioner in Peckham, founded the League of Coloured Peoples (1931) to campaign against racism. In 1934 Dr. C. L. Katial of Finsbury became Britain's first Asian mayor. A. J. Cronin, who was in general practice at 152 Westbourne Grove, was able to take up writing full time as a result of the success of his debut novel, *Hatter's Castle* (1931). His fifth novel *The Citadel* (1937) was a frontal attack on the greed of the Harley Street elite and did much to create a more favourable climate of opinion for the establishment of a National Health Service.

MAYFAIR

Posh from the first, Mayfair is a gilded rectangle of privilege and plutocracy, bounded by Oxford Street, Regent Street, Piccadilly and Park Lane. Bisected by Bond Street, its regular grid pattern is slashed through diagonally by the course of the hidden Tyburn river. Mount Street's name recalls a civil war artillery fort. Tiddy Dols restaurant was named for a seventeenth-century seller of gingerbread, who dressed and spoke like an aristocrat reduced to beggary. Shepherd Market, an elegant enclave of cafés and call-girls, memorializes Edward Shepherd, builder of Crewe House, the last surviving early Georgian mansion, now the Saudi embassy. As the name and size of Grosvenor Square imply, the Grosvenor family were pre-eminent in the development of the district and its scion, the Duke of Westminster, remains its main proprietor today.

Studded with embassies and punctuated with five-star hotels, in British movies Mayfair has been synonymous with *chic*, the natural habitat of couturier, furrier and perfumier, the habitual haunt of the famous and the glamorous, and society style-setters like Noel Coward

and Cecil Beaton. Lord Louis Mountbatten, Paul
Robeson, Somerset Maugham and Gordon
Selfridge were all residents, as before them were
Sheridan, Beau Brummell, Talleyrand and
William IV and his actress mistress Mrs. Jordan.
Elizabeth II was born here. Shelley, Disraeli,
George Eliot, Asquith and John Buchan were all
married at St. George's, Hanover Square. Novelist
Nancy Mitford worked in the Curzon Street
bookshop of G. Heywood Hill. The ashes of
haughty hostess Emerald Cunard were scattered
across Grosvenor Square. Dorothy L. Sayers'
fictional fixation, the aristocratic amateur sleuth
Lord Peter Wimsey, the absolute antithesis of her
real-life boorish husband, supposedly lived on
Piccadilly—at No. 221 (a Sherlockean tribute?).

F. D. Roosevelt,
Grosvenor Square

Style accompanies *chic.* Colefax and Fowler, pioneers of the
"English country house style", are just around the corner from where
William Morris' design business was founded. In Mayfair one may buy
antiquarian books at Maggs', fine ceramics at Thomas Goode's and
exquisitely crafted sporting guns at Purdey's, entrust one's hair to
Trumpers' or Nicky Clarke's, and dine at the Dorchester or the
Connaught .

Hanover Square, once inhabited by Tory generals who crushed the
Old Pretender's uprising in 1715, later became known for music rooms
where Liszt performed and Wagner conducted. Berkeley Square was
home to Clive and Canning. No. 44, designed by William Kent and to
many London's finest terrace house, now houses an exclusive gambling
establishment and Annabel's night-club.

Mayfair is "Little America". Embedded in Lansdowne House is the
grand circular room where the colonies' independence was formally
recognized. General Burgoyne, vanquished at Saratoga, lived in the next
street. Grosvenor Square, overshadowed by Eero Saarinen's very un-
Georgian US Embassy, has statues of Eisenhower and Franklin
Roosevelt and monuments to the war-time RAF American "Eagles"
squadrons and the victims of 9/11. In 1785-8 John and Abigail Adams
presided over the first American embassy at No. 9. In Bond Street
Franklin Delano Roosevelt shares a bench with Churchill.

Mayfair's often unregarded gems include the chastely neoclassical Grosvenor Chapel of 1730, where Florence Nightingale and Eisenhower both worshipped, and, in boldest contrast, Pugin's flamboyantly Gothic Jesuit Church of the Immaculate Conception of 1844, whose altar is a masterpiece of creative excess. The gardens between church and chapel, once a favoured dead-letter drop for Cold War spies, are lined with benches dedicated mostly to Americans, who have treasured this oasis of calm.

Chapter Seven
SPORTING LONDON

"In the afternoon we drove to the Bear Garden at Hockley in the hole to watch the fights that take place there, a truly English amusement."
Z. C. von Uffenbach, *Curious Travels in Belgium, Holland and England,* 1711

Upton Park tribute to World Cup winners of 1966

In making its bid to stage the Olympic Games of 2012 London could plausibly claim a sporting heritage stretching back over two millennia to the gladiatorial and military exercises of its Roman founders. Wembley, Wimbledon, Lord's, Twickenham and Hurlingham, and with a little territorial elasticity, Ascot, Epsom, Henley and Bisley, are London locations known around the world for sporting excellence. Sport has been central to the recreation of Londoners. Recording the exploits of sportsmen has provided employment for artist, writer and photographer alike. The Regency period, which saw the emergence of sporting journalism, also witnessed the heyday of the sporting print, a major genre of London artistic production. Even the sale and manufacture of clothing and equipment for sport became a significant feature of the capital's economy as large stores established "sports goods" departments and specialized outlets like Lillywhite's developed.

Masters of Arms

London has always had a large concentration of young men— apprentices and in-migrants—who needed to let off steam and show off. The sports enjoyed by the youth of medieval London were described enthusiastically by William FitzStephen as an essential part of the city's life. Apart from simple competitions of running and leaping they were largely martial—wrestling, duelling with quarter-staff, cudgels or sword and buckler, practising archery, throwing spears or running at the quintain. In winter youths strapped animal bones to their feet and skated on the frozen marshes of Moorfields, just north of the city walls. Combat sports were practised on a more elaborate scale by kings and aristocrats in the form of jousts and tournaments like the one held at Stepney Green to mark the coronation of Edward II in 1308. Other tournament venues included Smithfield (approached by Giltspur Street) and even London Bridge itself. Henry VIII, a fine archer and a keen jouster, had tiltyards at his palaces of Whitehall and Greenwich. The king fought encased in the superbly-articulated, specialized armours that can still be seen in the Tower Armouries. Italian styles of fencing with rapier and dagger were introduced in the sixteenth century, bringing the need for expert instructors. Henry VIII chartered them as a Guild of St. George in 1540. Military-minded gentlemen formed clubs to hone their skills. The long, narrow rectangle of Gerrard Street at the heart of today's Chinatown, was once a military exercise yard with its own fencing *salle*. In the eighteenth century London's foremost fencing school was run by the Italian master of arms Domenico Angelo in his academy at Carlisle House, off Soho Square. He taught George III. His son, Henry, taught Byron.

Combat sports that served as a preparation for real warfare survived long after they had lost their practical military value. Archery was revered as the key to historic victories over the French and was celebrated in the tales of Robin Hood. Elizabeth I's own tutor, Roger Ascham, wrote a treatise on archery, *Toxophilus*. The name of Newington Butts memorializes a regular shooting-ground. In the late eighteenth century interest in archery was revived in fashionable society. As a sport it had the attraction for the unmarried of being open to women as well as men and could therefore serve as an occasion for courtship. Participants were at little risk of injury or even of working up a sweat. Elegant clothes could be worn and even special "historically authentic" costumes devised. The Toxophilite Society was formed in 1781 and, receiving the insouciant patronage of the Prince of Wales, named the target colours, scores and distances for archery contests in his honour.

Theatre of Cruelty

The deliberate infliction of pain on animals was integral to many of the most popular "sports" of the early modern period. Throwing at cocks, for example, involved hurling sticks or stones at a tethered bird until its legs and wings were so badly broken that it could no longer evade missiles, at which point the assailant inflicting the final decisive damage could take the victim home for the pot. Baiting animals was deemed a spectacle fit for royalty and their honoured guests. In 1561 Henry Machyn recorded in his diary that there "was at Whyt-hall grett baytyng of the bull and bere for the in-bassadors of Franse... the wyche the Queen's grace was there and her counsell and many nobull men." In 1604 James I laid on a similar entertainment for the Constable of Castile, setting bears against greyhounds. The fact that bears rather than bulls were involved bespeaks lavish expense. Bears had to be imported and were virtually worthless when dead. A bull, by contrast, could be bought easily and its carcase sold on to butchers. The torments it had suffered were generally held to improve the flavour of its meat.

By Shakespeare's day the baiting of animals had become highly organized and highly profitable. The settings used to stage plays were used, and used more frequently, to stage the baiting of bears. The surviving accounts of the impresario Philip Henslowe reveal that he and his son-in-law Edward Alleyn made over twice as much at peak holiday periods from animal shows as from plays. Animal baiting was suppressed when the Puritans came to power in London in the 1640s, as Macaulay would caustically observe two centuries later, not because it inflicted pain on the animals but because it gave pleasure to the spectators. The baiting of bears and bulls, like other suppressed pleasures, was revived at the Restoration. By the eighteenth century animal-baiting attracted only the rough crowd and was chiefly confined to Hockley-in-the-Hole in Clerkenwell, a conveniently short distance from the live-meat market at Smithfield. Performances were periodically enlivened by stunts like tying fireworks to the tail of a dog and letting it loose among the spectators. Bouts involving animals were interspersed with human combats intended to draw blood. An inch cut was the usually understood minimum to mark a clear result. One such contest. witnessed in 1710 by a German visitor Z. C. von Uffenbach, matched a butcher against a "Moor" named George Turner, supposedly a professional fencing master. It ended when Turner's face was slashed open from the left eye to the chin, "with such force one could hear the sword grating against the teeth." The victor was borne away in triumph from what von Uffenbach recorded as "this truly English amusement".

Cock-fighting continued to attract all classes. In 1762 James Boswell, then a Scottish *ingénu* in London society, determined to experience what he conceived to be a typically English day. Dressed in suitably ruffianly style, he attended a cock-fight and also consumed copious quantities of beef and beer as essential adjuncts to the proceedings. Boswell's mentor, Dr. Johnson, conceded that cock-fighting and animal-baiting might, like drinking, raise the spirit of a company of men but concluded dryly that it would "never improve the conversation of those who took part in them." The name only of Cockpit Steps, between Birdcage Walk and Queen Anne's Gate, recalls the location of the original cockpit which was an adjunct to Whitehall Palace and was not finally closed until 1825.

The same shift in public attitudes that led to the abolition of slavery led also to legislation against baiting. The Society for the Prevention of Cruelty to Animals, formed in 1824, secured a ban on bull-baiting in 1835 and cock-fighting in 1840. Cock-fighting, being easier to conceal than bull-baiting, continued, with the added *frisson* of being forbidden. With the baiting of larger animals officially banned, ratting gained in popularity and was ideally suited to metropolitan conditions. Rats were all too plentiful around markets, stables and slaughterhouses and were liable to excite little pity even among the tender-hearted. A fenced enclosure could easily be fitted up in the courtyard or back-room of an inn and terriers matched against each other to see which could kill most rats in an agreed upon time. Writing ca. 1850, Henry Mayhew recorded that one London publican bought over 26,000 rats each year.

Thrill of the Chase

The peaceful glades of Epping Forest, stretching in patches through the suburbs of north-east London, remain as a reminder of its use as a royal hunting preserve. The London Chest Hospital in Bethnal Green occupies the site of the former hunting lodge of the bishops of London. The parks around the royal palaces at St. James', Greenwich and Richmond were originally hunting enclosures where the king could take daily exercise without the inconvenience of riding miles in search of stag or hare. Fox-hunting, once seen as *the* quintessentially English sport, developed from the mid-eighteenth century as newly-enclosed fields created a patchwork of hedges and ditches which made for an exciting ride punctuated by challenging jumps. Although "riding to hounds" reached its peak of popularity between 1780 and 1830 the advent of the railway, which many huntsmen feared would destroy the countryside and thus their pleasure, in fact made hunting more accessible to Londoners, as the novelist Anthony Trollope explained in 1868:

> *... a man... may work at his desk for four days a week and hunt the other two, sixty or a hundred miles from his home and get back to dinner with his family. Successful men of business have availed themselves so largely of this facility for getting air and exercise that hunting has been more than doubled instead of being crippled by the railroads.*

The same considerations applied to fishing, and in 1867 railway companies sponsored the publication of *The Rail and the Rod*, which identified angling spots that could be reached by rail within a thirty-mile radius of the capital. *The Field* magazine, established in 1853 by the author R. S. Surtees, creator of the fictional hunting obsessive, Jorrocks, found much of its readership among London suburbanites avid for the lifestyle of the country gentleman rather than actually living it.

Sport of Kings

Horse-racing was under active royal patronage from at least the reign of Charles II. Charles himself presented the first King's Plate prizes and personally rode a winner at Newmarket. (The king also introduced Londoners to the delights of yachting and skating, played real tennis and was a competent archer.) The first professional racing trainer, Tregonwell Frampton, was appointed by William III as manager of the royal stables, a post he held for over thirty years. The Ascot meeting was a royal occasion from its inauguration by Queen Anne in 1711. Interest in the sport was further increased as a result of the importation of Middle Eastern bloodstock. From the Byerley Turk (imported in 1682), the Darley Arabian (ca. 1702) and the Godolphin Barb (1724) were descended Herod, Matchem and Eclipse, from whom all English thoroughbreds can trace their lineage.

Because horses could not be transported over long distances without damaging their potential performance, before railways most race-meetings were brief, local affairs. Although Newmarket remained the mecca for breeding, racing and training, Tattersall's London sales-rooms was the prime centre for the inspection and sale of bloodstock. Two of the five "classic" races were established at Epsom, within easy reach of London, the Oaks in 1779 and the Derby in 1780. Derby Day at Epsom became the Londoners' great excursion, drawing crowds of up to a quarter of a million, of whom probably not one-tenth could see the actual race—or possibly cared to. William Powell Frith's immensely detailed 1858 picture of the occasion, *Derby Day*, features card-sharpers, pickpockets, drunks, lovers and gymnasts in spangled tights rather than horses and jockeys.

The Noble Art?

London can plausibly claim boxing as its own particular contribution to the pantheon of modern sports. In 1719 James Figg, recognized as first champion of all England, opened a pioneering academy at which he taught boxing and sword-fighting. Figg's disciple, Jack Broughton, a former Wapping waterman, formulated the first rules for boxing in 1743. These specified a thirty-second pause to recover from a knock-down, forbade striking an opponent who was down and banned hitting, or wrestling holds, below the waist. Broughton also invented boxing-gloves, known as "mufflers", which were, however, only worn for sparring. Real fights continued to be fought with bare knuckles. In Daniel Mendoza (1764-1836) London produced Britain's first sporting superstar. Born in Aldgate, "Mendoza the Jew" first learned to fight as a teenager to defend himself and his employer from gratuitous insults and harassment. A compact five foot six inches and never weighing more than a hundred and sixty pounds in an era when boxing imposed no restrictions on the relative weight of opponents, Mendoza should never, by any reasonable calculation, have been able to become champion of all England, as he was from 1792 to 1795. His secret was the recognition that speed and skill, and above all balance, could offset mere size and strength. It was Mendoza who pioneered swift footwork and matched it with combination punching that enabled him to damage and disorientate bewildered opponents before darting out of reach of retaliation. These insights he elaborated in *The Art of Boxing*, the first "scientific" treatise on the principles underlying "the noble art of self-defence". Mendoza the Jew became the first member of his religion to meet his sovereign. He was finally defeated by "Gentleman" Jackson, whose victory was achieved by the ungentlemanly tactic of holding Mendoza's pony-tail while pummelling him in the face. Mendoza thereafter confined his contests to the fives court, ran a successful boxing academy and retired to write his memoirs at pleasantly named Paradise Row, Bethnal Green, where his neat terrace house still stands.

Prize-fighting went into rapid decline in the 1820s after a series of scandals over fights deliberately thrown for bets or bribes. Royal and aristocratic patronage was rapidly withdrawn and the standing of boxing fell correspondingly in the eyes of the public.

Although bare-knuckle bouts were still being fought in the 1890s, the savagery (and corruption) of the ring was moderated by the establishment of the Amateur Boxing Association in 1880 and of the National Sporting Club in 1891. The President of the NSC, Lord Lonsdale, presented championship belts for the separate weight divisions established by the Club in its assumed capacity as the sport's governing body. Many NSC bouts took place in the luxurious surroundings of the Café Royal on Regent Street before a black-tie audience.

A new element entered London boxing in the late Victorian period with the establishment of boys' clubs run by volunteers from leading public schools like Haileybury and, most famously, Repton. Believing that boxing could channel and discipline street aggression to confer a sense of self-respect and deter young tearaways from crime, the *noblesse oblige* that took privileged youths to the slums enabled many lads to fight their way out of poverty. Repton's link with its eponymous club ended in the 1970s, but the club continues to nurture East End talent, most recently in the shape of Olympic heavyweight gold medallist Audley Harrison.

Although there were provincial fighters of note, a high proportion of British boxers continued to be drawn from the East End. The Jewish pre-eminence established by Mendoza was continued by Dutch Sam Elias, who trained on gin and invented the uppercut, and Barney Aarons, "the Star of the East". East End Jews continued to make their mark in the twentieth century through the careers of Ted "Kid" Lewis (born Gershon Mendeloff) and Jack "Kid" Berg (Judah Bergman). Lewis (1894-1970), the "Aldgate Sphinx", became Britain's youngest ever champion as a seventeen-year-old flyweight. In 1915 as world welterweight champion, he became the first British fighter to take a world title in the United States. He was also the first fighter to wear a protective mouthpiece. Berg (1909-91), the "Whitechapel Whirlwind", was junior light welterweight world champion at twenty-one and had a fighting career of over thirty years in the ring.

The Beautiful Game

"Soccer" comes from the public school slang for Association football. Different clubs and schools had developed their own distinctive ways of playing the game, but with the advent of railways it became possible to compete against more distant opponents who might not necessarily share the same rules. A common code was essential for the avoidance of ungentlemanly disputes with the referee or allegations of unfair play against an opposing side. Football in its modern form was first codified after a meeting, mostly of London clubs, which established the Football Association in 1863. The FA's founding London members included Barnes, Blackheath Proprietary School, Blackheath Crusaders, Crystal Palace, Forest (of Leytonstone), Kensington School, No Names (Kilburn), Perceval House (Blackheath), Surbiton and the War Office.

In its Victorian incarnation soccer was not easily distinguishable from the handling game which became rugby. The initial attempt to draw up agreed rules led to the withdrawal of one of the Blackheath clubs which insisted that a ban on hacking—deliberately kicking an opponent's shins—amounted to the prohibition of an integral part of the game. Competitive football continued to be dominated by clubs based on the public schools and such London-centred institutions as the army and the civil service until 1888 when the Football League was established by twelve clubs, all based in the industrial cities of the Midlands and the North, to arrange regular fixtures between them.

The professionalization of soccer depended on the existence of potential crowds able and willing to pay to watch a weekly match. This in turn depended on the general adoption of the five-and-a-half-day working week. At the same time there was a marked fall in the price of basic foodstuffs, especially imported grain, meat and butter, thanks to greater efficiencies of transportation in the 1870s and the advent of refrigeration in the 1880s. The resultant increase in disposable working-class incomes fuelled both the growth of professional spectator sports and also the proliferation of music halls, a boom in the building of vast public houses and the growth of chain store multiples supplying provisions, clothing and home-wares. Combined with the advent of compulsory elementary education, this rise in working-class spending-power also fostered the growth of a mass-circulation sporting press with London-based publications like *The Sportsman, Sporting Life* and the *Sporting Chronicle* each selling over 300,000 copies daily by the 1880s.

Professional football clubs were slower to develop in London than in the North and Midlands, often originating in church or works teams. In 1879 Fulham St. Andrew's was founded by St. Andrew's Sunday School. Tottenham was founded in 1882 as an off-shoot of Hotspur Cricket Club of Northumberland Park, whose players were looking for a winter recreation. The infant club was nurtured by the brewery that ran the White Hart pub and provided a ground in the lane which ran behind it. Brentford was an off-shoot of a rowing-club. Millwall originated in 1885 in the Isle of Dogs as a works team from Morton & Co, manufacturers of jam and canned foods. Queen's Park Rangers was founded in 1886 by an amalgamation of two church youth clubs. In the same year Arsenal was formed out of the great armaments complex at Woolwich, only moving to Highbury in north London in 1913. West Ham United evolved out of Thames Ironworks, the giant Blackwall-based firm of shipbuilders and engineers, with the active encouragement of the boss, Oxford-educated A. F. Hills. Playing initially as Thames Ironworks, the club was re-founded as West Ham in 1900, its first fixture being a gratifying victory over Millwall. Unusually, Chelsea was founded as a commercial venture after local businessman H. A. Mears failed to persuade Fulham to base their side at the former Stamford Bridge Athletics Ground. The amateur tradition in soccer, meanwhile, was upheld by the establishment in 1902 of the Arthur Dunne Cup and the emergence, unique to London, of a league system of post-school Old Boys' clubs, recruited mainly from the capital's suburban grammar schools.

Football crowds at professional matches, in London as elsewhere, were dominated by males from the skilled working class. The unemployed and the unskilled could rarely afford the entrance fee. The middle class did not care to attend, either supporting amateur sides or rugby. Crowd loyalties were territorial. If you lived in the East End you supported West Ham or Leyton Orient. On the opposite side of London loyalties were divided between Chelsea, Fulham, Queen's Park Rangers and Brentford. While some clubs like West Ham ("the academy of soccer") had a strong tradition of finding and nurturing local talent, there was a lively transfer market from the beginning; in this Scottish "professors", respected for their tactical subtlety, were especially prominent. This did not, however, affect the territorial basis of the team's identity, even when this became transparently fictional. When in 1901 delirious Spurs supporters hailed their "local" team for bringing home the FA Cup few probably paused to reflect that it consisted of five Scots, two Welshmen, an Irishman and three Northerners. Chelsea supporters probably did realize almost a century later that their club, true to its commercially-oriented origins, had the dismal distinction of fielding the first ever top side without a single player from anywhere in the British Isles.

This intense sense of soccer territoriality was a reflection of the loyalties that bound together the members of working-class sports teams based on a street, neighbourhood or parish. "Local derbies" between rival, especially neighbouring London clubs, like Spurs and Arsenal, were guaranteed to draw the largest crowds, and still do. At the other end of the scale of loyalty the annual England-Scotland match, first played in 1872, led to enthusiastic, if temporary invasions, of fans from north of the border. When war broke out in 1914 the strength of loyalties to specific soccer teams was ruthlessly exploited in the recruitment of volunteers for the trenches as young men rushed to the colours in the hope of finding themselves should to shoulder with an idolized Saturday hero.

The founding of the FA formalized the position of the dribbling game favoured by the leading London public schools—Eton, Harrow, Westminster and Charterhouse—in preference to the handling game preferred by provincial establishments such as Rugby and Marlborough. But this latter sport continued to have its London adherents. Although Guy's hospital had a rugby team as early as 1843, Blackheath, founded a decade later by former pupils of Blackheath Preparatory School, claims the longest continuous existence as a club open to all. Edwin Ash, founder of Richmond in 1861, was responsible in 1871 for the formation of the Rugby Union, established by representatives of thirty-two clubs meeting at the Pall Mall Restaurant to agree a code of 59 rules. In 1895 the problematic issue of payment, deemed essential for the economic survival of working-class players in the industrial cities of the Midlands and the North, led to a northern breakaway from the southern commitment to amateurism and the evolution of Rugby League as a distinctively professionalized sport. In 1907 the Rugby Football Union bought "Billy Williams' Cabbage Patch" and established a permanent venue for international matches at Twickenham, which also became the home ground of Harlequins RFC, although they have since moved across the road.

Swing, Swing Together

Rowing was originally a practical skill rather than a sport but it gave birth to one of the oldest annual events in London's sporting calendar— the race for Doggett's Coat and Badge. Thomas Doggett, an Irish comic actor who became manager of Drury Lane theatre, inaugurated the four-and-a-half-mile race from London Bridge to Cadogan Pier, Chelsea, in 1715 as a public affirmation of his loyalty to the recently established royal house of Hanover. Held on the first of August, the contest gained the victor a twelve-ounce badge of silver in the form of the white horse of Hanover and a fine scarlet coat to wear it on. Rowing continued to be the preserve of working watermen, many of whom also raced for purses. The inauguration of the annual Oxford versus Cambridge Boat Race, imparted a novel *éclat* to what was rapidly appropriated by the public schools and their clubbable alumni to become a socially exclusive sport, headed by the swanky Leander Club. Membership by invitation only and hefty subscriptions and expenditures on boat club dinners and club uniforms conspired to keep out social undesirables. The rules of Henley Regatta, first held in 1839, later explicitly excluded any person who had ever earned his living as "a mechanic, artisan or labourer".

Despite its monopolization by the elite, rowing continued to attract widespread spectator interest. Being a river sport it was in practice not possible to exclude spectators from a free spectacle. The annual University Boat Race, in particular, drew immense crowds and divided partisans of light and dark blue in even the slummiest parts of the capital. Boat race night became an annual saturnalia for inebriated undergraduate celebrants, attended routinely by the stoning of street-lamps, knocking off of policeman's helmets and retributory appearances at Bow Street Magistrate's Court.

Essence of Englishness
Varying types of bat and ball games were played in the Middle Ages, but cricket evolved as a competitive team game in the rural villages of southern England in the early eighteenth century. Contests involving picked teams, rather than regular village sides, began to be arranged by aristocratic sponsors to compete for large purses, often of hundreds of guineas. Occasionally bizarre matches were arranged between teams of disabled army and navy veterans, pitting the one-armed, for example, against the one-legged. By the 1740s cricket matches at the Artillery Ground in Finsbury could draw paying crowds of more than seven thousand. Although bowling was originally under-arm a batsman could still be intimidated as pitches were invariably uneven and treacherous before the invention of the lawnmower in 1830. The adoption of pads and gloves in the following decade was accompanied by a sanctioned switch to over-arm deliveries.

In 1752 a number of *habitués* of the Star and Garter Tavern in Pall Mall, who met to play cricket on fields adjacent to the White Conduit refreshment house at Islington, formed themselves into a club and began looking for a ground of their own. Thomas Lord, who was employed as a general factotum (and to undertake the tedious chore of bowling during practice sessions) took out a lease on a patch of land beside the by-pass which then marked the *de facto* northern boundary of built-up London. Lord's ground was opened in 1787 and in the same year some members of the White Conduit club broke away to form the Marylebone Cricket Club, which took its name from the location of its new ground and then, after beating its ancestor in its first fixture by 83 runs, subsequently reabsorbed it. The MCC was forced to move in 1811 when Lord's lease ran out and Dorset Square was built over the site of his ground. After moving the precious turf to a new site further north, it had to be moved yet again in 1814 to make way for the construction of the Regent's Canal. Finally settling at St. John's Wood, the MCC became acknowledged as the supreme authority on the conduct and rules of the game, not just in England, but wherever cricket was played.

Outclassed
London's historically large concentrations of wealthy residents and unattached young people created an economic and social base for a number of sports and clubs that, at least initially, had few parallels or imitators outside the capital.

Although all eligible Londoners between the sixteenth and the eighteenth centuries were in theory obliged to serve in the militia, the authorities were chary of the widespread distribution of firearms. It was, however, still possible to shoot wildfowl in eighteenth-century Bloomsbury. Today's Museum Tavern in Great Russell Street was originally the Dog and Duck. French invasion scares prompted the formation of volunteer rifle companies, which met annually for reviews on Wimbledon Common for drilling and shooting competitions organized by the National Rifle Association until it relocated the contest to Bisley in 1890.

The exclusive Hurlingham Club was established in 1869 primarily to arrange the shooting of live pigeons released from traps. The name of Hurlingham, however, soon became synonymous with polo. Introduced from India, the first game was played on Hounslow Heath in 1870 between Lancers and Hussars and re-exported to English expatriates in Argentina and the United States. The Hurlingham Club rapidly acquired a status analogous to that of the MCC as the world headquarters and ruling body for the sport.

Whether lawn tennis was invented in Birmingham or London, it was quickly taken up, like croquet, as an ideal pastime for suburbanites with large grounds laid to lawn. When the All England Croquet Club, founded at Wimbledon in 1869, decided to adopt tennis as well, it admitted a cuckoo that swiftly took over the nest. In 1877 the club name was changed to the All England Croquet and Lawn Tennis Club, and in 1882 to the All England Lawn Tennis and Croquet Club. In 1888 it spawned the Lawn Tennis Association, which became the game's governing body. The first Wimbledon tournament, held in 1877 with the support of *The Field* magazine, attracted just two hundred spectators. By 1884 it had become popular enough for a men's doubles and a ladies singles championship to be added.

Hockey was pioneered at Blackheath as a winter game for cricketers. In 1886 a Hockey Association was formed, chiefly from clubs based in London's wealthier suburbs. Golf was supposedly first played in London in 1608 on Blackheath by King James I. Blackheath Golf Club, founded by London Scots in the mid-eighteenth century, claims to be England's oldest. The club's betting book makes it clear that, like cricket at that time, games were generally played for a stake, often a gallon of claret. A century later a second London course was established at Wimbledon by Scottish members of the Volunteer rifle movement. Improvements in suburban railway services led to the proliferation of golf courses, especially north and west of London from the 1880s onwards.

Billiards, first recorded in the sixteenth century, was taken up as a gentlemanly pastime in London clubs and even before that in coffee-houses. Colsoni's Chocolate House is recorded as having two billiard tables as early as 1693. The game gained greatly in popularity in the nineteenth century thanks to the introduction of the rounded leather cue-tip, cue chalk and, in 1835, the manufacture by Thurston's of the india-rubber cushion. By 1837 the firm of Thurston and Kentfield was manufacturing tables with slate rather than wooden beds. Billiards thus acquired a new precision and, thanks to its favour with Prince Albert, a new *cachet*. In imitation of the royal retreat at Osborne on the Isle of Wight, grand London houses began to acquire a special billiard room, which became an exclusively male retreat. Snooker was introduced from India, where it had been devised in the officers' club at Ootacamund, a snooker being the regimental nickname for a subaltern prone to landing himself and his men in impossible situations and thus finding himself "snookered".

Another imperial importation, this time from Canada, was the canoe, leading to the formation of a Royal Canoe Club at Teddington in 1866. Roller skating burst onto the social scene in 1875. By 1876 fifty rinks had been established. Gymnastic expertise had to be imported to London. A purpose-built gymnasium was built by German expatriates at St. Pancras in 1859. The "games mistress" was invented by the Swedish pioneer of physical education Martina Bergman-Osterberg, who established her training college at Hampstead.

While working-class districts of London supported their own amateur cricket and soccer teams they had no truck with middle-class sports such as tennis, golf or hockey, which in any case required expensive equipment and access to specialized facilities. Working-class competitiveness, driven more by the need to express comradeship than to provide a counter-point to desk-work, was often expressed in sports and pastimes alien to London's bourgeoisie but widely followed by the working class of other great conurbations—darts, bowls, quoits, skittles and the racing of pigeons or whippets—pastimes that were often organized from public houses and whose outcomes provided the opportunity for betting. Involving little physical exertion but often requiring patience and cunning, these activities appealed to the middle-aged and older generations and perhaps for these reasons, as much as their proletarian associations, have been neglected by historians of sport.

The popularity of pigeon-fancying, dog-racing and betting on horses, along with allotment gardening and the keeping of caged birds, confirms that London's millions shared the deep rural attachment of their betters. The development of extensive tram networks and the advent of the pneumatic tyre and the "safety bicycle" in the 1880s gave younger generations access to the countryside on summer evenings and weekends. In 1891 a London Federation of Rambling Clubs was established. Competitive cycling established a home at Herne Hill in south London but failed to retain the mass following it would soon acquire in Europe.

Sport had few female adherents until the emergence of independent girls' schools which modelled themselves on boys' public schools and were determined to set equally demanding standards. In the capital the pathfinder came in the unlikely shape of Miss Buss, founder of the North London Collegiate School, which had a gymnasium and added swimming, skating and athletics to its curriculum. The rationale for female participation in sport was derived as much from its capacity to meet the peculiar physiological needs of adolescent girls as from the more traditional character-building arguments. Hockey and the fearsome Canadian sport of lacrosse came to be thought of as particularly suitable for schoolgirls. Tennis, badminton and cycling continued to appeal to those who were no longer at school. Maintaining appropriately modest dress under conditions of exertion remained problematic. "Bloomers" shocked to the extent that in 1899 the editor of the *Rational Dress Gazette* was struck with a meat-hook while cycling through Kilburn.

Further, Higher, Faster
The establishment of the modern Olympics by the French aristocrat Baron de Coubertin was largely inspired by his admiration for the British cult of sport, but the British initially took little interest in his project and were represented only by a scratch team at the first revived Olympiad at Athens in 1896. The second, held in Paris as part of the monster *Exposition* to usher in the new century, was a farrago of muddle in which amateur, professional and demonstration events were jumbled together. The 1904 Games, held in St. Louis, Missouri, were virtually inaccessible to anyone but Americans. It was intended that in 1908 Rome should be the host but the devastation of Naples by an earthquake in 1906 forced the Italians to withdraw. Britain stepped into the breach, despite initially having neither a suitable location nor even a budget. An appropriate venue was found at the White City, Shepherd's Bush, which had been constructed by the Hungarian impresario Imre Kiralfy to host a spectacular Franco-British exhibition. Next door the world's first purpose-built Olympic stadium was erected in ten months, complete with the first purpose-built Olympic pool.

Fifteen hundred competitors from nineteen nations then took part in what was the first Olympiad to be organized by trained sports administrators. Regrettably there were numerous accusations of partiality levelled at the umpires, especially by the American contingent which virtually came to the point of rupturing all future sporting contacts. The tragic hero of the Games was Italian marathon runner Dorando Pietri, who entered the stadium a full half mile ahead of his nearest rival. Dazed with exhaustion, he meandered in a delirium until directed towards the finishing line by bewildered officials—and was disqualified for receiving assistance. Queen Alexandra subsequently presented Pietri with a consolatory silver cup. The royal family was also responsible for having the odd few hundred yards added to the traditional twenty-six miles of the marathon course—so that they could see off the competitors from a window of their apartments in Windsor Castle.

A Golden Age

The period from the 1920s up to Britain's soccer World Cup victory in 1966 is often presented as a Golden Age of British sport. Attendances at sporting fixtures achieved unprecedented numbers. British competitors could win at Wimbledon and bring home a clutch of gold medals from the Olympics. Sporting heroes still tended to be self-effacing in public and respectable in private. There was certainly a widening of access for both participants and spectators. The collapse in the price of agricultural land in the 1920s encouraged the laying-out of suburban golf-courses and tennis courts as catalysts for the development of commuter estates. Large employers with paternalistic managements like Shell and London Transport took advantage of the same situation to provide extensive and well-equipped sports clubs for their workers. In an era of depression and mass unemployment sport was perceived as a panacea for soothing class tensions. The Serpentine in Hyde Park was opened as a public swimming place. London boroughs extended the provision of tennis courts, running tracks, "lidos" and other forms of public play space. Hackney Marshes provided over a hundred football pitches for East End soccer enthusiasts. By 1929 the London County Council had acquired 350 pitches—but still not nearly enough to satisfy a thousand applicant teams.

Wembley Stadium, created for the 1924 Empire exhibition, became to soccer what Lord's was to cricket—the sacred shrine for international performance *par excellence*. Its inauguration in 1923 as the home of the FA Cup final, however, came close to major catastrophe. Built to a capacity of 127,000, it was besieged by a crowd of would-be spectators estimated at 210,000. Thousands spilled onto the pitch, but disaster was almost miraculously averted by the single-handed efforts of

PC George Scorey on his white horse, Billie, who rode in ever-widening circles for forty minutes pressing the invaders back into the stands. Although 900 minor injuries were sustained there were no fatalities. Bolton Wanderers went on to beat West Ham 2-0.

New spectator sports relying on novel technologies were introduced. Greyhounds began chasing an electric hare at White City in 1927. Motor cycle racing without brakes—"speedway"—was another spectacle geared to weekday evenings when there was little competition from other established spectator sports. Radio coverage brought a new dimension of enjoyment into the homes of millions. Lord Reith, the first Director-General of the BBC, intuited the profound significance of sporting occasions in drawing together a society disoriented by the dissolution of old certainties. Despite the costs and technical difficulties involved, priority was given to the organization of "outside broadcasts". The first coverage of a boxing contest, between Ted "Kid" Lewis and Georges Carpentier, took place as early as 1922, the year in which the BBC began broadcasting. This was followed by coverage of the Boat Race, but for some years broadcasters were confined to events of strictly limited duration, rather than extended encounters like Test Matches or Wimbledon.

The 1948 Olympics
The 14th Olympiad was scheduled to have taken place in Britain's capital in 1944. Despite the continuation of rationing so severe that competing teams were obliged to bring their own food, and despite the setback to the entire economy caused by the unexpectedly severe late winter of 1947, the event went ahead successfully in 1948. Defeated Germany and Japan were not invited to participate and the USSR chose not to. Nevertheless the 14th Olympiad was the largest to date, involving fifty-nine countries. Visiting teams were austerely accommodated in colleges and barracks. The proprietors of Wembley Stadium, the main venue for events, made it available free of charge and a new Olympic way was built at a cost of £120,000. The US topped the final medals table, followed by Sweden and France. But the star of the games was a Dutch mother of two, Fanny Blankers-Koen, who won four golds and was declared Victrix Ludorum, the first woman in Olympic history to be so nominated. The complete disruption of British sport by the Second World War doubtless underlay the

disappointing performance of the host nation, though fourteen silver medals implied that a recovery was under way.

Extra Time

The year of the 14th Olympiad (1948) was also the year in which Londoner Freddie Mills became world light heavyweight champion, Arsenal won the League, and the matchless Don Bradman made his last Test appearance at the Oval, only to be bowled out second ball for a duck. Superficially these headline events suggested that the pattern of pre-war sport was being re-established. Football, boxing and cricket certainly continued to command the largest followings but the predominant post-war trend was to be towards greater diversity. New sports emerged. 1948 also witnessed the foundation in London of the British Judo Association and the first Devizes-Westminster canoe race—"the Mount Everest of the kayaking world". In 1951 there was the first London to Brighton running race and, at Ruislip Lido, the establishment of Britain's first water skiing club. As part of the same trend what had once been minority sports, like squash, acquired a much broader following, and what had formerly been firmly middle-class pastimes, notably tennis and golf, became accessible to a newly-affluent working class.

Boxing, once second only to football in popularity among working-class men, lost its mass appeal, despite the success enjoyed by such Londoners as Charlie Magri, Terry Spinks, John H. Stracey, Nigel Benn, Frank Bruno, Audley Harrison and most famously, Henry Cooper, the first boxer to be knighted. Wrestling, after a brief period of popularity on television, likewise dwindled to a minority interest.

Cricket finally abandoned the feudal forelock-tugging implicit in the Gentlemen v. Players fixture, played for the last time in 1962, but it took until 1998 for the MCC to admit women members. The founding of the Lord's Taverners in 1950 brought a new light-heartedness to the game as showbiz personalities and sports journalists played alongside guest professionals to raise money for cricketing charities. But, cricket, too, looked to be losing its appeal until it began to reach out to potential new fans by means of one-day matches and limited-over competitions which dramatically upped the pace of the game. Excellent television coverage, symbolized by Lord's prize-winning, futuristic Media Centre building, also helped. Cricket's revival seemed assured in the summer of 2005, which was dominated by a riveting Test series against Australia as England finally regained the Ashes after eighteen long years in a thrilling last match at the Oval.

Although the first all-London F.A. Cup final of the twentieth century only took place in 1967 (Spurs 2-Chelsea 1), London clubs continued to command ardent support. But the supporters were changing as the massed ranks of middle-aged working men were infiltrated by the young and the affluent. Organized hooliganism disfigured "the beautiful game" for decades, eventually leading to the long-overdue modernization of grounds into all-seater venues. After Jimmy Hill of Fulham successfully challenged the wage-ceiling which had limited players to the take-home pay of a skilled artisan the floodgates opened to enable top professionals to earn as much per week as their bank manager was likely to earn in a year. Glitz replaced grit as the hallmark of the game as footballers became icons of fashion and objects of obsessive media attention.

Fulham, Charlton, Queen's Park Rangers, Crystal Palace, Millwall and even Wimbledon all enjoyed phases of glory. West Ham won the Cup in 1964, 1975 and 1980 and supplied the captain and both goalscorers for the England team which beat Germany 4-2 in the World Cup Final at Wembley in 1966. Spurs won both the League and the Cup in 1960, won the Cup again in 1961, 1981 and 1982. In 1972 they took the UEFA Cup in the first-ever all-England final and ten years later won it again. Arsenal, however, has remained the most consistently successful London club and has even moved to a brand-new stadium. Chelsea, meanwhile, has replaced Spurs as their main rival.

Professionals were finally admitted to the Wimbledon tournament in 1968 but it took until 1995 for professionalism to be accepted in rugby. Venerable sporting venues disappeared. Harringay Arena closed in 1958. The White City was demolished in 1983. Two decades later decaying, twin-towered Wembley itself went, at last to be replaced by a stadium worthy of the twenty-first century. Wimbledon likewise underwent a major make-over. Speedway, still popular in the provinces, disappeared altogether from the capital. Greyhound racing attempted to reinvent itself as a smart evening out, combining fine dining with a flutter. The annual London Marathon, first held in 1981, rapidly established itself as a global event and national institution. In 2002 Britain's Paula Radcliffe won the women's event in her debut performance and in 2003 broke the women's world record. Four-fifths of the runners following in her footsteps were, however, "fun-runners", dressed as teddy bears, waiters, gorillas etc. raising some £35,000,000 for charity in what has become the world's greatest annual fund-raising event.

London's success in securing the Olympic Games of 2012 seems certain not only to promote the regeneration of the dismal, weed-choked desolation of the Lower Lea Valley, but also to provide a further boost for the role of sport in London's life. With an annual turnover of £4.7 billion, sport already accounts for one per cent of the region's economy. Some 683,000 Londoners belong to the clubs and teams which utilize the capital's five hundred sports halls, pools, tracks, pitches and rinks and provide employment for fifty-five thousand people in sports-related activities. From 2012 they will also have access to an 80,000-seater Olympic Stadium, designed by Iraqi-born superstar architect Zaha Hadid, an Aquatics Centre with two fifty-metre pools, a 12,000-seater Velodrome and two further "multi-sport" arenas—all to be set in the largest park created in Europe for a hundred and fifty years.

OF BABEL
A Linguistic Interlude

Two of the paintings on the back of the three sixteenth-century copper-plate maps of the City (see p.80) happen to be of the Tower of Babel. The close-packed streets of London's riverside and city centre are thus literally backed by an incarnation of linguistic chaos. The dramatist Thomas Dekker wrote of Gresham's Royal Exchange that "at every turn a man is put in mind of Babel, there is such a confusion of languages." Shakespeare once lodged in a French-speaking London household and exploited the confusions of mutual incomprehension between English and French to comic effect in two scenes in *Henry V.*

More than three hundred languages are spoken in London today. *East End Life,* the free weekly news-sheet produced by the London Borough of Tower Hamlets, has different sections in English, Bengali and Somali. Local councils, National Health Service Trusts and public libraries routinely publish information in Chinese, Punjabi, Gujarati

Mosque, Brick Lane

and Hindi. The Citizens Advice Bureau advertises its existence in languages from Albanian through Farsi to Vietnamese. London is a, if not the, world centre of publishing in Arabic, particularly of opinions critical of Arab governments.

For the scholar of languages the streets of London offer a ready-made laboratory, a living data-bank. In Shaw's *Pygmalion* Professor Higgins finds a congenially learned companion in Colonel Pickering, a retired Indian Army officer and expert on the languages of the Raj. Edwardian clubland would have been populated by dozens of such types, former missionaries, "Old China hands", colonial judges and district commissioners. Higgins himself claims to be able to identify varieties of cockney to within six streets and triumphantly locates Eliza Doolittle as a denizen of Lisson Grove. Cecil Beaton's superb set for the film version of Shaw's play, *My Fair Lady*, knowingly adorns the wall of Higgins' study with Lord Leighton's dashing portrait of the orientalist and pornographer, Sir Richard Burton. Allegedly the master of twenty languages, from Portuguese to Pashto, Burton successfully passed himself off as an Afghan doctor to become one of the first non-Muslims to make the pilgrimage to Mecca. Burton now lies beside his wife in an overgrown Roman Catholic cemetery at Mortlake, resting in a tent-shaped tomb with a glass observation panel and a ladder at the back to enable the curious to peer down at their dust-laden coffins.

Eighteenth-century London produced a real life Professor Higgins in Sir William Jones. At Harrow he learned Latin, Greek, French and Italian and later added Arabic, Hebrew, Persian, German, Spanish, Portuguese and the rudiments of Chinese to his range. His first book was a translation from Persian into French. Although Jones found the law uncongenial, he became a judge in Calcutta so that he could become rich enough to marry. Already a Fellow of the Royal Society and a member of Johnson's Literary Club, in India Jones founded the Asiatic Society of Bengal, which pioneered the scholarly study of Asian cultures, religions and languages. In tackling Sanskrit Jones noticed numerous similarities with ancient Greek, thus discovering their common membership of the great family of languages known as Indo-European. In doing this he founded a new discipline—comparative philology. A statue of this mighty scholar was erected beneath the dome of St. Paul's within five years of his early death. Jones is depicted with massive tomes containing the corpus of the Hindu law-giver Manu. The asoka tree, now an Indian national symbol, was named *Jonesia asoka* in his honour.

London's heritage of multilingualism is a direct consequence of its status as a "mart of many nations", compounded by its role as a haven for refugees and capital of a global empire. Given the world-wide dominance of English today as a *lingua franca* of commerce, computers, medicine and aviation, it is easy to forget that five centuries ago it was literally a marginal tongue, spoken only by one people on one part of an archipelago on the edge of Europe. English at that time had scarcely achieved any fixed form. That it eventually did so was the product of two factors—printing and London.

William Caxton spent thirty years as a merchant based in Bruges, representing the interests of English merchants in the Low Countries and Rhineland. Encountering Gutenberg's invention of printing with movable type, he mastered the process in Cologne and brought a press back to England as a retirement project. Establishing himself in the shadow of Westminster Abbey in 1476 (there is, alas, no plaque to mark the spot), Caxton became the first English publisher—but which English to use? Caxton's problem is illustrated by an anecdote he recounted to explain it. Two merchants leave London for the Continent but have scarcely got past Gravesend when a storm forces them to land in Kent. They approach a farmhouse to buy some eggs but are indignantly repulsed by the farmer's wife who says she cannot understand French. The travellers eventually make clear what they want, to be told that if they had asked for "eyren" in the first place they would have got them sooner. Accepting that such a common word as "egg" was not understood less than twenty miles from the capital, Caxton nevertheless fixed on the speech of London, now known to scholars as the East Midlands dialect, to become the standard for printed English and thus, in effect, for polite speech.

If Caxton felt forced to fix on a standard for English, three centuries later Samuel Johnson came to the conclusion that it could not be fixed. As Johnson explained in the *Preface* to his great *Dictionary*, he had begun the enterprise with the express purpose of providing permanent meanings and usages for the vocabulary of English but the experience of compilation had convinced him that the language was in its nature ever-changing, inveterate in its coinages, in its absorption of foreign words and in its redefinition of existing ones.

Despite the local dominance of English, many of London's immigrant communities continued to maintain a linguistic distinctiveness, sometimes at their peril. During the Peasants' Revolt of 1381 and again on "Evil May Day" in 1517, the industrious Flemish, identified by their speech, were slaughtered in the streets by resentful mobs. In the 1730s the historian William Maitland declared of Soho that "many parts... so greatly abound with French that it is an easy matter for a stranger to imagine himself in France." It was estimated that during that period forty per cent of the inhabitants of Soho habitually spoke French. An English diplomat, assigned to a Continental posting, is known to have polished his command of the language prior to departure by six weeks' "immersion" there.

Although French may have remained an essential instrument of diplomacy and commerce and a key to polite intercourse and learning, it did not necessarily meet with the approval of the metropolitan rabble. Voltaire, a passionate Anglophile, while domiciled in Maiden Lane in 1726-7 once spent a pleasant period sauntering through the Inns of Court only to find that, when he was identified as a Frenchman, he was swiftly surrounded by a hostile crowd. Climbing up a lamp-post in refuge the philosopher daringly harangued his would-be tormentors with a challenge: "Am I not unfortunate enough not to have been born among you?" By the time he had finished speaking the crowd was applauding.

The ultra-respectable German bankers of Victorian Denmark Hill spoke impeccable English for business purposes and also sustained a German choir and organized festivals in honour of Goethe and Schiller. German-speaking artists could likewise flourish at court, where Victoria and Albert habitually conversed in German. The royal couple played duets with Mendelssohn; Winterhalter painted them; Boehm sculpted them and was knighted for it (and became the secret lover of Victoria's sculptress daughter, Princess Louise). To the end of her days Victoria retained a marked preference for ministers who were prepared to speak to her in German.

Ashkenazi speakers of Yiddish first came to London in substantial numbers in the eighteenth century, but it was the influx of the 1880s which established a Yiddish-speaking community capable of supporting a Yiddish theatre and a Yiddish press. This was in the face of the best endeavours of the Jews Free School in Bell Lane which, with the fervent blessing of established Anglo-Jewry, sought to preserve the heritage of Judaism as a faith while dismissing Yiddish as a language and a culture with contempt. Nevertheless the Pavilion Theatre at Whitechapel continued to attract audiences for Yiddish drama until the 1930s. The impoverished parents of the future showbiz moguls, Lords Grade and Delfont, newly translated from Odessa to Brick Lane, turned to the Yiddish stage to augment their sweatshop earnings. Yiddish also found a powerful partisan in the anarchist Rudolph Rocker. A German Catholic by birth, he set himself to learn Yiddish as an act of ideological commitment, embracing it as the common speech of the oppressed and editing an anarchist weekly in Yiddish, *Der Arbeiter Fraint* (*The Workers' Friend*), which only ceased publication in 1950. This was printed in the East End by the Narodny Press, which also printed the Yiddish verse of the unwordly Avram Stencl, whose reputation was revered throughout the diaspora.

From Yiddish cockneys took "nosh" (food) and "gelt" (money), from Romany "pal" (originally meaning "brother") and the abrupt address "Oi, mush" (literally "Here, face"), from Hindi "buckshee" (free, surplus, "going begging" from *bakhsheesh* meaning "alms"), "shufti" (look) and "doolally" (mad, demented, from the army mental hospital at Deolali, near Bombay). The cockneys' own distinctive contribution to English has been the development of rhyming slang, generally believed to have evolved from the *argot* used by costermongers to screen their various deceptions and dishonesties from customers, policemen, officials and outsiders generally. The superficial impenetrability of much rhyming slang depends on the fact that, because so many expressions are contracted or truncated, they do not seem to have anything to do with rhyme. You have to know that "butcher's" (look) is short for "butcher's hook". "China" (mate) is a contraction of "China plate". "Tom" is jewellery from "tomfoolery". "Tea leaf" (thief) is, however, never abbreviated.

Many lexical items in rhyming slang have evolved through even more radical processes of removal or compression. "Bottle and glass" (arse) becomes "Aristotle" (to rhyme with bottle) which is then contracted to "Aris". New words are often inspired by famous personalities; drawling TV presenter Alan Whicker (nicker—a pound), racing-driver Ayrton Senna (a tenner—ten pounds), Dudley Moore (a score—twenty pounds), Lee Marvin (starving), Britney Spears (beers) and Nelson Mandela (a specific brand of lager—Stella (Artois)). From a previous generation Gregory (Peck) for cheque and Ruby (Murray) for curry have proved too useful to be discarded. Rhyming slang also survives vigorously in Australia, along with other cockney patterns of greeting and swearing, although this is scarcely surprising considering the cockney origin of many of Australia's early—and involuntary—immigrants.

NOTTING HILL

Notting Hill is synonymous with Europe's largest party, the annual Carnival which, on the last weekend in August, draws a million revellers to its Victorian streets and squares. Over the half century of its existence Carnival has transcended its Caribbean roots to become a multi-ethnic, multi-faceted, gay and lesbian celebration of counter-culture. For the rest of the year Notting Hill is content to be *the* London address for the glamorous and the gifted. Uniquely among the capital's residential areas it even has its own insider's guidebook to local living—listing over a hundred eating and drinking

Carnival dancer

establishments, sixty plus fashion outlets, seventeen galleries, eight hairdressers, six jewellers, specialist bookshops for gastronomes, travellers, gardeners, etc.

The area takes its name from a turnpike gate and was once known as Kensington Gravel Pits. Farmland until the 1820s, then briefly and abortively laid out as a race-course, Notting Hill proper was built up with the ornate stuccoed mansions of the Ladbroke estate, complemented by exclusive gardens, setting a new standard for suburban elegance. Between 1820 and 1885 some thirteen thousand houses were built over what is technically, though seldom colloquially, known as North Kensington. Not quite convenient enough for City businessmen, the area attracted lawyers, retired military men, widows living off annuities and a smattering of artists. Appropriately it became the birthplace of the British nanny and was also the home of the family on whom J. M. Barrie modelled the Darlings in *Peter Pan*. Notting Hill High School for Girls became an early centre of educational excellence for females. There was also a strong Roman Catholic presence, with no fewer than six convents, two churches and a college. Originally Irish, today this has a marked Iberian tinge, with a Spanish school and shops and Portuguese patisseries.

Socially speaking, the slide started in the inter-war period when the sub-division of mid-Victorian mansions began. Others were turned into hostels or hotels. When, in the 1940s, cartoonist Osbert Lancaster returned to the scenes of his childhood, what had been "the very acropolis of Edwardian propriety" had been reduced to a wasteland of residential decay—grubby, ragged curtains behind cracked windows, peeling paint, rotting woodwork. A refuge for refugees, the area was also a haven of last resort for Caribbean immigrants denied decent housing elsewhere. Slum landlord Peter Rachman's formula of exploitation and intimidation made him a millionaire and his name a synonym for misery. Worse was to come with inter-racial street-fighting, misleadingly labelled "riots", in 1958 and consequent neo-fascist mischief-making.

The turn-around came in the sixties as Portobello Road antiques market took off as a leading weekend attraction. The Ladbroke estate achieved Conservation Area status in 1968. By the 1970s David Hockney and John Cleese were local residents. By 1999 the Hugh Grant/Julia Roberts movie *Notting Hill* merely confirmed an already established mirage of classless classiness. In reality, the typical resident of Notting Hill is likely to be a flat-dwelling, fitness-conscious, *Guardian*-reading graduate, earning at least twice the average national wage. Not necessarily glamorous—but probably gifted.

Chapter Eight
VICTORIAN VALHALLAS: THE MAGNIFICENT SEVEN

"For there is good news yet to hear and fine things to be seen,
Before we go to Paradise by way of Kensal Green."
G. K. Chesterton, "The Rolling English Road", 1914

Karl Marx tomb, Highgate Cemetery

Necropolis Needed

Britain's second census, conducted in 1811, revealed that London had become the first city in the western world with a population of more than a million. In the 1820s the population of the metropolis grew by a further staggering twenty per cent. More living meant more dead in a city where most traditional churchyards had long since reached capacity. The half-acre churchyard of St. Anne's, Soho, was reckoned to contain over a hundred thousand burials. The result was corruption—literal and physical as well as personal and financial. A youthful Dickens exposed the scams worked by greedy sextons who would routinely smash coffins to cram yet another burial in on top of them. Ecclesiastical architect Francis Goodwin drew up elaborate but abortive plans for a Grand National Cemetery, embellished with pseudo-Athenian temples. Another scheme envisaged the construction of a gigantic pyramid on Primrose Hill, into which five million corpses would be slotted into cubicles like some pharaonic beehive.

London's emerging burials crisis was brought to an unanticipated climax by the outbreak of Britain's first cholera visitation in 1831-2, which added an additional ten thousand corpses to the capital's normal annual death-toll. This happened to coincide with the accession to power of a Whig government eager to expose the nation's life to the cleansing breezes of commerce and competition. Suspicious of all monopolies, the reformers were ready to deprive religious bodies of their monopoly of the disposal of the dead and to turn it into a business. When Parliament was petitioned to authorize the establishment of graveyards on the fringes of the metropolis in the interests of public hygiene the result was the creation of the "magnificent seven" in what were then rapidly developing suburbs.

Ask the average Londoner which is the city's most famous cemetery and he/she would probably say Highgate, where the massive memorial to Karl Marx has been drawing a steady stream of atheistic pilgrims since its erection in 1956, at the height of the Cold War. But London's most important cemetery for the famous is at Kensal Green, where over eight hundred of the incumbents have merited entries in the *Dictionary of National Biography*, more than twice as many as at Highgate—and including the editor of the *DNB*, Sir Leslie Stephen, father of Virginia Woolf. Kensal Green was the first of the commercial cemeteries to open, in 1833, and boasted state-of-the-art technology with a hydraulic lift to serve its catacombs. Consumer choice was paramount, with bereaved families offered the option of catacomb, mausoleum, brick-lined vault or traditional earth grave in a landscaped setting planted with eight hundred specimen trees. A decade after its opening the cemetery achieved a new eminence when George III's sixth son, the scholarly and reclusive Duke of Sussex, chose Kensal Green over Windsor, having been appalled at the shambles attending the interment of his brother, King William IV. Royal endorsement conferred a *cachet* that soon made the cemetery the resting-place of choice for Victorian *eminenti*: the Brunels, father and son, Thackeray and Trollope, Charles Babbage, pioneer of computing, Thomas Wakley, founder of *The Lancet*, W. H. Smith, eponymous founder of an empire of newsagent-booksellers and Major Wingfield, inventor of tennis. Among the eminent also lay those who contributed to the gaiety of London life: celebrity chef Alexis Soyer, the tightrope-walker Blondin, who once cooked an omelette while balanced half-way across Niagara Falls, and the trick-rider Andrew Ducrow, who spent £3,000, the price of a modest church, on a tomb of his own design, "erected by genius for the reception of its remains."

In the adjacent St. Mary's cemetery, opened for Roman Catholics in 1858, lie Cardinals Newman and Manning, the Swiss-Italian Gatti dynasty, who ran a metropolitan empire of continental cafés and ice-cream parlours, the celebrated Crimean war nurse Mary Seacole—recently voted the greatest Black Briton of all time—and some twelve and half thousand Irish who fled the Great Hunger of the 1840s and found work in the nearby brickfields, gasworks and railway yards while their wives and daughters slaved as skivvies and laundresses for the bourgeoisie of Bayswater and Brompton. A monument of unexpected grandeur commemorates named Belgian soldiers who died in the Great War, presumably battle casualties evacuated to expire in London hospitals. Kensal Green continues to have its attractions. The ashes of the playwright Terence Rattigan were brought from the Caribbean to be interred here in his family vault. Freddie Mercury of Queen was cremated here, although his ashes were taken to be scattered at Mumbai (Bombay).

The cemetery at West Norwood, opened in 1837, has no such galaxy of the great as Kensal Green can claim but it does have sixty-five monuments listed Grade II or Grade II* and the last resting-places of Mrs. Beeton, author of the essential vade-mecum of Victorian housewifery, the *Book of Household Management*, Baron Julius de Reuter, founder of the international news agency and sugar tycoon Henry Tate, donor of the gallery which bears his name.

The proprietors of Abney Park cemetery at Stoke Newington, opened in 1840, rejected consecration, aiming to attract a Nonconformist clientele. For reasons which now seem opaque they dignified their enterprise with a massive Egyptian gateway inscribed with hieroglyphs which translate as "The Gates of the Abode of the

Mortal Part of Man". Occupying the former grounds of two seventeenth-century mansions, the cemetery originally benefited from the attractions of an arboretum with over two thousand different species of trees. Success, in the shape of over three hundred thousand interments, ensured that the woodland was steadily destroyed to make way for grave plots. A large statue of hymn-writer Isaac Watts (*Our God, Our Help in Ages Past, Jesus Shall Reign*) serves as reminder of his residence in long-vanished Abney House. Fittingly for a bastion of Nonconformity, Abney Park is the earthly resting-place of the founder of the Salvation Army, William Booth (1829-1912), whose funeral brought London to an unexpected standstill when half a million spontaneously lined the streets to show their respects when he was "called to glory". Perhaps a little incongruously, Abney Park also contains the remains of the original "Champagne Charlie" ("Champagne Charlie is my name, Champagne drinking is my game"), George Leybourne, as well as those of Albert Chevalier, the doyen of stage cockney comedians. Elsewhere lies London's first fire chief, James Braidwood, one of only two fatalities of the great Tooley Street conflagration of 1861.

The Friends of Nunhead Cemetery, which also opened in 1840, modestly concede that it is the least known of the "magnificent seven" but claim that it does have at least sixteen species of butterflies nowadays. Perhaps the most distinguished occupant is Sir Polydor de Keyser (1832-98), the Belgian waiter who became Lord Mayor of London. The Friends have published a biographical dictionary of some four hundred others. A shabby clerk, maddened with grief at the death of his lover, gives voice to a tormented monologue in Charlotte Mew's poem "In Nunhead Cemetery".

Tower Hamlets cemetery, opened in 1841, is even more overgrown than Nunhead and with over seven thousand burials per acre, even more overcrowded. Within a decade of its opening four-fifths of the burials here were at public expense, the families of the deceased being too impoverished to pay for interment, let alone the sort of elaborate plumed-horse, multi-hearsed carnival of death so beloved of the East End's elite of ex-boxers, money-lenders, criminals and publicans. By 1889 over 247,000 corpses had been crammed in here. There are, unsurprisingly, few names of distinction. Wildlife importer William Jamrach, supplier of exotic beasts to circuses, zoos, the Kaiser and the Sultan of Turkey, also made the goldfish a favourite cockney parlour pet. Legendary pub-owner and ex-boxer Charlie Brown accumulated a bewildering display of bric-a-brac, curiosities and stuffed animals, brought by thirsty sailors from the ends of the earth, which made a London landmark of "Charlie Brown's"— officially the Railway Arms, but no one ever called it that. The headstone of Will Crooks (1852-1921) has been renewed in recognition of his signal services to the East End. Self-educated and self-assured, Crooks so regularly harangued local workers outside the dock gates that his pitch became known as "Crooks' College". A proud epitaph proclaims:

A COOPER BY TRADE HE BECAME
A GUARDIAN OF THE POOR
A BOROUGH COUNCILLOR
A MAYOR OF POPLAR
A LONDON COUNTY COUNCILLOR
A MEMBER OF PARLIAMENT
A PRIVY COUNCILLOR
He lived and died a servant of the people.

Collective graves house the remains of departed "Brothers" from London's Charterhouse and victims of the *Princess Alice* disaster of 1878, when six hundred day-trippers drowned in raw sewage off Barking Creek after their pleasure-cruiser was sliced in two by another ship.

Highgate
Opened in 1839 on a steep, sprawling hillside, Highgate proved so successful that an extension was opened in 1855. The eastern extension is now regularly accessible to visitors, the original, western part less frequently so. In 1862 the poet Dante Gabriel Rossetti buried his wife, Lizzie Siddal, here after she had taken her own life and, in a melodramatic gesture, threw a volume of unpublished verse into the grave with her. Five years later he had the body exhumed to retrieve his poems. Architects Edward Blore, Sir James Pennethorne and S. S. Teulon are all buried here in what Pevsner compliments as "the most atmospheric of London's great Victorian cemeteries". So are Mr. Chubb

of lock fame and Mr. Cruft, who invented the dog-show to promote Spratt's dog-biscuits.

The monstrous tomb of Karl Marx is an obvious highlight. In its shadow is a memorial to black activist Claudia Jones, a moving spirit behind the Notting Hill Carnival. Opposite there is a modest headstone for that journalistic scourge of the Establishment, Paul Foot. Surrounding tombs of left-wing exiles from repressive regimes in Iraq, Afghanistan and the Horn of Africa attest to contemporary London's role as a refuge for asylum-seekers. Nearby lie the evolutionist philosopher Herbert Spencer and novelist George Eliot and her lover, the critic G. H. Lewes—a ready-made egg-head seminar to last for eternity. If they wanted to add a few more voices for variety, they could invite in scientist Michael Faraday, lesbian novelist Radclyffe Hall, polymath TV presenter Dr. Jacob Bronowski, pioneer TV chef Philip Harben , actor Sir Ralph Richardson and Douglas Adams, author of the quirky cult classic *The Hitchhiker's Guide to the Universe*. In more muscular mode one might also recall the presence here of bare-knuckle pugilist Tom Sayers and "Squire" Osbaldeston, the fiery cricketer and dare-devil horseman who gambled away a fortune of £300,000. The MCC erected an impressive monument to the fiendish bowler Lillywhite—but left his name at that; in death, as in life, only amateurs were to be honoured with initials. A monument designed by Lutyens honours William Friese-Greene as "the inventor of Kinematography" and includes his Patent No. 10,131 in his epitaph. Bankrupted twice by his efforts to improve the movie camera, Friese-Greene died with less than two shillings in his pockets. The film industry at least rallied to give him a big send-off.

Visitors might care to note, within a few steps of the entrance to the western cemetery, a headstone marking the *temporary* resting-place of American art teacher Ernest Fenellosa. As an imported foreign expert in Japan in the 1880s, when the craze for "things Western" was at its height, he persuaded the Japanese education authorities that introducing Western-style art teaching did not necessarily mean junking the indigenous heritage. When they learned that their mentor had died and been buried in a land not even his own, sorrowing Japanese disciples fetched him back to his spiritual home and had him interred overlooking Lake Biwa. And do not miss Nero the lion on top of the grave of menagerie master George Wombwell.

Brompton: From the Ends of the Earth

Whereas the other great commercial cemeteries became abandoned, decayed and overgrown and have had to be rescued by volunteer associations of "Friends", Brompton, established in 1837, has the unique distinction of having been compulsorily purchased by the state, bought in 1852 for just half what it cost to create. Through the quirks of institutional history it has become technically a branch of the Royal Parks Department, though it does also have a supporters club of Friends. Apart from having, in relation to its area, probably the most interesting selection of graves and monuments, Brompton also has the great advantage for the visitor of being the most accessible of the Victorian Valhallas from central London, being just two minutes walk from West Brompton station on the District Line. And, unlike Highgate, there is no admission charge.

A stroll through Brompton's aisles and avenues is a world tour in miniature. There are epitaphs in Latin and French, Polish and Amharic, the tombs of an Irishman born in Matamoros and an Australian born in Fyzabad and memorials to men who served in the Tsarist army and the Indian Forestry Service. Others commemorate the man who organized Edward VII's baggage and the naval pilot who brought down a Zeppelin and then, while wounded, fixed his own plane after it had crash-landed from the force of the explosion. Here lies George Borrow, who tried to sell Protestant Bibles in Catholic Spain and Orthodox Russia and wrote the first dictionary of the Romany language. Other globetrotters include pioneering war correspondents W. H. Russell, who coined the phrase "the thin red line", and G. A. Henty, who became a prolific author of "ripping yarns" for boys. Elsewhere in Brompton rest Sir Frederick James Halliday, who claimed to have witnessed the last suttee (widow-burning) in India, and Sir Henry Cole, who organized the Great Exhibition of 1851 and invented, but did not bother to patent, the Christmas card.

Long Wolf, a Sioux chief with Buffalo Bill's Wild West Show, who died of bronchial pneumonia while on tour in 1892, lay at Brompton for over a century until his remains were repatriated to a probably happier hunting-ground in South Dakota in 1997. Here still lies Louis Leonowens—"dear little Louey"—the son of Anna, the governess of *The King and I* fame. He returned to Thailand to found a timber exporting company which still trades under his name. (Anna, who eventually founded the Nova Scotia College of Art and Design, lies in Montreal.) Nearby, in a grave surmounted by a granite obelisk lies "Jucoi Nagayori Asano", who died in 1886, just twenty-one years old, an incidental casualty of Japan's craze for Westernization. Asano had probably been sent to study in London by a father whose Western-style title of Marquis identifies him as a member of the country's modernizing elite. The obverse of the obelisk acknowledges that its Japanese inscription was provided by Lieutenant-General Viscount Tani, another modernizer who had distinguished himself during the last samurai rebellion in 1877 and had subsequently become minister of agriculture and commerce. Opposite Asano's grave lies Zygmunt Morozewicz, O.B.E., a Cavalier of the Order of Military Virtue, Poland's equivalent of the Victoria Cross. Two hundred paces further on lies Rear Admiral Nicholas Wolkoff, A.D.C. to His Late Majesty Tsar Nicholas of Russia.

Earthly Powers
Hundreds of Brompton's permanent residents have their adventures and achievements recorded in terse lapidary summaries. Opposite the tomb of the prolific Victorian portrait sculptor Matthew Noble stands the great granite tomb-chest of Colonel Harry Byrne, who fought in Italy under Garibaldi, served as a captain in the American Civil War and, in his sixties, as a colonel in the second Boer War. Nearby is the curious monument erected for General Alexander Anderson of the Royal Marines, an iron table bearing twelve cannon balls, three gnomically labelled Beyrout, Gaza and Syria. To the south of Byrne's tomb is the family vault of the Thesigers. Here Frederick Thesiger, Baron Chelmsford, who lost an army of 1,500 men to assegai-wielding Zulus at Isandhlwana in 1879, rests alongside the actor Ernest Thesiger, a closet gay who wore women's jewellery under his clothes and painted his toenails green.

The achievements and attachments of earthly existence are recorded as eternally valid among those who "fell asleep", "passed over" or were "called home". Thus we learn that Thomas Lloyd was editor-in-chief of a long defunct journal of commentary *The Statist.* Beside him is Louis Campbell-Johnston, founder in 1920 of The British Humane Association for "the promotion of benevolence for the good of humanity". A Fellow of the Society of Antiquaries of Scotland lies fittingly beneath a Celtic cross. Beneath another lie the third son of the third Lord Saumarez and the fourth and fifth sons of the first Baron Machermorne, observing in death the finely marked social precedences of the Edwardian era. Other headstones record professional rather than social eminence, like a CV for the recording angel. Sir Robert Rawlinson, Chief Engineering Inspector to the Local Government Board, had also been Sanitary Commissioner to the British Army in the Crimea, Administrator of the Lancashire Cotton Famine Fund and President of the Institute of Civil Engineers. Sir Richard Charles Bart was Serjeant Surgeon to H.M. King George V and a Knight of Justice of St. John of Jerusalem—and also G.C.V.O., K.G.S.I., LL.D., M.D., F.R.C.S. and I.M.S.

Women are for the most part praised for their domestic virtues—"for forty-one years devoted wife", "a most brave and loving little mother of six", "for forty-seven years the faithful and beloved nurse". "Her children rise up and call her blessed" is an oft-repeated phrase. A few feisty females do, however, grab the attention. The striking statue of Blanche Roosevelt (Tucker) is on a suitably commanding corner site for a diva. The first American woman to perform in Italian at Covent Garden, she also sang for Gilbert and Sullivan but abandoned her brief stage career to marry an Italian aristocrat, then took up novel-writing to produce *Stage-struck, or, She Would Be an Opera Singer*, followed by biographical studies of various male friends, including Longfellow, Verdi and Doré. Blanche Roosevelt's literary career is, however, omitted from her epitaph, as, understandably, is her position as the mistress of Guy de Maupassant. The rose she holds to her ample bosom may be a pun on her name—Roosevelt is Dutch for Rosefield, her initial stage name being a pseudo-Italianized version of this, Madame Rosavilla. The grave of Emmeline Pankhurst, leader of the militant suffragette movement, is strikingly unpolitical in its symbolism. Her headstone is almost mystical, a Celtic cross bearing a haloed Christ with a hand raised in blessing, surmounted by to two angels bearing a chalice upwards towards the receiving hand of the Almighty.

"The Greatest Doctor of All Time"

At the station end of the cemetery is a monument with a chequered history all of its own. Erected to Dr. John Snow "in remembrance of his great labours in science and of the excellence of his private life and character", it was restored in 1895 and again in 1938 by Members of the Section of Anaesthetics of the Royal Society of Medicine and anaesthetists in the United States of America. Destroyed beyond repair by enemy action in 1941, it was then replaced by a replica erected by the Association of Anaesthetists of Great Britain and Ireland in 1951. From all of this the onlooker might reasonably deduce that Dr. John Snow was a pioneer of anaesthetics, which indeed he was, being primarily responsible for the introduction into British medical practice of both ether and chloroform. In 1853 Snow administered chloroform to Queen Victoria during the birth of Prince Leopold and in 1857 did so again at the birth of Princess Beatrice. The innovation met with the monarch's unqualified approval: "soothing, quieting and delightful beyond measure". Royal endorsement contributed greatly to the widespread acceptance of anaesthetics on the grounds that it was good enough for the Queen.

Snow is, however, nowadays best remembered as an epidemiologist. As a teenager he had served as an unqualified volunteer during the first cholera outbreak of 1831-32. Prevailing medical theory attributed the disease to "miasma", or contaminated air. But Snow believed the miasmic doctrine unfounded, having himself tended numerous sufferers without catching it from their breath. He also observed that the disease spread worst among miners working long shifts underground, without access to privies, who ate their food with unwashed hands. Following the return of cholera in 1848-49, Snow published an essay arguing that the disease was spread by ingestion rather than inhalation. The Institute of France awarded him a princely £1,200 in recognition of his discovery, but reactionary British colleagues remained sceptical, provoking Snow to produce a second edition, based on data gathered in Soho during the third cholera outbreak of 1854. Snow's pioneering exercise in medical mapping recorded the physical distribution of cholera deaths and identified the source of the water normally consumed by 658 of the 860 local victims. If, he reasoned, infection spread through the air the distribution of victims should be random, but in fact it proved to be patterned and localized. Snow also noticed that men working in the local brewery never caught the disease; because they were allowed to drink the beer they made for free, they never touched water. The local workhouse was likewise virtually exempt because it had its own well. Snow correctly identified a contaminated pump in Broadwick Street as the source of infection and had its handle taken off. Cholera deaths in the locality declined at once. Having published some 89 scientific papers, Snow died at just forty-five. Ironically for a strict teetotaller, he is commemorated in the name of the pub overlooking the site of the Broadwick Street pump. An extensive website is maintained by the University of California (www.ph.ucla.edu/epi/snow.html) to honour the man voted "the greatest doctor of all time" in a UK poll organized by *Hospital Doctor* magazine in 2003.

Final Curtain
A few footsteps from Snow's last resting-place is a huge gravestone on which the carving looks as fresh as if it had been done yesterday. As the granite almost certainly came from Scotland the cost must have been enormous but the occupants could certainly afford it. The splendidly named Sir Squire Bancroft (1841-1926) and Lady Bancroft were a theatrical couple who graduated from the boards to management. As handsome as his name, the habitually monocled Bancroft—actually Sir Squire Bancroft Bancroft—specialized in drawing-room comedies and retired after twenty years, with a nest-egg of £180,000. As much the "swell" off-stage as on it, Bancroft devoted his forty-one years of retirement to composing lengthy volumes of memoirs and serving as President of the Royal Academy of Dramatic Art. Nothing on the grave hints at the profession which made his fortune save the opaque inscription *From Shadows And Fancies To The Truth*.

Towards the northern end of Brompton's main axial avenue the passer-by is bidden "Of Your Charity Pray for the Repose of the Soul of Tom Foy The Comedian", usually known as "The Yorkshire Lad". Former sailor William Charles James Lewin was better known as "Breezy Bill" Terriss and punningly by fellow-Thespians as "No. 1 Adelphi Terrace". Terriss made his name playing handsome heroes and became hugely popular with an adoring public, devastated when he was stabbed to death by a madman at the stage-door of the Adelphi Theatre.

One of the most extravagant, indeed theatrical, memorials in the entire cemetery, graced by the sorrowing figure of a lissom female, is dedicated to the memory of Sir Augustus Henry Glossop Harris, the manager of Drury Lane, whose bust still stands outside that theatre.

The tomb of Henry Pettit bears a portrait of a sad-eyed man with a droopy moustache and droopy necktie. He was the author of numerous melodramas with titles like *A Woman's Revenge* and died of typhoid at forty-five. Brandon Thomas once remarked that he wanted to be remembered as a great actor but would be known only as the author of the farce *Charley's Aunt.* He was right. The grave of the Austrian tenor Richard Tauber is still lovingly maintained more than half a century after his death. Surrounded with glowing crimson geraniums, it is visited by admirers on his birthday, 16 May, each year.

Confined to Barracks

On the western side of the cemetery is an enclosed area entirely given over to military burials. It includes a monument to the Brigade of Guards. To its north is another marking the burial site of 2,625 Chelsea Pensioners interred there since 1854. Chelsea Pensioners by definition died full in years. Violent death in combat is the prerogative of the young. Most of Brompton's war graves memorialize officers of the grander regiments, Guards, Hussars etc. Memorials to fliers are a reminder of the risks run by "knights of the air" who carried no parachutes. Even a stalled engine could prove fatal. Memorials to ordinary private soldiers are few. Benjamin Williams was killed on 9 November 1918, just two days before the Armistice. His parents would have received the dreaded War Office telegram while their neighbours rejoiced at victory. Nearby another headstone pays eloquent tribute to Constance Baker, "An Ideal Wife and Mother Aptly Termed for Services Rendered during the Great War Mother of the Wounded".

The award of a Victoria Cross is recorded on the gravestone of the widow of the Reverend James William Adams, a forty-year-old Irish chaplain with the Indian Army and one of only five civilians ever to receive Britain's highest gallantry award. In 1879, during the second Afghan War, several men of the IXth Lancers had tumbled into a deep ditch, filled with freezing water, where they thrashed helplessly as a merciless enemy closed in on them. Adams plunged in waist-deep, dragged the men free and escaped on foot. Twelve further recipients of the Victoria Cross also lie buried in Brompton. Four were given for actions undertaken in the course of the Crimean War, when the award was first instituted. One of these was won by Private Samuel Parkes who, in the course of the famous "Charge of the Light Brigade", single-handedly defended his dismounted trumpet-major, first of all against two Cossacks and then against six Russians. Six more VCs were won in the course of the Indian Mutiny, one by Thomas Hancock who would die in Westminster Workhouse aged 48 and be buried in an unmarked common grave. Medical orderly Joseph Farmer won his VC for his part in the disastrous action at Majuba Hill in 1881 during the first Boer War when he held a white flag over the wounded until he was shot through the arm and then used his other arm until he was shot through that one, too. Farmer's headstone is a boulder taken from the scene of his gallantry.

Name Games
Like many writers, Beatrix Potter, who lived a short walk away in the exclusive residential development known as The Boltons, looked for names for her characters in cemeteries—hence Squirrel Nutkin, taken from the Nutkins family vault. There are other Brompton names which cry out for literary appropriation but are still going begging: Princess Violette Lobanov-Rostovsky, Alma Ernestine Berger, mother of the Countess of Clancarty, Ludwik Napoleon Bodar-Rousseau, Sissie des Voeux, John Ralph Engledue, Wortley William Baggal, Andrina Founereau and Amari Sebastiano, Maria Mutton and Alexandra de Goguel, *née* Comtesse de Toulouse-Lautrec. Many headstones helpfully provide nicknames. Jane Zarzhetsky was apparently known familiarly as Mampie and Mary Balmer as Morabhai, while George Louis Edward Raggett was called Gee-Gee by his intimates. Lyulph Pape was known as Tommy.

Some names acquire a life of their own as they become synonymous with national institutions, such as Sotheby's auction house and the Cunard shipping line. Both their eponymous founders lie in Brompton. S. Leigh Sotheby met an early end drowning in the River Dart. Canadian-born Sir Samuel Cunard was the pioneer of regular transatlantic steamship services. "Banting" is a term now all but lost to the English language, although it is still in use in Swedish. Coined to describe what would now be called dieting, the word recalls an undertaker's thirty-year battle against obesity. William Banting might otherwise have gone down only as a minor footnote in history as the maker of the Duke of Wellington's coffin. Passing the two hundred pound mark, the five foot five inch sixty-two-year-old began to suffer from increasing deafness and so consulted Dr. William Harvey, an ear-nose-and-throat specialist of Soho Square. Harvey diagnosed Banting's obesity as the cause of his defective hearing and also of numerous other ailments which afflicted him. His solution was to make Banting cut out the staple elements of conventional Victorian "plain fare"—bread, beer, beans and butter, pork, potatoes, milk and sugar—and to substitute red meat, fish, fruit and non-root vegetables. Within a year Banting lost almost fifty pounds and twelve inches from his waistline. In delighted and disinterested gratitude he published at his own expense *A Letter on Corpulence Addressed to the Public* to spread the gospel according to Harvey, giving away the first edition of a thousand copies and then a second of fifteen hundred. Banting next found himself in possession of a best-seller as a third edition sold sixty thousand copies at a shilling each. The pamphlet was soon translated into French and German and pirated in the USA. Banting maintained his weight loss and lived to be eighty-one. Dr. Harvey, meanwhile, found himself the object of professional hostility from medical colleagues who cavilled at his daring to step beyond the boundaries of his own expertise and criticized his failure to provide a scientific explanation of why his forerunner of the Atkins diet worked—although it did.

Eye-Catchers

Professor Nikolaus Pevsner, doyen of architectural critics, was in no doubt that "the most remarkable tomb in the cemetery" was designed for the ship-owner and artistic patron Frederick Leyland by Sir Edward Burne-Jones, best known as a designer of stained-glass windows and painter of mythological scenes. Leyland's last resting-place consists of "an exquisite Romanesque marble shrine inlaid with bronze floral scrolls, standing on short columns, with pitched copper roof and surrounded by art nouveau iron railings." A dozen yards away is another pseudo-medieval casket raised on columns, peculiarly appropriate for an artist who painted in the Pre-Raphaelite style. Valentine Cameron—"Val"—Prinsep was Frederick Leyland's son-in-law and, thanks to his wealthy wife, was able to dabble with writing novels and plays, both of which he did successfully. Handsome, effortlessly charming and powerfully built, Prinsep was an enthusiastic officer of the volunteer militia company known as the Artists' Rifles. George du Maurier, who had been a student in Paris with Prinsep, made him the model for the character of Taffy in the hit play adapted from his novel *Trilby*.

Last Innings

Among the artists, actors, architects and authors there are also men of muscle and nerve. The tomb of bare-knuckle pugilist "Gentleman" John Jackson is surmounted by a moody-looking lion. Near the south exit the tomb of rower Robert Coombes is surmounted by an upturned stone scull and draped with a stone blazer. Although barely nine stones in weight Coombes became the champion oarsman of both Thames and Tyne and was also coach to the Cambridge University crew. But the ending of his professional career plunged him into poverty, obscurity and an early death in Maidstone madhouse. Percy Lambert, whose grave is marked by a broken motor car wheel, was the first man actually to drive a hundred miles in just one hour. He promised his fiancée that he would give up racing when they got married and went out at Brooklands for one last record-breaking spin, which was indeed his last.

The name of John Wisden is synonymous with cricket or rather the cricket-lover's Bible. A tiny, slight figure, "the Little Wonder" was a ferocious bowler who in 1850, playing for the North versus the South, clean bowled all ten of the opposing batsmen in a single innings, a feat unequalled in first class cricket before or since. During a tour of America Wisden took six wickets with six successive balls. In 1855 he opened a shop selling cigars and cricket gear and from this "Mecca for cricket lovers" began to publish his annual *Almanack* in 1864. The first edition was an eclectic effort, mixing up cricket results with useful information about coinage and canals and a potted history of China. The 1865 edition contained the scores from all the previous season's first class matches. In 1867 he began to include the dates of cricketers' births and deaths and from 1870 onwards the *Almanack* contained descriptions of matches. Since then *Wisden* has become established as the authoritative work of both reference and commentary, with collectors eager to pay thousands of pounds to acquire the early volumes. Finally, no one rests here more appropriately than local businessman Sir Henry Mears, founder of Chelsea football club, whose massive stadium dwarfs the cemetery's circuit walls.

NICKED!
A Criminal Interlude

*"Whoever indeed considers the Cities of London and Westminster...
the great irregularity of their Buildings, the immense Number of
Lanes, Alleys, Courts and Bye-Places, must think that, had they
been intended for the very purpose of concealment, they could scarce
have been better contrived... the whole appears as a vast Wood or
Forest, in which a Thief may harbour with as great Security, as
wild Beasts do in the Deserts of Africa or Arabia."*

Henry Fielding, 1751

Dick Turpin, a Victorian interpretation

Crises of Criminality

In Tudor times population was rising fast, faster still in London, though
this was only dimly understood. Inflation, scarcely understood at all,
was making most of the rich richer while raising the cost of everyday
items of food and drink. The poor, if they could get work, worked
harder for less. Wars, against the Scots, French, Irish and Spanish,
discharged hardened men, many disabled, more disgruntled, onto an
already overcrowded labour market. Casual violence was a common

feature of city life when almost all men routinely carried side-arms. The playwright (and disillusioned ex-soldier) Ben Jonson killed a fellow-actor at Hoxton in what he alleged was a "duel". Pleading guilty, he got off with a brief imprisonment. Careful analysis of seventeenth-century court records for Southwark reveals that the murder rate was six times as high as it is today. Dr. Johnson, a great bear of a man, routinely carried a cudgel and claimed to have beaten off four footpads with it on one occasion. Horace Walpole complained that one was "forced to travel even at noon as if one was going into battle." In his day even members of the royal family were robbed in plain daylight. Until the coming of gas lighting in the 1820s the streets were even more hazardous by night.

In the early eighteenth century population growth stalled and improvements in farming produced consistent surpluses of grain that were readily convertible into gin. Whence came the "gin mania" likened by modern commentators to a crack cocaine epidemic and famously depicted by Hogarth in his contrasting prints depicting the miseries of Gin Lane, identifiable from the eccentric spire of St. George's as being around Seven Dials, as against the jolly comforts of honest Beer Street. Gin-drinking on a monumental scale was not only held responsible for general lawlessness but did for a while seriously threaten to reverse the growth of London's population, so lethal were its effects.

In the following generation the celebrated Bow Street magistrate Sir John Fielding blamed excessive immigration for the crime wave of his day: "... if some restraint could be laid on the imported Irish it would be another means of preventing a great many robberies... There are certainly a much greater number of Jews and Irish than can possibly gain subsistence by honest means."

London's role as a centre for highly-skilled manufacture and sophisticated commerce contained the implicit possibility of perverting legitimate expertise to dishonest and fraudulent ends. The locksmith becomes the cracksman, the printer a forger or pornographer, the honest merchant a con-man. On London's docks the borderline of crime was blurred by complex systems of "fees", bribes and kickbacks which routinely eroded the value and volume of goods between their arrival and their final delivery to the purchaser. Easily divisible products like tobacco or spices were most vulnerable. The proportion deemed to have been "spoiled" in transit could soon become a fixed percentage to be skimmed off every shipment, regardless of condition. Craftsmen in the royal dockyards were allowed to carry out off-cuts as "chips"; frustrated supervisors eventually put their collective foot down to decree that a "chip" could not be more than three feet long. Middle-class moralists like Defoe and Hogarth, who had known both poverty and prosperity, knew that in London the opportunity for crime and the temptation to commit it were everywhere and the line between vice and virtue was all too easy to cross. When Moll Flanders first steals a bundle of clothes it is on impulse, not by design—that comes with experience. When she steals a gold necklet from a small child she waylays Moll blames the parents for their foolishness in allowing the child out alone with such a valuable item and congratulates herself for not actually killing her victim to conceal her crime.

London's role as Britain's largest port made it the great point of arrival for goods, like silks, lace or brandy, which were low in volume and high in value. It also ensured the constant presence of discharged sailors and rootless newcomers ready for recruitment into the ranks of crime. The reforming magistrate Patrick Colquhoun (1745-1820) calculated that by 1800 three thousand ships were unloading over three million packages a year and that the West India merchants alone were being plundered to the tune of a quarter of a million pounds annually. Thanks to his persuasiveness London finally acquired its first adequate defences against such predators—high-walled, deep-water docks and a professional river police, the capital's first constabulary.

The theatricality of London life favoured the deliberate adoption of false personae. In Wilkie Collins' *No Name* (1862) the ever-plausible Captain Wragge maintains a meticulous data-base of individual identities ("Skins to Jump Into")—dead but documented—which he could assume or discard at convenience. Styling himself a "moral agriculturalist; a man who cultivates the field of human sympathy", Wragge is a total relativist: "Narrow-minded mediocrity... calls me a Swindler. What of that? The same low tone of mind... calls great writers, scribblers—great generals, butchers... It entirely depends on the point of view." Eventually he makes a legal, if not entirely legitimate, fortune from a placebo laxative promoted by shameless and massive advertising: "I have shifted from Moral Agriculture to Medical Agriculture. Formerly I preyed on the public sympathy; now I prey on the public stomach."

Wragge epitomizes a long line of real life London tricksters, stretching back at least to Chaucer's day, when ale-wife Alice, who sealed a false bottom into her quart pot with pitch, was paraded with her fraudulent measure. Two Stratford women bakers, repeatedly convicted of selling short-weight loaves, were themselves conned by one William who claimed to be a sergeant sent to arrest them but let them off with a warning after extracting a "fine". Two perfectly fit men who pretended to have lost their power of speech and begged for alms, "making a horrible noise, like unto a roaring," earned an hour each in the pillory for three days.

In a series of pamphlets on the art of "Conny-Catching" Robert Greene (?1560-92) categorized in detail the specializations of the Tudor underworld: "anglers" lifted items from open windows with a crooked stick; "conny-catchers" cheated innocents at cards or dice; "abram men" counterfeited insanity. "Schools" for inducting juveniles into the art of cutting purses existed at least two centuries before Dickens described Fagin and the Artful Dodger teaching Oliver Twist how to pick pockets in their "Thieves' Kitchen" on Saffron Hill. Criminals gave themselves mutual protection through hidden signs of recognition and a slang or "cant" impenetrable to the uninitiated. *The Devil's Cabinet Broke Open* (1658) alleged that robbers wore a glove hanging by one finger from their belt, cheats left every other doublet button undone and cut-purses put an inconspicuous but visible white mark on their hat-band. The clever criminal also knew the ins and outs of the complex and arbitrary nature of English law. Stealing a horse meant death but obtaining one by deception risked only a forty shilling fine and a turn in the pillory. Much, quite possibly most, of this genre of writing was catch-penny sensationalism rather than objective reportage but it reflected a widespread fear of crime while simultaneously feeding it.

London crime was never more organized than by the "thief-taker general" Jonathan Wild (?1682-1725) who, over the course of a dozen years, sent at least a hundred men to the gallows before meeting his own end there. Wild's denunciation of his victims was usually the result of disobedience to his orders or a means of disposing of rival operators who declined to join his task-force. Many valuables were purloined, not by thieves on the streets, but by trained domestic servants, hired out by Wild's own staff agency, to help at receptions and balls that were too large for trusted household domestics to handle alone. His much-applauded success as a recoverer of stolen goods rested on his skilful and systematic organization of their theft in the first place. The scale of Wild's operations was international. Wigs, watches, snuff-boxes and swords that he was unable to sell back to their owners at a profit were shipped off to Holland for resale.

Highwaymen operated on the approaches to London wherever travellers were forced to cross stretches of uncultivated land. In Ben Jonson's day this could be as close in as St. John's Wood; by 1793 the hazardous areas were Hounslow Heath and Finchley Common. Highwaymen considered themselves the aristocrats of crime and in criminal court routinely proclaimed their profession as "gentleman". Many were ex-officers, trained to the saddle and to arms, accustomed to danger and disdainful of paid work. There was nothing gentlemanly about the notorious Gregory Gang, which included the celebrated Dick Turpin (1706-39). They operated the other way around from most highwaymen, basing themselves in the labyrinthine East End and riding out into Turpin's native county of Essex to attack isolated houses and farms where they would terrorize and torture the inhabitants until they revealed their valuables. Turpin's sordid and vicious exploits became so much the stuff of legend that a century after his execution (for horse-stealing) his name was still known to every transportee in the penal colonies of Australia. The popular novelist Harrison Ainsworth (1805-82) set the seal on Turpin's falsely heroic status by inventing his famous (and entirely fictional) ride to York in the novel that launched Ainsworth's literary career, *Rookwood.*

Between April 1888 and February 1891 there were eleven "Whitechapel murders", of which five, committed between August and November 1888, have been attributed to "Jack the Ripper". All remain unsolved to this day. The name of Jack the Ripper was signed on a letter and a postcard sent to the Central News Agency claiming responsibility for the murders. Chalk graffiti appeared on a wall in Goulston Street, proclaiming "The Juwes are The men that Will not be Blamed for nothing." The speed and accuracy with which many of the victims were mutilated, coupled with their proximity to the London Hospital and to London's main area of Jewish settlement, prompted much speculation that the murderer (or murderers) was either medically trained or a Jewish ritual slaughterer. Other suggested candidates range from members of the royal family to the Queen's physician, Sir William Gull, the writer George Gissing, the Impressionist painter Walter Sickert and even the eminently righteous Prime Minister William Gladstone. The investigating officers narrowed their suspicions down to four prime suspects: Kosminski, a poor Polish Whitechapel Jew; Michael Ostrog, a Russian con-man and thief with a history of mental illness; Dr. Francis Tumbelty, an American quack who jumped bail and fled Britain in November 1888, after being arrested for gross indecency; and Montague Druitt, a barrister who committed suicide in December 1888. The wider interest of the Whitechapel murders lies in the attention they drew to the East End and the deprivation suffered by its inhabitants, an outcome swiftly exploited by local philanthropists, missions and settlements which benefited from the publicity generated by police investigations, coroners' inquests and background "colour" pieces peddled by a prurient press. Interest in the Ripper was rekindled in 1913 by the publication of Marie Bello Lowndes' *The Lodger*, which appeared in thirty-one editions, was translated into eighteen languages and was used as the basis for five films, including Alfred Hitchcock's first cinematic effort.

A former choirboy, Boy Scout and veteran of the Great War, John Reginald Halliday Christie (1899-1953) was twice sacked for dishonesty before serving three terms for theft and being convicted twice for violence. After ten years apart from the wife he deserted, Christie re-settled with her at 10 Rillington Place, a short cul-de-sac in Ladbroke Grove. Incredibly in view of his record, Christie served with the police during the Second World War and won two commendations. While living at Rillington Place he murdered at least seven women, including his wife, in order to commit acts of peri-necrophilia, sexual intercourse with the dying. In 1950 Christie was also responsible for a grotesque miscarriage of justice when his perjury condemned to the gallows his illiterate and mentally deficient neighbour Timothy Evans, for the supposed murder of his infant child and wife, upon whom Christie had himself attempted an abortion that proved fatal. Christie became a vagrant until his successor at Rillington Place discovered the body of one of his victims, one of three papered over in a wall recess. Christie was found, tried and hanged.

Evans was granted a posthumous pardon in 1966, thanks largely to the efforts of broadcaster and author Ludovic Kennedy, whose book, *10 Rillington Place*, proved highly influential in changing parliamentary opinion in favour of abolishing the death penalty. The same title was used for American director Richard Fleischer's 1971 film version of Christie's story. The film was shot in the house next door to No. 10 in what had been renamed Rushton Close and was shortly afterwards demolished to make way for the Westway. Its approximate location is now marked by Bartle Street and Rushton Mews.

SOHO

Once synonymous with sin and strip-clubs, Soho has reinvented itself as a gastronomic redoubt, with two hundred and fifty eating-places crammed into one square mile. Kettner's, founded by Napoleon III's Austrian chef, was once patronized by Whistler and Wilde. The Algerian Coffee Shop may be even older. Gerrard Street's Chinatown is, however, post-war. Other venerable foodie landmarks include the Hungarian Gay Hussar, L'Escargot, Pâtisserie Valérie and The French House, specializing in uncompromised provincial cooking.

Bounded by Oxford Street, Regent Street, Covent Garden and Leicester Square, Soho was developed after the Great Fire of 1666 by opportunistic speculators as an upmarket residential district to rival St. James'. The exuberant plaster ceilings of the House of St. Barnabas, a women's refuge since mid-Victorian times, are a reminder that it was built for the Beckfords, whose fabulous fortune came from sugar and slavery. Newton, Hogarth, James "Athenian" Stuart and Sir Joshua Reynolds are among the *eminenti* who have lived on Leicester Square. Other Soho residents have included Dryden, Mozart, Burke, Canaletto, Casanova, Shelley, Hazlitt and Sir Joseph Banks.

The influx of immigrants who have shaped Soho's cosmopolitan character began with Cretan Greeks in the 1680s. French Huguenots made the area renowned for silver-smithing and making wigs, velvets, mirrors and furniture. Chippendale set up shop in St. Martin's Lane, while Sheraton was in Wardour Street, and Wedgwood had his London showroom in Greek Street. A French-speaking enclave abutting fashionable Mayfair and St. James', Soho was also peopled by teachers of polite accomplishments like foreign languages, music, fencing and dancing. The Huguenot legacy echoes yet in Sir Aston Webb's Huguenot church on Soho Square, an essay in terra-cotta Gothic.

By the mid-nineteenth century Soho had lost its social *cachet*. Soho

Bohemian life on Old Compton Street

Square had become home to Crosse and Blackwell's pickle factory and to manufacturers of billiard tables, black lead and artists' colours. There was also a house of ill-repute catering to voyeurs and flagellants. Golden Square was populated by itinerant musicians, then colonized by dealers in woollens and worsteds. In Dean Street refugee Karl Marx lived in two-roomed squalor with his brood of sickly children. Oddly, half a dozen specialist hospitals were established in the area. Creative endeavours were still represented by the music publishing firm of Novello and such novelties as London's earliest advertising agency and a pioneering school of judo. John Logie Baird gave the first demonstration of television in an upstairs room in Frith Street. Wardour Street became a centre for a film industry whose commercial ethics made it renowned as the only London street to be shady on both sides.

By the 1960s pimps and pornographers, with the active connivance of the police Vice Squad, had made Soho a byword for sleaze and sexploitation. Threats by planners to demolish everything for a dystopian vision of fast-flowing traffic corridors, aerial walkways and tower-blocks galvanized local residents to found the Soho Society in 1972. This not only stymied the scheme but rolled back the sex trade to tolerable proportions, freeing commercial premises to cater for other appetites. Old Compton Street's purveyors of lager, leather and lingerie ensure that an aura of raffishness remains.

Chapter Nine
AT HOME

"It is not in the showy evolutions of buildings but in the multiplicity of human habitations which are crowded together that the wonderful immensity of London consists."

Samuel Johnson

Sir John Soane's house, Lincoln's Inn Fields

Georgian

Georgian taste favoured a stripped-down classicism, even plainer outside than in, with decorative detailing largely confined to doors and windows. Instinctively built to a human scale, typical terraced townhouses served as offices or shops with minimal alteration.

Samuel Johnson lived at numerous locations off Fleet Street and worshiped at St. Clement Danes, at the rear of which his own statue now stands. He doubtless also bought tea, to which he feared he was fatally addicted, at Twining's historic shop a few steps away. Johnson's surviving house at 17 Gough Square, which he occupied from 1748 until 1759, contains the attic room in which he dictated to six secretaries the forty thousand plus entries of his great *Dictionary* and the ten times larger number of quotations from English literature which he selected to illustrate the proper use of the words he had defined. Having himself endured many years of severe poverty as a hack writer, Johnson was something of a soft touch and ended up supporting a dozen dependents and servants, none of them particularly proficient in the household arts. Johnson's house today, however, has none of the chaotic squalor, dust and broken furniture remarked on by Sir Joshua Reynolds when he came to visit.

The "little country box" out at Chiswick, which was the rural retreat of William Hogarth (1697-1764), would offer but a blighted sanctuary now, given the constant roar of traffic from the nearby roundabout which bears his name. Set at an angle to the present main road, the house was built around 1700, acquired by Hogarth in 1749 and occupied by the artist, his wife, mother-in-law and sister. Set behind a high brick wall, it retains a delightful garden and a mulberry tree dating from the period of Hogarth's occupancy. The house contains some two hundred of his engravings, the largest collection on permanent display. Hogarth himself lies a few minutes walk away in the burial ground of the parish church of St. Nicholas, which he shares, ironically, with his enemy, William Kent.

An even shorter stroll in the other direction from St. Nicholas' takes one to Chiswick House. Modelled on Palladio's Villa Rotonda at Vicenza, it was designed by Richard Boyle, the third Earl of Burlington (1694-1753) in 1725-9. Lord Hervey waspishly dismissed it as too small to be lived in but too large to hang from one's watch-chain. It was, indeed, not meant to be lived in—it had no kitchens. (Burlington himself lived in an adjacent house, demolished in 1758.) Chiswick House was rather meant to be posed in, to serve as a gallery for the owner's tasteful treasures, to be a place of entertainment for the likes of Handel and Rysbrack and to stand as an exquisite exemplar of the architectural style which its creator hoped to see generally adopted throughout Britain. The spectacular plaster ceilings are the work of William Kent, Burlington's protégé—and, it was believed by many, something much more intimate as well. A scale model of the building can be seen in the British Galleries at the Victoria and Albert Museum. In 1788 wings were added to Chiswick House by James Wyatt so that it could be lived in—or rather died in, because both Charles James Fox and George Canning did just that and in the very same room (though not simultaneously). Chiswick House was also visited by two American presidents, Adams and Jefferson, the latter when he was building his own Palladian residence at Monticello.

Chiswick House was later used as a psychiatric hospital before being restored after 1928. Wyatt's wings were removed in 1952. The gardens are also historically important. Laid out by Kent and Charles Bridgeman, they were among the first in England to break with the formal geometric symmetries of the Continental style in favour of a more "natural" look, imitative of an idealized English countryside. Though long neglected, the gardens still contain statues brought from Hadrian's villa at Tivoli, a gateway by Inigo Jones, a bridge by Wyatt and a conservatory attributed to Sir Joseph Paxton, the designer of the Crystal Palace. This attribution is entirely plausible as Chiswick House was, from 1753 to 1892, a London home of the Dukes of Devonshire, and Paxton had started his professional career as their gardener.

In 1713 Johann Mattheson observed that "whoever wishes to be eminent in music goes to England. In Italy and France there is something to be heard and learned; in England something to be earned." Georg Friedrich Handel (1685-1759) had already taken the hint and a decade after Mattheson uttered his dictum was able to move into a newly-built house at 25 Brook Street, which remained his home until his death. It was therefore in this residence that Handel composed *Zadok the Priest* for George II's coronation in 1727, *Messiah* and the *Music for the Royal Fireworks*, which was first rehearsed in the house. When Handel moved in the house was new and the street was considered to be "for the most part nobly built and inhabited by People of Quality." Other Brook Street residents included Edward Shepherd, who built much of Mayfair (hence Shepherd's Market), the influential architectural critic Colen Campbell, whose *Vitruvius Britannicus* served as a pattern-book for mansion-builders eager to display their classical credentials, Prime Ministers Pitt the Elder and Henry Addington and Sir Jeffrey Wyattville, who Gothicized Windsor Castle for George IV. One of the few surviving features of Handel's house as it was in his day is a fine dog-leg staircase. Three marble fire-surrounds salvaged from Tom's coffee-house in Covent Garden have been installed as part of the restoration programme. The house also bears a plaque marking it as a residence of rock legend Jimi Hendrix in 1968-9.

Considering that he is reckoned to have ridden more than 250,000 miles to deliver over 40,000 sermons one could be forgiven for thinking that 47 City Road, the home of John Wesley (1703-91), might have been more noted for his absence than his presence. In fact he only lived there for the last eleven winters of his life. Built by him in 1779, the house contains his Prayer Room and the bedroom in which he died. Wesley is buried behind the adjacent Chapel.

Any fame attaching to 18 Folgate Street derives not from an historic occupant but from Californian artist Dennis Severs (1948-99) who bought it in 1979 and spent the rest of his life developing it as the setting for a fabricated experience of eighteenth-century Spitalfields life as lived by a family of successful silk-weavers. The family he invented, of supposed Huguenot origin, was called Gervais, anglicized to Jarvis, and had bought the house as new in 1724. Visitors, guided by Severs, were taken on a room-by-room tour, from cellar to attic, during which they would be tantalized by the sense that the elusive "inhabitants" were actually just in the next room—always the next room—a deception skilfully achieved through lighting, draughts of air, sound-effects (originally conveyed through speakers plundered from discarded TV sets) and even the smells of food, coffee, candles and chamber pots. Each room was arranged to constitute a still life drama. Some of the decor consisted of authentic period items, much was artfully contrived by Severs from cleverly disguised or recycled modern materials. What Severs vehemently denied was that anything about the experience he created was fake; its authenticity depended on the imaginative sympathy of the participants. The frivolous, the inattentive or the disruptive could expect to be berated and summarily ejected. Denis Severs' house was bequeathed to the Spitalfields Trust and the tours continue. The epitaph on Severs' grave proclaims the conviction by which he ordered the home which became his life's purpose—Aut Visum, Aut Non, "either you see it or you don't."

Regency

The Regency style, like its eponymous patron, was classical in its inclinations but tended to become unbuttoned and exuberant in its expression, obscuring lapses of taste with generous layers of stucco, like make-up on a rock star past his prime.

If there had been a Royal Institution of British Architects in his lifetime Sir John Soane (1753-1837) would surely have been its president. He was Professor of Architecture at the Royal Academy. Soane's statue, positioned in the sort of simple but strikingly geometric setting characteristic of his architecture, adorns his slighted masterpiece, the Bank of England. Soane himself rests in the burial ground adjoining Old St. Pancras Church, in a Greek Revival monument he actually designed for his wealthy wife. But Soane's real monument is the remarkable house created for himself at 13 Lincoln's Inn Fields. Soane originally bought No. 12 in 1792 and completely reconstructed it. Avid collectors, the Soanes acquired the eight canvases of Hogarth's *The Rake's Progress*, works by Watteau and Canaletto and dozens of antique vases, busts and statues. No. 13 was bought and rebuilt to house them and their ever expanding treasures and occupied in 1813. Mrs. Soane died in 1815 but Soane continued to amass acquisitions including Hogarth's *Election* series, Reynolds' notebooks and Robert Adam's entire archive of nine thousand drawings and designs, bought at a bargain basement price of two hundred pounds. In 1824 Soane added No.14 to accommodate his ever-growing hoard. The following year he held open house for three days to show off the sarcophagus of Seti I, bought for two thousand pounds after the British Museum had declined it as too dear. By the time of Soane's death his collection had become increasingly eclectic, including not only canvases by contemporaries such as Turner and Fuseli, but also antique gemstones, Indian manuscripts, drawings by Piranesi, Wren's watch and Napoleon's pistols. Soane then secured a special Act of Parliament to ensure that his home and collections were preserved for posterity as a public museum.

The Hampstead residence now known as "Keats' House" was built in 1815-6 as Wentworth Place, an asymmetrical pair of semi-detached houses with a shared garden. Keats, having lost one brother to death and another to emigration within a year, was invited to live with the

Shakespeare scholar Charles Armitage Brown in the smaller of the two houses. In 1819 a Mrs. Brawne moved into the other one with her daughter, Fanny, to whom Keats became engaged. Many of Keats' best-known poems were written in this house and his "Ode to a Nightingale" was composed under a plum tree in the garden. Keats left for Italy in 1820 in the hope of recovering his failing health but never returned. Keats' House, now in the care of the Corporation of the City of London, hosts a variety of events, ranging from poetry evenings and study days about the Romantics to tea parties themed around Teddy Bears, the Mad Hatter and the 95th Rifles, the real regiment associated with Bernard Cornwell's fictional rough diamond Richard Sharpe.

Victorian

> *Early Victorian architectural practice was dominated by "the battle of the styles" between a revived Gothic and an historicist classicism newly informed by scholarship. Later eclecticism ranged from the neo-rusticity of the "Arts and Crafts" movement to the syncretic flamboyance of a retro manner that was less "Queen Anne" than "Wrenaissance".*

"The Sage of Chelsea", Thomas Carlyle, lived at 24 (then 5) Cheyne Row, Chelsea, from 1834 until his death in the first-floor drawing-room almost half a century later. It was one of a red brick terrace block built in 1708. Upon finding his future home Carlyle described it enthusiastically to his wife Jane as an "excellent old house... eminent antique... wainscotted to the very ceiling and has all been new-painted and repaired... And then as to room, Goody!... Three storeys beside the sunk storey." The sunk storey (basement) was where Carlyle and Tennyson later smoked their pipes into the chimney to avoid the wrath of Mrs. Carlyle. From the Carlyles' point of view the house had an even greater attraction—it was cheap, a fact which Carlyle, an historian, explained in historical terms: "Chelsea is unfashionable; it was once the resort of the court and the great; hence, numerous old houses in it, at once cheap and excellent." Jane proved to be a devoted wife, resourceful home-maker and witty hostess to visitors such as Darwin, Ruskin and Mazzini. Carlyle did his writing in an attic eyrie which, after almost twenty years of being distracted by noises from neighbours and the street, he unsuccessfully tried to soundproof in 1852-3, the unintended result of his alterations being to magnify sounds coming from the river. Carlyle's house remains much as it was at the time of his death, complete with original furniture, pictures and books, and even his hat, hanging on its peg.

Of the ten different London homes of Charles Dickens only one survives. The site of his ample former house at 1 Devonshire Terrace, on the Marylebone Road, is marked by a carved panel bearing the likenesses of Mrs. Gamp, Barnaby Rudge, Mr. Micawber and others. A blue plaque marks the site of his last marital abode, a sumptuous mansion on Tavistock Square. This even had its own mini-theatre where Dickens acted out family entertainments with literary chums like Wilkie Collins and Douglas Jerrold. The splendid library, lavishly furnished with mahogany fittings and thick-pile carpets, provoked George Eliot to observe archly that it was the ideal working-place for a writer who was so well-known for his sympathy with the plight of London's poor. In fact, Dickens found his library so unsympathetic to composition that he hired a bare room miles away in New Cross to write in—a far cry from his youth when he could join in the conversation of a family dinner party while drafting the next episode of *Oliver Twist*, "the feather of his pen still moving rapidly from side to side."

As a bachelor Dickens had occupied a suite of three rooms in Furnivall's Inn, just opposite Staple Inn, near which Pip finds his lodgings in *Great Expectations*. The site of Furnival's Inn is now covered by the vast Flemish Gothic headquarters built for the Prudential Assurance Company Ltd. A bust of Dickens stands in a shrine-like portico on the north side of the main courtyard. Dickens' first marital home survives at 48 Doughty Street, just north of Gray's Inn, where he had worked as a most reluctant legal clerk in Raymond Buildings. When he moved into his new home in 1837 Dickens felt he had arrived. At eighty pounds a year his house cost him more than twice as much as the Carlyles were paying in Chelsea. Doughty Street was then gated and patrolled by a top-hatted commissionaire who saluted him smartly and called him "Mr. Dickens". It was while living in Doughty Street that Dickens completed *The Pickwick Papers* and wrote *Oliver Twist* and *Nicholas Nickleby*. Dickens' daughters Mary and Kate were born in the house and, to his profound grief, his sister-in-law Mary died there. The family had been out to the theatre and when, after half an hour, Mary had still not come down from changing her dress, they found her dying. Dickens was unable to write for a fortnight, the only time in his career that this ever happened. Mary is supposedly the model for many of his idealized female characters. Dandyish in his personal turn-out, Dickens was something of a domestic despot in matters of household organization, demanding that all pictures be straight and cushions plumped.

When Charles Darwin (1809-82) returned from his five-year circumnavigation aboard HMS *Beagle* he would ideally have liked to settle in Cambridge but reluctantly concluded that a scholar committed to science needed the resources of the "dirty, smoky" metropolis. On marriage Darwin settled in Gower Street, Bloomsbury, for five years until the sight of armed troops marching up to Euston Station to be transported northwards to overawe Chartist demonstrators so alarmed him that he sought refuge for himself and his family in the peaceful Kent village of Downe. Darwin's Gower Street home is now gone but the site is appropriately occupied by the biology laboratories of University College. Darwin lived at Down (*sic*) House from 1842 until his death. Reclusive by nature, he seldom left the village and wrote all his major works there; but he must have kept the local postman very busy because he maintained a huge correspondence which can now be accessed online. Down House is a museum devoted to Darwin's life and work, a theme much enlarged on in a gallery devoted to Evolution in the Museum of Natural History. One should not, however, imagine Darwin confined to a peaceful, book-lined sanctuary thinking Great Thoughts. The rambling former farmhouse and extensive grounds served him as a laboratory to test out hypotheses, often with his own children conscripted as assistants. To prove to a sceptical Joseph Hooker that plants could be carried to remote islands by sea currents, Darwin filled his basement with tanks of sea-water, immersing 87 kinds of seed in them for 137 days to demonstrate that they could even cross the Atlantic. In his aquarium Darwin once hung a pair of severed duck's feet, employing his children first to count the water snails attaching themselves and then to wave them in the air for hours to simulate the duck migrating, with the snails still alive after twelve hours' flight. At the suggestion of his eight-year-old son Darwin immersed a dead pigeon in a seawater tank for thirty days and then successfully germinated seeds from its putrid crop. In the garden he once dusted bumble-bees with flour and then, having disposed his children in a strategic network, got them to count how many flowers each one visited.

The early childhood of William Morris was passed in what was virtually a chateau on the edge of Epping Forest. The death of his father, a City stockbroker, caused the family to move to more modest accommodation in the shape of Water House, Walthamstow, which is now a gallery devoted to his life and work. Exhibits include the knight's helmet made as a visual aid for the painstaking painting of the Oxford Union (which turned into a fresco fiasco), the loom used by his daughter, May, an expert weaver and needlewoman, and the satchel Morris himself used during his revolutionary socialist phase to carry copies of his propagandist journal *Commonweal*, which he sold on street corners. There is also a superb pencil drawing of a Gothic cathedral doorway by Morris' mentor, Ruskin, furniture by his Scottish admirer Mackmurdo and paintings by his disciple, Frank Brangwyn. After leaving Oxford, Morris and his life-long friend Edward Burne-Jones moved into the former lodgings of their then hero, Dante Gabriel Rossetti, in Red Lion Square. Here they lived amid post-graduate clutter and attempted their first essay in craftsmanship—a gigantic settle which they made too big to manoeuvre up the staircase. The house still stands but is in private occupation.

It was William Morris' marriage that prompted the revolution he effected in English domestic decor. As a teenager Morris had been repelled by the machine-made products that had won plaudits at the Great Exhibition, considering them the debased expression of a degrading and exploitative economic system. When Morris came to set up his own home he could find nothing to suit his taste or requirements—so he had one built and filled it with furniture and textiles made by himself and his friends. Red House, at Bexleyheath, Kent, was built in 1859 to the designs of Philip Webb, whom Morris had met while failing to become an architect in the office of G. E. Street. Modelled on the sort of home that might have been occupied by a prosperous Flemish burgher of the thirteenth century, it was constructed, true to principles which Morris would later rationalize and elaborate at length, out of local materials and by local labourers. The interior decor represented an early attempt to implement Morris' later dictum to have nothing in one's house that one did not know to be useful or believe to be beautiful. The Morris idyll at Red House lasted just five years. Although only ten miles from his workshop in Queen Square, Bloomsbury, the Bexleyheath location obliged him to undertake a two-hour journey to get there and was simply incompatible with running his design business. Red House was, therefore, sold at a thumping loss, for half of what it had cost to build. Passing into private occupation, it remained largely inaccessible to the public until its recent, fortunate acquisition by the National Trust.

Among Morris' many overlapping careers was a highly successful one as an interior decorator, undertaking commissions for private clients, like the wealthy and cultured Ionides family of Holland Park, and for official bodies, like St. James' Palace and the Victoria and Albert Museum where the Gamble Room, which popularized his three-fold division of domestic walls by a dado and picture-rail, can still be seen. Upstairs in the British Galleries are examples of Morris wallpapers, textiles and rush-bottomed Sussex chairs. Morris himself acted as a consultant on textiles to the Museum and it was on his advice that one of its glories, the immense Ardabil carpet, was purchased.

Morris' last London home, Kelmscott House, at 26 Upper Mall, Hammersmith, had been badly neglected when he took it over in 1877 but his fellow socialist, George Bernard Shaw, witnessed a miracle of transformation: "Nothing in... this magical house... was there because it was interesting or quaint or rare or hereditary... Everything that was necessary was clean and handsome; everything else was beautiful and beautifully presented." The house remains in private occupation but the setting is well worth seeing, not least because the riverside at Hammersmith is where, in Morris' futuristic fantasy *News From Nowhere*, the narrator, Hammond, wakes up in the 1950s to find a social revolution has been carried out to abolish poverty, policemen and Parliament—but not apparently housework, which is still done by women, though joyfully. From Kelmscott House a modest and very pleasant riverside ramble will then bring the walker to Hogarth's house.

Leighton House, Holland Park Road, is more an art gallery than a home and as such reflects the splendour of the social position achieved by Frederic Leighton (1830-96), the first painter to be ennobled (although it was a close-run thing; he was literally on his death-bed). A nomadic childhood had made Leighton fluent in four languages and brought him the friendship of such glitterati as the writer George Sand and the actress Fanny Kemble. Thackeray, another friend, prophesied to Millais that Leighton would become President of the Royal Academy before Millais did—and was proved right. Leighton had fine features, a good tenor voice and a (selective) willingness to please. Fellow artist George Du Maurier called him "one of the world's little darlings who won't make themselves agreeable to anything under a duchess." Leighton's painterly career got off to a flying start in 1855 when Queen Victoria paid six hundred pounds for his first major work, *Cimabue's Celebrated Madonna is carried in Procession through the Streets of Florence*. Ruskin, the century's most influential critic, praised it as "very important and very beautiful". It now hangs above the foyer steps of the National Gallery. As a painter Leighton tended to draw his subject-matter from classical antiquity and, to a lesser extent, "the East". His polished social skills and command of languages eminently fitted him for the position of President of the Royal Academy, and he also served as a keen colonel of the Artists' Rifles. Henry James caricatured Leighton in a short story as Lord Mellifont and he also features in Disraeli's *Lothair* as Gaston Phoebus. One of Leighton's obituarists cuttingly summarized him as "often as nearly great as a man without creative genius can be." A splendid recumbent bronze effigy of Leighton is in the north nave aisle of St. Paul's but his house is a more revealing monument. The first (1864-66) phase alone cost nearly five thousand pounds, about the same as a modest-sized parish church. In Pevsner's words the "reticent exterior conceals the most sumptuous and colourful nineteenth century artist's house in London." Leighton continued to embellish and enlarge the building for thirty years. The main studio, decorated with a cast from the Parthenon frieze, is over fifty feet long and has separate back stairs access for discreet use by models and dealers. The fabulous Arab Hall (1877-79), inspired by the palace of La Zisa in Palermo, incorporates Iranian tiles, Syrian glass and Egyptian woodwork dating from the thirteenth to the seventeenth centuries. The alabaster capitals were carved by Sir Joseph Boehm from designs by the children's illustrator, Randolph Caldecott. Walter Crane contributed a mosaic in a mock-Persian mode. Apart from Leighton's own paintings Leighton House also contains works by Watts, Burne-Jones and Millais and tiles by William de Morgan.

Edward Linley Sambourne (1844-1910) was a passionate amateur photographer and a cartoonist for *Punch* for forty-three years. Almost fifteen thousand of his photographs and a thousand products of his pencil still survive, as does his marital home at 18 Stafford Terrace, Kensington. A virtual time-capsule of middle-class comfort and "artistic" taste, the house contains original William Morris wallpapers and paintings by Sir Luke Fildes, who was a family friend. Other members of the Sambourne circle included the artists G. F. Watts and Walter Crane, writers Rider Haggard and Bret Harte and the librettist W. S. Gilbert. After the Sambournes' deaths No. 18 passed to their son Roy, who left it virtually untouched until his death in 1946. It then passed to his sister, Maud Messel, whose daughter Anne, mother of Lord Snowdon, used it as an occasional *pied-à-terre* and party venue. It was at her Guy Fawkes celebration in 1957 that she proposed forming a society to campaign on behalf of what was then regarded as the hideously unacceptable art and architecture of the Victorian period. With the enthusiastic support of Sir John Betjeman and Professor Nikolaus Pevsner thus was the Victorian Society born, with 18 Stafford Terrace serving as its first headquarters.

Moderne

Continental in inspiration, and usually in execution, the International Modern movement proved a bird of passage, its exemplars striking but invariably solitary islands of stark exoticism amidst an ocean of neo-Georgianism and pseudo-Tudor "by-pass variegated".

Adjoining the surviving Great Hall of medieval Eltham Palace stands a 1930s fantasy, part Roman temple, part Cunard liner, built by John Seely and Paul Paget for Stephen Courtauld and his socialite wife Virginia ("Ginny") as a breathtaking setting for their glamorous parties. Above the entrance is a sculpture of Hospitality—a woman with fire, food and drink. The over-the-top bathroom would have served for a Hollywood movie-set. Everything became somewhat run down when the building was used by the Royal Army Education Corps (1945-92) but it has been stunningly restored by English Heritage. Superficially Art Deco, the Courtauld House is, upon closer examination, a mysterious melange of styles and symbols: an Ionic colonnade, Tudor mullions and gables, towers with sloping medieval rooftops, metal Crittall windows. The north facade is a loose imitation of Wren's south facade at Hampton Court. There is a neoclassical squash court. The six figures of chessmen on the roof are said to represent historic owners of the site—kings, queens, bishops, a knight, a Cromwellian colonel (the castle) and a farmer (the pawn). The gardens include references to China, Japan and Italy, the interior decor to Kew, Venice, Stockholm and, in keeping with the playful knowingness of all these aesthetic and cultural keys, to *Alice in Wonderland.*

The last home of Sigmund Freud (1856-1939) at 20 Maresfield Gardens, Hampstead, was only occupied by him during the last year of his life, when he was dying of cancer of the jaw and cheek. It contains a reconstruction of his study and consulting room, complete with the iconic couch and a selection of luxurious Oriental rugs. The furniture, brought from Austria, ranges from fine Biedermeier tables and chests to eighteenth-century painted peasant pieces. Freud's extensive collection of classical antiquities, running to nearly two thousand items, testifies to the breadth of his learning and interests, much of his own theorizing having been stimulated by his reflections on the insights afforded by classical mythology. Freud's daughter Anna (1895-1982), pioneer of child psychology, continued to live in the house until her death. In accordance with her wishes, the house became a museum and research centre devoted to her father's life and work.

Hungarian architect Erno Goldfinger (1902-87), like Freud a refugee from Continental fascism, achieved a doubtless unwanted posterity from having his name stolen by his friend Ian Fleming to use for a ruthless criminal mastermind, though some of his more unforgiving critics might have thought that his most notorious creation, Trellick Tower in North Kensington, was indicative of a similar ruthlessness. Vilified by the tabloid press and stigmatized in half a dozen novels, it has been reinvented to become a residence to be envied, with Grade II listed status. The house Goldfinger designed for himself in 1940, and in which he lived for the rest of his life, is one of a group of three in Willow Road, Hampstead, and contains art works by his friends, Henry Moore, Max Ernst and Bridget Riley and, courtesy of the National Trust, is open to visitors. The headquarters building Goldfinger designed for Sanderson Wallpapers at 50 Berners

Street, Marylebone, is now the ultra-modernist Sanderson Hotel.

Dessert

For those whose taste for domestic interiors remains unquenched the British Galleries at the Victoria and Albert Museum offer such delights as the exuberantly gilded Music Room from Norfolk House, St. James' Square, and a model of the astonishing Red Room, entirely panelled in scarlet glass, designed by Robert Adam for Northumberland House. The Geffrye Museum at Kingsland Road, Shoreditch, offers a panorama of English living-rooms over four centuries. Housed in handsome almshouses built in 1715 for the widows of ironmongers, the museum was originally intended to instruct craftsmen working in the cabinet-making trade of the surrounding Shoreditch area.

The preservation of historic houses has been a pretty haphazard business, except where, as in the case of Soane and Freud, the previous owners made their own arrangements. The survival and refurbishment of Keats' and Carlyle's homes owe much to American enthusiasm. Macaulay's home, Holly Lodge, on Campden Hill, was demolished in 1968 to make way for an extension to Queen Elizabeth College; ironically the College has itself been absorbed into King's College and its buildings converted to residential use. Nearby Thorpe Lodge, the former home of the celebrated Governor of the Bank of England, Montagu Norman, was noted for its De Morgan tiles, Japanese motifs and seventeenth-century Italian fireplace; it now survives as a Sixth Form Centre for Holland Park School. The home at 88 Mile End Road of the world's most celebrated navigator, Captain James Cook, eventually ended up as a kosher butcher's premises. Condemned in 1960 as unsafe, it was offered to the governments of Australia and British Columbia but neither was willing to finance its relocation and so it was demolished in 1977.

MADE IN LONDON
An American Interlude

America was invented in London—at least that is where the money came from. The histories of the city and the continent have been intertwined ever since. What kept the early colonial settlements going through their first precarious decades of existence was trading with London, drawing reinforcements of settlers via London and importing from London the guns, tools and implements crucial to survival. When the Pilgrim Fathers arrived in Massachusetts they were greeted by an English-speaking Patuxet native, Squanto (Tisquantum), who had once lived on Cornhill. Squanto's skills as interpreter, diplomat, guide and technical adviser were to prove vital to the survival of the Plymouth Plantation.

Ben Franklin

Less than a decade after the settlement of Jamestown, Virginia, the visit of "princess" Pocahontas caused a sensation in London when she was presented at court. Social success exacted a fatal price as Pocahontas contracted smallpox and was buried at Gravesend before she could return home. Captain John Smith, whose life Pocahontas is supposed to have saved, lies in the south aisle of St. Sepulchre at Newgate where a brass epitaph and stained glass window proclaim the fame of the

"Governour of Virginia and Admiral of New England". Outside the church of St. Mary-le-Bow, Cheapside, stands a suitably swaggering statue of bearded, booted Smith, a copy of the Virginia original.

St. Bride's, Fleet Street, is also closely connected with the early settlement of America. Here were married the parents of Virginia Dare, the first English child to be born in the New World. Her bust stands above the church's font. Edward Winslow, three times Governor of the Pilgrims' Plymouth settlement, was married in St. Bride's. The imposing oak reredos crafted as part of St. Bride's post-war restoration is a memorial to Winslow and the Pilgrim Fathers. A few hundred yards from St. Bride's stood the correctional institution known as Bridewell Hospital. In 1619 its governors were asked to send seventy-five boys and twenty-five girls "to help populate Virginia." Another hundred were sent in 1622. Given the appalling death-rate among the early settlers one wonders whether they might have fared better as feral predators back on the streets from which they had been taken.

Maryland was founded by the Roman Catholic George Calvert, Lord Baltimore, who never actually got there. He is buried in the church of St. Dunstan in the West, Fleet Street. His son, Cecil, second Baron Baltimore, secured the colony's charter. His memorial can be seen in St. Giles-in-the-Fields.

The colonies' first institution of higher education was founded by John Harvard. A bookish young man he had inherited his mother's pub, the Queen's Head in Borough High Street, and was considered a man of substance in Massachusetts. Dying of consumption the year after he arrived there, he bequeathed half his fortune, just short of eight hundred pounds, towards the building of a college. The school acknowledged Harvard's munificence by naming itself in his honour. Southwark Cathedral has a Harvard chapel, with a stained-glass window, donated by Harvard alumnus and US Ambassador Choate in 1905, bearing the arms of Harvard College and Emmanuel College, Cambridge, of which Harvard was an alumnus. Harvard alumni are known to have been dining fraternally in London since at least the early eighteenth century. The Harvard Club of the UK claims that there are almost five thousand Harvard alumni living in Britain.

William Penn was born at Tower Hill, baptized and schooled in the church of All Hallows by the Tower and, following his conversion to Quakerism, variously imprisoned for publishing an unlicensed pamphlet, unauthorized open-air preaching and refusing to take the oath of allegiance. Given this track record the attractiveness to Penn of finding religious freedom in the New World is evident. The colony he founded was called Pennsylvania in honour of his father, war hero Admiral William Penn.

The diocese of London extended across the Atlantic. Bishop Compton was a keen plant-collector who doubtless rejoiced to plant England's first magnolia in the garden of his summer palace at Fulham. London's ubiquitous plane trees are another importation, being an Oxford-bred hybrid of American and Oriental varieties. This horticultural traffic went in both directions. The cotton seeds that founded Georgia's plantation economy came from the Chelsea Physick Garden. Georgia owes its foundation to the death in debtor's prison of a friend of General James Oglethorpe. Oglethorpe engineered a parliamentary enquiry into prison conditions which confirmed that many inmates were more victims of misfortune than perpetrators of evil. It was consequently proposed to establish a penal colony to offer defaulters and minor offenders a positive alternative to incarceration. Oglethorpe appointed two recent Oxford graduates, John and Charles Wesley, to provide spiritual guidance for his new settlement. They were not up to the task and returned home chastened. John had, however, been profoundly impressed by the fervour of the Moravians he had encountered and on returning to London sought out Moravian congregations there. It was at a Moravian meeting in Aldersgate that Wesley experienced an epiphany by which his heart "felt strangely warmed" by a sudden certainty of his salvation. From this the Methodist movement developed, not to challenge Anglicanism but to revitalize it. Only in the decade before Wesley's death did Methodism organize itself as a separate church, the split being precipitated by Wesley's determination to provide priests specifically for service in newly independent America, contrary to the refusal of the bishop of London to make such provision.

Wesley's early follower George Whitefield attracted such numbers to his chapel on Tottenham Court Road that it had repeatedly to be enlarged. Adopting a more severely Calvinist doctrine than Wesley, Whitefield broke from him to play a major role in the "Great Awakening", which brought a spiritual frenzy to America's frontier settlements. Believing that every truly religious person needed to experience a rebirth in Jesus, he can be considered the progenitor of the "born again" Christian. The American Church in London now very fittingly occupies the former site of Whitefield's chapel. Beside it the, at first glance oddly-named, Eisenhower Documentation Centre now stores business records in former bunkers, deep beneath the platforms of Goodge Street Underground station, where the timetables for the D-Day invasion were worked out.

Americans, especially from the Middle Colonies and the South, sent their sons to be educated in London, many of them to Westminster School. Many came as young men, preparing for a career in colonial courts and legislatures, to listen to study law at the Inns of Court. The connection between the Middle Temple, Virginia and the Carolinas was especially strong. At least five signatories of the Declaration of Independence were Middle Temple men.

Benjamin Franklin first came to London in 1724 to train as a printer in the former Lady Chapel of St. Bartholomew the Great. He returned to London three decades later as the representative of five colonies. Franklin's lodgings at 36 Craven Street survive and can be visited. He found congenial company at the long-vanished North Briton coffee-house in nearby Cockspur Street. Franklin was deeply involved in the acrimonious public debate which preceded the American Revolution. On the very eve of his departure from England the Earl of Chatham came to Craven Street in person in a last-ditch attempt to broker an agreement to head off a "civil war in the empire". Franklin predicted to the elder Pitt that the conflict would last ten years and that the Americans would win.

Chatham's dramatic collapse during a House of Lord's debate on the American crisis would be depicted in detail in a vast canvas by John Singleton Copley, one of the *atelier* of American artists who gathered in London under the aegis of Benjamin West. Appointed History Painter to HM George III, West occupied a large house, studio and gallery at 14 Newman Street. As a result of his colonial origins and metropolitan eminence he became responsible for introducing a succession of American painters to the London art scene, including steam-boat pioneer Robert Fulton and Samuel Morse, inventor of the telegraph code. On the death of Sir Joshua Reynolds West succeeded him as President of the Royal Academy. On his own death he was buried in St. Paul's Cathedral. By an odd coincidence, when Whistler first arrived in

London he took rooms in Newman Street, which remained a favoured address for painters. Whistler was only one of another coterie of American artists who settled in late Victorian London. John Singer Sargent was for twenty years the most fashionable (and expensive) of London "Society" portraitists. Upon Sargent's death his executors were surprised to find that the urbane sophisticate had designed an intensely religious memorial for himself, now to be seen in the crypt of St. Paul's Cathedral.

The statue of Abraham Lincoln in Parliament Square was initially the outcome of an American proposal to mark the passage of a century of peace between the two great English-speaking peoples. This may have caused some puzzlement as few British schoolchildren are ever taught about the War of 1812. Nevertheless the conflict has left its lapidary echoes. In the south transept of St. Paul's stands a statue of General Pakenham and his comrade-in-arms, killed in the course of the British defeat in the battle of New Orleans. Above the entrance to the crypt is a monument to the man who burned the White House.

Also in the crypt of St. Paul's is a memorial to the first American to be killed fighting for Britain in the Second World War. Billy Fiske, son of a Chicago banker, at sixteen captained the American bobsleigh team that won the gold medal at the 1928 (first ever) Winter Olympics. He later dabbled in films and married an English aristocrat. Serving, very appropriately, with 601 ("Millionaires") Squadron at Tangmere, Sussex, Fiske made a kill on his first operational flight. Crash-landing his Hurricane on 16 August 1940, he was rescued by his ground-crew but died of burns. His memorial, a few feet from Nelson's sarcophagus, bears his RAF pilot's wings.

Another by-product of the War of 1812 was America's national anthem. The British bombardment of Fort McHenry in Maryland inspired Francis Scott Key to compose a poem in praise of the lone American flag flying over the battered stronghold. Published as *The Defence of Fort McHenry*, the words were later appropriated to become *The Star-Spangled Banner*. It is, perhaps, seldom appreciated that the poet's vantage-point of the incident was from the gundeck of a British warship or that the tune to which his words were set—*To Anacreon in Heaven*—had been written around 1780 as a drinking-song by John Stafford Smith, musical director of the Chapel Royal in St. James' Palace.

William Waldorf Astor came to Britain in 1892 because he thought his American homeland was becoming far too democratic to be comfortable for a wealthy man. After a quarter century of social campaigning to get himself accepted into the English establishment he finally succeeded when the outbreak of the Great War gave him the chance to contribute lavishly to charities for refugees, orphans and convalescents. In 1917 he became the first native-born American to become a member of the House of Lords as Viscount Astor of Hever.

In 1907 mining engineer Herbert Hoover moved into Red House, Hornton Street, Kensington, and established a London-based consulting firm to promote oil exploration. As the Royal Navy had just opted to switch from coal to oil his timing was impeccable. By 1910 Hoover was worth $3,000,000 but still living in his modest eight-room house. Hoover became a public figure on the outbreak of war in 1914 when 150,000 neutral Americans—visitors, businessmen, students and a Wild West show touring Poland—were stranded in Europe. As the head of a relief committee based in the Savoy Hotel Hoover used his superb talent for administration to organize and finance the repatriation of 120,000 compatriots in six weeks. His brilliant direction of this ambitious and worthy project raised his public profile and personal popularity to set him on the road to the White House.

London society maintained a distinct *froideur* towards Americans in the immediate post-Revolutionary period. As first minister to represent the infant republic John Adams established his legation at what is now 9 Grosvenor Square. Standing at the far end of the square from the modern US Embassy, the building now overlooks the monument to the British victims of 9/11. By the time Washington Irving came to London relations were altogether more cordial. He met the influential publisher John Murray and, through him, Sir Walter Scott. With Scott's encouragement Irving published *The Sketch Book of Geoffrey Crayon Gent* (1820), which contained both a celebrated essay on Westminster Abbey and *Rip Van Winkle*. It made him famous on both sides of the Atlantic.

Notwithstanding Macaulay's sneering gibe "who reads an American book?" American writers have received warm welcomes in London. Harriet Beecher Stowe was lionized, *Uncle Tom's Cabin* selling three times as many copies in Britain as in the USA. Louisa May Alcott was taken to the House of Commons to hear John Stuart Mill and introduced to Gladstone, Dickens and Mazzini. Nathaniel Hawthorne wrote an affectionate account of *Our Old Home*. Mark Twain came determined to write a hostile book about the British but was so charmed by his reception that he abandoned the idea. Years later he returned to live in Tedworth Square, Chelsea. Henry James came to London and not only stayed but became a naturalized Briton. The encounter between wealthy expatriate Americans and the perils and confusions of London "Society" became a recurrent motif of James' work and also reflected reality. In the half century before the Great War over a hundred American heiresses married into the British aristocracy, Winston Churchill's mother, Jennie Jerome, being among the first. Ezra Pound lived in London from 1908 to 1920, initially in a first-floor room at 10 Kensington Church Walk, rented for eight shillings a week. Pound's literary acquaintance included D. H. Lawrence, Robert Frost, Hilda Doolittle and W. B. Yeats. Pound was a generous champion of avant-garde young artists, promoting the work of T. S. Eliot, whom he encouraged to settle in England.

If literature has provided one major component in a shared transatlantic culture, the stage has provided another. Black minstrel singers introduced a genre widely imitated in London's music halls. The first Peter Pan was a 37-year-old American actress, Nina Boucicault. Paul Robeson first appeared in London in 1922, found fame with the song *Ol' Man River* in the 1928 production of *Show Boat* and was acclaimed for his *Othello* in 1930. In *Song of Freedom* he played a London docker who discovers that he is the heir to an African chiefdom. A blue plaque was placed on Robeson's Hampstead home at 1-2 Branch Lane in 2002 and there is a theatre named in his honour at Hounslow.

Senator Joe McCarthy's anti-Communist campaign benefited Londoners in persuading victims of his machinations to resettle in England. Harmonica virtuoso Larry Adler wrote the music for the oh-so-English film comedy *Genevieve*. Film director Joseph Losey created a sinister dissection of class and corruption in his collaboration with Harold Pinter on *The Servant* (1963), Actor-director Sam Wanamaker became the driving force behind the campaign to reconstruct Shakespeare's Globe Theatre and is commemorated by a memorial tablet next to the Shakespeare window in Southwark Cathedral. The capital has returned the compliment by exporting to Hollywood such

London-born talents as Charlie Chaplin, Alfred Hitchcock, Bob Hope and Elizabeth Taylor.

SOUTHWARK

London's first suburb has been variously renowned for prelates, prostitution, printing, prisons and provisioning. Much favoured for riverside residences by ecclesiastical aristocrats in the Middle Ages, Southwark retains in the ruined dining-hall of the palace of the Bishop of Winchester a gaunt reminder of former glories. The Bishop, who once took profits from a string of local brothels, had his own prison for obstreperous customers. Known as the Clink, it gave its name to the institution of prison itself. Dickens' father was imprisoned for debt in the Marshalsea, of which one wall still survives.

Packed with industrious Flemish immigrants, Southwark's riverside parishes became a leading industrial area in the early modern period, turning out clocks and coffee-grinders, delftware and glassware. The first English Bible to be printed in England was produced in Southwark in 1535. By the eighteenth century brewing had become dominant as Southwark became the focal point of the hop trade and a major producer of the heavy, dark beer known as porter, a London speciality. In the nineteenth century the provision trades became prominent with the large-scale production of flour, bacon, cocoa and vinegar. Sainsbury's in particular took advantage of the proximity of the "breakfast wharves" of Tooley Street to relocate major food-processing operations here.

Eighteenth-century Hopton's Almshouses in the shadow of Tate Modern are a reminder that there were once a dozen similar institutions in the area. Further south, around the open spaces of St. George's Fields, the availability of cheap land attracted philanthropists to establish the Bethlehem Hospital for the insane, the Magdalen Hospital for the reformation of prostitutes and other institutions for the instruction of the blind and of indigent orphans.

Southwark's Gothic cathedral only attained that status in 1905, having previously been the parish church and, before the Dissolution, the Priory of St. Mary Overie. It is the last resting-place of Chaucer's fellow poet Gower and of Bishop Lancelot Andrewes, who chaired the committee of forty scholars which produced the King James Bible. A

The Globe Theatre

The Globe Theatre does not stand on the exact site of its Shakespearean predecessor but with a few hundred yards of it. The original Globe was built in 1598-9 by Cuthbert and Richard Burbage, recycling timbers from the original Theatre at Shoreditch. Unroofed but galleried, it was a summer venue where the baiting of bulls and bears was organized as well as the production of Shakespeare's plays. In 1613 the firing of cannon at the premiere of Henry VIII set the thatched roof alight and burned down the theatre. The only casualty was a swpectator whose breeches caught fire until they were extinguished with a bottle of ale. Re-opened in 1614, the Globe waws closed by Parliament in 1642 and demolished in 1644.

Following a lengthy campaign by American actor-director Sam Wanamaker CBE (1919-93), the Globe was triumphantly rebuilt using as far as possible the authentic materials and techniques employed in the original, and reopened in 1996.

side chapel is devoted to the memory of John Harvard, while another chapel is dedicated to sufferers from AIDS and HIV. Beside an elaborate stained-glass window dedicated to Shakespeare is a memorial to actor-director Sam Wanamaker for his work with the Globe Theatre. This, in turn, acted as an unforeseen catalyst for the rejuvenation of the entire South Bank so that a string of visitor attractions now stretches from the London Eye past the Millennium Bridge and via Vinopolis, a replica of Drake's *Golden Hind* and HMS *Belfast* to Tower Bridge and the Design Museum.

Chapter Ten
MOST OF LONDON: THE SUBURBS

"The richest crop for any field
Is a crop of bricks for it to yield
The richest crop that it can grow,
Is a crop of houses in a row."
Tarbuck's *Handbook of House Property*, 1875

"Artistic" house, Bedford Park

Most Londoners live in suburbs and have done so for the last couple of centuries. By the time of the first census in 1801 the population of the City of London proper represented barely a tenth of the population of the metropolis as a whole. Yet in literary and cultural terms the suburbs have been generally ignored or deplored, largely on grounds of snobbery—hostility towards their lower middle-class residents, towards speculative builders, towards their *faux* vernacular architecture and the equally phoney lifestyle it allegedly represents. Sir Walter Besant (1836-1901), a prolific chronicler of the capital's history, accused the suburbs of being "without any society; no social gatherings or institutions, as dull a life as mankind ever tolerated." Women in particular he saw as victims, as they "lost all the London life—the shops, the animation of the streets, their old circle of friends; in its place they found all the exclusiveness and class feeling of London with none of the advantages of a country town." Writing a century later, the usually urbane Lord Norwich was equally dismissive in his *Architecture of Southern England.* Bexleyheath was "darkest suburbia" and Brentwood "outer suburbia *par excellence*". Hanif Kureishi's *The Buddha of Suburbia* (1990) excoriated his childhood home as the realm of the "miserable undead... when people in Bromley drowned they saw not their lives but their double-glazing flashing before them." Chislehurst was the abode of "people obsessed with velvet curtains, Martinis and electric lawnmowers."

Kentish Town has been described by the normally enthusiastic Ed Glinert as "a depressing slice of suburbia". But, as Gillian Tindall's brilliant exposé of its lost past, *The Fields Beneath,* has shown, the suburbs have their own rich histories. In *Nature near London* (1883) Richard Jefferies (1848-87) celebrated the richness of wildlife to be found in the Surrey suburbs. In 2001 the Museum of London's exhibition on London's art world hailed Hampstead, Twickenham, Richmond and Camden Town alongside Marylebone, Chelsea and Soho as "Creative Quarters". The poet Stevie Smith is indelibly associated with Palmer's Green. The world's first blood donor organization was run from an Edwardian terraced house in Peckham. Churchill's last refuge bunker was located at Dollis Hill. Malawi's dictator Dr. Hastings Banda was once a GP in Harlesden. Serial murderer and ex-Army butcher Dennis Nilsen buried the dismembered body parts of a dozen of his victims in the garden of his home at Cricklewood.

Victorian snobs claimed that a suburbanite could be recognized on sight, but defining a suburb is more problematic. Len Reilly, historian of south London, defines a suburb as "a new residential development on a greenfield site" and, more poetically, as the result of "a cascade of aspiration through the labour market", the outcome of the interaction of population growth and migration and changes in household structure and the separation of work and home which accompanied industrialization. Alison Light has defined modern suburbia in cultural terms, as the stronghold of "Conservative modernity", a self-obsessed universe of leisure and loneliness, of servantless shrines to domesticity, guarded by gnomes and gazebos, proclaiming a calm contentment denied to supposedly less happy breeds confined to the horrors of the inner city or the rural idiocies of village life. More cynically, a suburb has been defined as an area developed by cutting down the trees and then naming the streets after them.

Arguably Roman Southwark was London's first suburb. By Chaucer's time that area was as notorious for its brothels as it was celebrated for its inns. Shakespeare's Southwark retained these characteristics but had also become a burgeoning industrial area, teeming with immigrant craftsmen engaged in brewing and printing and the manufacture of glass and pottery. According to the *Oxford English Dictionary*, Shakespeare's contemporaries employed the word "suburb" to mean "a place of inferior, debased and especially licentious habits of life".

Although areas like Clerkenwell could still retain the air of an aristocratic *quartier* in Stuart times, repeated Elizabethan and Jacobean attempts at restraining suburban sprawl by legislation and fines had so far failed that James Howell could remark in *Londinopolis* (1657) that "the suburbs of London are much larger than the body of the City, which make some compare her to a Jesuit's hat, whose brims are far larger than the block." Downstream from the Tower, inland from both sides of the river as far as Ratcliffe and Rotherhithe, there had developed what H. J. Dyos, Britain's first professor of urban history, characterized as "a nether world of dungheaps, stinking trades, bloodsports, gallows, low taverns, prostitutes, foreigners, thieves, the poor and the mob". Only a couple of miles inland, however, the social climate was distinctly more salubrious. Derek Morris' painstaking study of Mile End New Town in the mid-eighteenth century reveals it as up-market, well-policed and well-heeled. Hackney, Bethnal Green and Bow had numerous academies for the education of young ladies, youths preparing for Oxbridge and Dissenters preparing for ministry and mission, all safe from the distractions and temptations of the metropolis. A proliferation of almshouses and asylums likewise confirmed the notion of the suburb as guarantor of physical and moral purity.

To the west of London William III's adoption of Kensington Palace as a residence established the nucleus of a court suburb around it. During the following century upstream settlements such as Hammersmith and Chiswick became favoured as semi-rural retreats from stress. The poet Alexander Pope, actor David Garrick and aesthete Horace Walpole all favoured Twickenham. Dr. Johnson's long-suffering hostess Mrs. Thrale, however, sounded a warning note:

> *Streatham does very well for a Summer Villa, but the consciousness that one should hate to dye there, would make me live in it with a kind of odd Anxiety one knows not how to describe—like being Abroad.*

A detailed account of the *Environs of London*, covering parishes within a twelve mile radius of the City, was published in 1792-6 by clergyman Daniel Lysons (1762-1834). His work remains of value two centuries later and can be supplemented by the proliferation of water-colour views produced during the same period by artists such as Thomas Gurtin, Paul Sandby and George Morland. As yet undeveloped areas like Camberwell and Notting Hill attracted colonies of young artists eager to sketch the picturesque scenes then still visible within an hour of Charing Cross. That would change very soon and very rapidly. William Cobbett observed that "cockneyfication" began at Beckenham as lines of terraces dribbled along the main arteries into London.

Ralph Horwood's 1812 map of London delineates a built-up area of about fifteen square miles, roughly three miles from the north (Islington) to the south (Walworth) and twice as far across, from Paddington to Limehouse. By 1900 the sprawl stretched from Tottenham to Croydon, from Brentford to Barking. Starting at any extremity would by then require a walk of at least fourteen miles to emerge the other side into something resembling open countryside. Areas favoured a century previously as rural retreats, such as Islington and Camberwell, had now become boroughs, each with a population larger than that of Newcastle or Nottingham. Nineteenth-century London grew twice as fast in area as in population. Suburbanization reflected both the disproportionately rapid growth of the middling classes and the lowering of transport costs thanks to stage coaches in the 1820s, buses from the 1830s, trains from the 1840s, the Underground from the 1860s, horse trams from the 1870 and by 1900 motor buses, electric trams and the deep-level Tube. The demolition of residential accommodation in central districts to make way for wharves, warehouses, workshops, gasworks and transport facilities operated as a push factor to displace the poor outwards.

The advent of horse-drawn trams in the 1870s was, if anything, even more important than the railway in encouraging commuting. Before the advent of the electric tram and train, however, commuters in many suburbs would have been outnumbered by those who worked in the immediate locality as domestic servants, shop staff, building craftsmen, teachers, as the employees of banks, public utilities, transport companies, catering outlets, the postal service or local government or in such major London industries as brewing, printing and clothing.

If the outer suburbs are defined as the area beyond the boundaries set for the Metropolitan Board of Works or its successor the London County Council but within reach of its transport system, in 1861 they accommodated 400,000 people, equal to 12 per cent of the metropolitan population. By 1911 the figure stood at 2,700,000, equal to 37 per cent of the whole. In the 1880s the four fastest-growing English urban areas were all in outer London: Leyton (133 per cent in that decade), Willesden (122 per cent), Tottenham (95 per cent) and West Ham (59 per cent). Rather than being bourgeois these suburbs were distinctly artisan in character. By the 1890s the ring of explosive growth had moved further out to Ilford (278 per cent) and East Ham (194 per cent), followed by Acton, Edmonton and Wimbledon. In the following decade the lead was taken by Merton and Morden (156 per cent), Wembley (137 per cent) and Purley (128 per cent), followed by Ealing, Southall, Chingford and Coulsdon.

The Battle for Style
Although most suburban building was the work of small-scale speculators, short on cash and long on optimism, the best aspired to the architectural vision represented by the exquisite *cottages ornées* of John Nash's Park Village on the edge of Regent's Park or by the stately and individualized walled mansions of the Eyre estate in nearby St. John's Wood. The latter represented a decisive break with the uniform terraces, squares and circuses of Georgian Bath or Bloomsbury. The

development of St. John's Wood as a neighbourhood of villas set in generous grounds encouraged a craze for horticulture that was decisively advanced by the appearance in 1826 of John Claudius Loudon's *Gardener's Magazine*, the first specialized publication in the field. Loudon proclaimed unashamedly that one of the major purposes of a garden was "to display the taste and wealth of the possessor." In 1838 he published *The Suburban Gardener and Villa Companion*, a standard text for the horticulturally ambitious. By then Dickens had already lampooned this new cult in *Sketches by Boz*:

> *If the regular City man... can be said to have any daily recreation beyond his dinner it is his garden. He never does anything to it with his own hands but he takes great pride in it notwithstanding... He always takes a walk round it before he starts for town in the morning... his delight in his garden appears to arise more from the consciousness of possession than actual enjoyment of it. When he drives you down to dinner... he orders the French windows of his dining-room (which of course look into the garden) to be opened and... descants at considerable length upon its beauty and the cost of maintaining it.*

Loudon advocated replacing sombre yews and dreary conifers with sycamore, plane or almond trees, complemented by limes, laurels and laburnums. The Chinese practice of grouping bedding-plants in blocks gained favour. The invention of the lawnmower in 1830 encouraged householders to lay down more garden to grass. Loudon's own invention of the curved glazing bar led to the construction of stylish conservatories and hothouses.

The Ladbroke estate at Notting Hill epitomized the mixture of profit and peril that accompanied the development process. Charles Henry Blake (1794-1872), having made his fortune in India, determined to increase it by building on a fine hill-top site and employed the noted artist-architect Thomas Allom (1804-72) to design a range of handsome houses and lavish communal gardens. The outbreak of the Crimean War (1854-6), followed by the Indian Mutiny (1857), choked off the then prevailing building boom, so that Blake was forced to sell his own imposing home at 24 Kensington Park Gardens only five years after moving into it. A rapid recovery from

1859 onwards saved him from bankruptcy and he soon turned to the energetic promotion of a railway line to connect Hammersmith with the main route running into Paddington. Acting in cahoots with the company chairman, Blake secretly bought, for £838 per acre, some 130 acres of farmland over which the proposed route would have to pass. He and his co-conspirator then demanded from their own fellow-directors a staggering ten thousand pounds an acre for it but settled for £2,150— and then resigned in disgrace. None of this stopped Blake from going on to develop hundreds more properties in the environs of what became the hugely successful Hammersmith and City line and living out a comfortable retirement in Eastbourne.

Commuting and Community

"To young people...I would strongly recommend a house some little way out of London. Rents are less; smuts and blacks conspicuous by their absence; a small garden, or even a tiny conservatory... is not an impossibility; and if Edwin has to pay for his season-ticket, that is nothing in comparison with his being able to sleep in fresh air, to have a game of tennis in summer, or a friendly evening of music, chess or games in the winter, without expense."

Mrs. Panton, *From Kitchen to Garrett,* 1888

The economist J. R. McCulloch observed in 1851 that "the picturesque hills of Surrey, near Dulwich and Norwood, are studded with the villas of citizens who retire there from the bustle of town" and credited as a major cause "the easy communication afforded by the omnibuses and coaches which run... till late at night." In fact Dulwich still had a residential density of only one person per acre a decade later, when Camberwell had fifteen and Peckham twenty-four. Apart from Southwark south London had remained remarkably rural until the opening of the Vauxhall (1816), Waterloo (1817) and Southwark (1819) bridges. John Ruskin grew up in a Camberwell home with a rear garden of three acres with its own orchard, meadow, stable, pigsty and a byre for three cows. A. R. Bennett's memoir of *London and Londoners in the Eighteen-Fifties and Sixties* recalled a Camberwell whose quietly respectable streets were enlivened daily by milkmen dressed in country smocks and girls crying fresh watercress. Summer brought vendors of fresh cherries and strawberries, gypsies selling brooms and pegs and water-carts to lay the dust on thoroughfares not yet macadamized. Scavengers with horse-drawn carts collected cinders for recycling into bricks, rags to make paper, paper to make cardboard, bones to make glue and kitchen-waste to fatten pigs. The suburbs thus created a living for the residents of less salubrious quarters. In the same way the kitchen waste of the residents of Notting Hill was recycled by the pig-keepers of Notting Dale while their dirty linen provided employment for the laundresses of Kensal Town.

The railway had initially been conceived for inter-city communication; its potential for intra-urban transportation was only gradually understood. When the Great Western Railway was opened to traffic the first stop out of its terminus was at Slough, fourteen miles to the west. Only in the 1860s, a quarter of a century after the opening of the capital's first station at London Bridge, did railways begin to affect suburbanization. As historian H. J. Dyos declared, "the locomotive was in truth practically middle-aged before it appeared in Camberwell." It lowered the social tone of the neighbourhood. When in 1863 Herne Hill became a major junction for the line between London, Chatham and Dover and a loop line joined Denmark Hill to Victoria and London Bridge in 1866, the area was rapidly engulfed by streets of cheap houses. Camberwell's building frenzy peaked in 1878-80 when some 416 firms or individual builders were engaged in erecting 5,670 "close-set nests of bricks and mortar" as the *Building News* so delicately put it. Inevitably not all could prosper. In 1881 of 4,800 houses recently built in East Dulwich some 40 per cent remained untenanted, forcing rent reductions of up to 15 per cent.

Bedford Park

"Now he who loves aesthetic cheer
and does not mind the damp,
May come and read Rossetti here
by a Japanese-y lamp.

Thus was a village builded
for all who are aesthete,
Whose precious souls it fill did,
with utter joy complete.

For floors were stained and polished,
and every hearth was tiled,
And Philistines abolished,
by culture's gracious child."

St. James's Review, 1881

Bedford Park is commended in *The Buildings of England (London 3: North West)* as, if not quite the first ever garden suburb it is often claimed at be, then at least "the first example where the relaxed, informal mood of a market town or village was adopted for a complete speculatively built suburb." The originator of the project was Jonathan T. Carr (1845-1915), a cloth merchant with aesthetic inclinations and entrepreneurial impulses. In 1875 he bought 24 acres at Acton Green on what was then the western edge of London. The site was rich in mature trees, thanks to Dr. John Lindley (1799-1865), the first professor of botany at University College, curator of the gardens of the Royal Horticultural Society and the occupant of eighteenth-century Bedford House, whose grounds stood at the core of the new community. The *Lady's Pictorial* noted perceptively that "the first thought of the proprietor was how to spare the greatest number of trees and build artistic houses among them that might look as though surrounded by the growth of centuries." A station, Turnham Green, opened in 1869, gave access to the City within thirty minutes, but the City-bound commuter was not the ideal intended resident. Carr's prospectus, lauding the locality as "The Healthiest Place In The World", asserted that his estate "represents the first endeavour to secure, in the erection of houses at moderate rents, good construction, with attention to artistic effect, coupled with most complete sanitary arrangements, both in their drainage and perfect freedom from sewer gas." Each house, regardless of cost, would have a garden and a "Bath Room" with hot and cold water. Communal amenities would include not only the usual church and public house, but also a clubhouse, art school, tennis courts and kindergarten.

The project's first consulting architect was E. W. Godwin (1833-86), whose *avant-garde* credentials were guaranteed by having been chosen by Wilde and Whistler to design their Chelsea residences. Adverse criticism of the internal planning of Godwin's draft designs led to his dismissal in favour of Richard Norman Shaw (1831-1912). Shaw was further commissioned to design St. Michael and All Angels church, the club, stores and Tabard Tavern, as well as Carr's own commanding Tower House (now lost). Dubbed "Queen Anne revival", a convenient, but not particularly accurate, epithet, Shaw's style was actually an eclectic fusion of English and Flemish motifs emphasizing gables, pediments and monumental chimneys and contrasting bold rubbed-brick features, tile-hanging and terra-cotta embellishments with white-painted balconies, balustrades and bay-windows. Equally distinctive was his banishment of such highly typical features of mid-Victorian urbanism as stucco, basements, iron railings and tall rear extensions.

Shaw's "Type D3" of 1879 cost £1,400 to build. Three main downstairs rooms were complemented by a kitchen with scullery, pantry, larder and downstairs WC plus a generous hall flanked by two lobbies. There were five first-floor bedrooms plus a bathroom, a separate WC and two further attic bedrooms. By 1880 Shaw was ready to turn over his interest in the project to his pupil and protégé, E .J. May, a local resident, who continued with his master's style but concentrated on producing much larger houses on bigger plots for individual purchasers, a change of emphasis that reflected the success of the venture in attracting the "right sort" of purchaser. Early residents of Bedford Park included the architect C. F. A. Voysey (who designed 14 South Parade), artists Lucien Pissarro and Jack Yeats and the dramatist Sir Arthur Pinero. As early as 1882 the fiery preacher and prolific author, the American-born, Moncure Daniel Conway, another local inhabitant, could observe that "to those who dwell here the world is divided into two great classes—those who live at Bedford Park and those who do not." The Architectural Association paid a visit to the site as early as 1877 and in 1880 its "quaint and pretty architecture" was praised by William Morris himself. The *St. James's Gazette*, however, lampooned the houses as looking like boiled lobsters. Gilbert and Sullivan also made satirical reference to the project, and G. K. Chesterton utilized Bedford Park, as the thinly disguised Saffron Park—a not very coded reference to a supposedly favoured hue among Aesthetes—in his anarchist fantasy *The Man Who Was Thursday* (1908). (The anarchists in question, supposedly plotting world domination, *all* turn out to be undercover policemen.)

Shaw's style was to be widely imitated—at the Duke of

Devonshire's nearby Grove Park Estate, at Bush Hill Park Estate, Enfield (1878), Heathfield Park, Willesden (1883), Duke's Avenue, Muswell Hill (1906) and, most notably, by the work of his former assistant, Ernest Newton at Camden Park, Chislehurst (1893-1916). By the 1950s Bedford Park had become run-down and, in the eyes of some, ripe for redevelopment. Acton Council's demolition of a Shaw house acted as a wake-up call. Led by architect and local resident Tom Affleck Greeves, the Bedford Park Society was founded in 1963. In 1967 it achieved a landmark success with the listing of 356 designated properties as Grade II. An official concept of a "Conservation Area" status did not then exist. Bedford Park became one of the first in the country in 1969.

Hampstead Garden Suburb

Lying at the northern edge of Hampstead Heath between Golders Green and East Finchley, Hampstead Garden Suburb was founded in 1907 by Dame Henrietta Barnett (1851-1936), wife of Canon Barnett, the East End settlement pioneer who had established Toynbee Hall. Fearing that the proposed northward extension of the Underground would bring the "ruin of the sylvan restfulness of... the most beautiful open space near London", she organized a lobby group, the Hampstead Heath Extension Council, to prevent the eighty acres of Wylde's Farm being engulfed by "rows of ugly villas such as disfigure Willesden and most of the suburbs of London." Having raised the cash to save the Heath Extension and handed it over to the London County Council for safekeeping, Henrietta Barnett sketched out plans in the *Contemporary Review* for a model settlement and established a trust to create a community to accommodate "persons of all classes of society and standards of income" and especially to welcome the handicapped. It was hoped that even working people would have "the opportunity of taking a cottage with a garden within a 2d fare of Central London." If the labouring classes could live in proximity to the cultured it was hoped that they might be exposed to "the contagion of refinement". There would be an Institute to promote cultural uplift but no public houses were to be allowed. Housing density would be limited to eight per acre, the houses being separated by hedges or fences, not walls. Roads would be tree-lined and at least forty feet wide. Noise should be avoided— even that of church bells.

The planning of the layout and design of houses and public buildings was entrusted to Raymond Unwin and Barry Parker, who had recently established Letchworth Garden City in Hertfordshire. The eminent country house specialist Edwin Lutyens (1869-1944) became Consulting Architect and was responsible for Central Square. M. H. Baillie Scott contributed Waterlow Court (1907-9), a complex of fifty-one flats around a cloistered quadrangle. Intended for single professional women, it included a communal dining room to save residents from the labour of feeding themselves at either end of a busy working day. Unwin matched this concept with The Orchard (1909, demolished 1970), a complex of fifty-seven flats for elderly residents sharing communal baths, washhouses and baking ovens.

Unwin himself lived at Wylde's Farm, which had been the home of the landscape painter John Linnell in the 1820s and was threatened with demolition to make way for a car park for a proposed Underground extension. In 1906 Unwin moved in, converted the barn into a drawing office and stayed until 1940. The war brought building to a halt and the post-war inflation of building costs effectively killed off the experiment in creating a mixed-class community. The American essayist Logan Pearsall Smith wryly noted the prevalence of "societies for Mothercraft and Handicraft and Child Study... lectures on reincarnation, the Holy Grail and the teaching of the Holy Zoroaster". George Orwell often came to the home of his friends, the Fierzes, at 1B Oakwood Road to change into grubby clothes before heading off to the slums and it was there that he typed the first draft of *Down and Out in Paris and London* in 1933. Direction of new development was taken over by J. C. S. Soutar and limited to the building of conventional neo-Georgian houses for sale, although there were also specialized units of courtyard flats for ex-servicemen. Shops, cafés and cinemas were still kept out. Despite this and although much of Lutyens' scheme remained unrealized, in 1951 Pevsner could still describe the outcome as "the aesthetically most satisfactory and socially most successful of all twentieth century garden suburbs."

Homes for Heroes

During the First World War two estates for "key workers" were built by the Office of Works to the designs of its architect Sir Francis Baines (1877-1933). The Progress Estate of a thousand houses at Well Hall,

Eltham, was built in 1915 for munitions workers at Woolwich Arsenal. The much smaller Roe Green Village in Brent, an estate of 270 flats and houses, was built in 1917-9 for workers at the Aircraft Manufacturing Company on a site previously used by the Kingsbury Polo Club. The architect provided a "village green" with an inn as a focus, plus a doctor's house and half a dozen shops. As the plant employed 4,400, Roe Green can only have accommodated a privileged few. Although these two initiatives represented an extraordinary response to the needs of war-time both were thoughtfully laid out and proved highly influential among architects employed by local councils in the post-war period.

When the Great War ended Prime Minister Lloyd George rashly promised that Britain's victorious armies would return to "Homes Fit for Heroes". Walter Long, President of the Local Government Board, elaborated the rationale underlying this pledge: "To let them come home from horrible, water-logged trenches to something little better than a pigsty here would, indeed, be criminal... and a negation of all we have said during the war, that we can never repay those men for what they have done for us." Cynical contemporaries interpreted government-subsidized house-building as "the antidote to Bolshevism".

The need for housing to accommodate returning warriors was anticipated by the eccentric architect Ernest George Trobridge (1884-1942) at Kingsbury, not far from the Roe Green estate. Trobridge's Slough Lane estate of 1921-2 consists of highly individual houses in an Arts and Crafts mode adapted to demonstrate their designer's commitment to the philosophy of the eighteenth-century Swedish mystic Emanuel Swedenborg. Entrances, hearths and the sheltering roof, tiled or thatched, were all given exaggerated emphasis to achieve what has been called "the *ne plus ultra* of suburban rural escapism". Anticipating a shortage of building materials Trobridge patented a construction method utilizing green elm, exhibiting it to great acclaim at the 1920 Ideal Home Exhibition. Unfortunately the area failed to attract newcomers until a station was opened at Kingsbury in 1932. Another group of later Trobridge houses, accompanied by flats, is in Buck Lane. Tudor Gates features herringbone brickwork and twisted chimneys. Rochester Court has stone facings inspired by Rochester Castle. Other blocks of flats feature drawbridge entrances and chimneys disguised as turrets.

Metro-Land
"Through Amersham to Aylesbury and the Vale,
In those wet fields the railway didn't pay."
John Betjeman, "Metroland"

The Metropolitan Railway or "Met" had electrified its services as far as Harrow and Uxbridge by 1906 but it was not until 1925 that electrification reached out as far as Watford and Rickmansworth, opening up for development a large, fan-shaped swathe of agricultural land north-west of London stretching through Middlesex, Hertfordshire and Buckinghamshire. Stanmore was reached in 1932. Steam services carried the connection out as far as Amersham and Aylesbury. The Met itself built "Harrow Garden Village" in 1930-34 in anticipation of the opening of Sir Charles Holden's Rayners' Lane station. The company's main efforts, however, were directed towards getting others to do the actual work of building.

A prolonged poster campaign elaborated a rural idyll of spacious houses in small communities, with mature trees and ever-radiant skies. Later the Underground itself joined in to promote less remote destinations. Kingsbury Hill was noted as being less than six miles from Marble Arch and ten minutes from Baker Street by electric train. An artwork poster featuring Golders Green ("A Place of Delightful Prospects") featured a pseudo-Tudor house of masterful ambiguity— detached or one half of a pair bisected by the poster edge? In the verdant front garden a man in early middle-age scatters fertilizer from a bucket onto an improbably rampant herbaceous border. His status as the house-owner, rather than a professional gardener, is clearly implied by his formal dress—creased trousers, waistcoat—lacking only a jacket to be correct for "the office". His wife sits knitting in a deck-chair on the lawn, a bonny infant at her feet. In the background half a dozen neatly dressed figures stroll along a broad, traffic-free, tree-lined avenue, while a speeding train closes the perspective. No other houses are visible. A photographic poster for "Coulsdon Heights", sub-titled "A Charming Corner of the Estate", featured a fashionably dressed couple in city clothes pausing to admire the bosky prospect over a stile in a wooded lane with not a single building of any sort in sight.

This Happy Breed

Paradoxically the metropolitan building boom of the 1930s was the product of depression. Demand for housing was fuelled by the ambitions of an expanding lower middle class of clerks, teachers, petty bureaucrats and employees in commerce, transport and leisure. By 1930 the population of Greater London was increasing by more than a thousand persons per week. The percentage of unemployed remained in single figures. Southerners with work in shops, offices or the factories making vehicles or electrical goods aspired to a new sort of life in a new sort of home. On the supply side there were few bottlenecks. Labour displaced by mass-unemployment in the north, Scotland and Wales came south in search of work. Interest rates were low. Building societies cut their required deposit from 25 per cent to 10 or even 5 per cent. In real terms houses would never be so cheap again nor so readily available. Greater London prices began at around £400—about double the annual income of a white-collar or even skilled manual worker. House-building sustained a broader recovery in the metropolitan economy, creating a demand for bricks, timber, glass, paint and fittings, many of which were manufactured or at least processed in the region. New homes meant new furniture, kitchen and garden equipment and electrical goods. Department stores outside the West End, like Bowman's of Camden Town or Roome's at the far eastern end of the District Line, in Upminster, catered for housewives with no need to work and time to devote to the beautification of their abodes. New communities meant new shops, schools and cinemas, creating still more new jobs in building and staffing them.

Sticks or Bricks?

Three major architectural styles dominated the housing of the inter-war period. The sub-Georgian vernacular of the pioneering garden suburbs was favoured by the mandarin architects working for the London County Council and London's boroughs. The Modern was promoted by a small clique of home-grown internationalists like Maxwell Fry and refugees from Continental persecution such as Gropius, Goldfinger and Lubetkin. Speculative builders favoured an eclectic "Tudorbethan", and so did their clients. The neo-Georgian that proliferated on council estates was often a stripped-down version, devoid of individualizing detail in such matters as roof-lines or fenestration. The gigantic

Becontree estate sprawling across the borders of Dagenham, Barking and Ilford actually had over ninety different designs of dwelling but virtually all were built at the same height, in the same materials.

A few outstanding examples of "Modern" homes were built, mainly for very wealthy individual clients in self-consciously arty suburbs like Highgate and Hampstead. Most Modern homes were in fact "Moderne", i.e. still built by traditional methods using traditional materials but masked by superficial features such as curved walls, flat or green-tiled roofs, with steel balconies and windows. Constructed of brick, rather than ferro-concrete, they remained conventional in their internal arrangements. Mediterranean and maritime in their inspiration, such houses looked, to the conventionally-minded masses, just about acceptable at the seaside but seemed strangely out of place in the suburbs, as though stranded by a departed tide.

"Mock-Tudor" was more a malleable mode than a single style, permitting builder and client to indulge in an orgy of individuation by combining porches, gables, oriels, half-timbering, tile-hung or roughcast panels, diamond-paned leaded-lights and stained-glass windows with galleon, floral, cottage or sun-burst motifs. The result was a statement, more proprietorial than architectural, which to the casual passer-by may have been all but indistinguishable from its neighbours—cartoonist Osbert Lancaster knowingly dubbed it "bypass Tudor variegated"—but the result remained deeply satisfying to its initial purchaser. Above all, this type of house, though deeply bastardized in its descent from the high-flown elegances of Norman Shaw or Charles Voysey, was valued for what it was not: neo-Georgian. What was the point of making half a lifetime of sacrifices to buy one's own home if it could be mistaken for a council house?

Cosy, cottagey, comfortable and convenient, the new residences of the new bourgeoisie aroused the contempt of the cultural cognoscenti. They were reviled as small houses for small families of small-minded people. Writing in 1927, J. B. Priestley denounced the

square little boxes that look as though they have been nailed on to the landscape... so ugly that even time will not beautify them... I do not understand why there is such a general passion now for building semi-detached or detached little houses... I am convinced that it is this detachment that is responsible for a great deal of ugliness.

Supposedly egalitarian writers such as Orwell were equally scathing.

Few of these critics presumably were housebound themselves. Housewives, however, appreciated the long-overdue "luxury" of hot and cold water on both floors, electric power for cooking, lighting and appliances and the company of music from the wireless while their husbands were out at work and their children at school. Even minor design features improved lifestyles in small but significant ways. Children could be left to play safely in a back garden with high fences and overlooked by "French windows" and a bright kitchen. Door-handles at shoulder-height kept infants out of the "best" front room. Bay windows brought in more light and permitted discreet evaluation of unwanted callers. New patterns of socializing emerged only hesitantly. Shopping usually required a trek to a "parade" of specialist outlets rather than "popping into" a corner shop to exchange gossip. Many women did suffer from social isolation, cut off by distance from female relatives and often by their own sensitivity or snobbery from their neighbours.

The Suburb as City

> *"It ain't all honey*
> *And it ain't all jam,*
> *Walking round the 'ouses*
> *With a three-wheeled pram. "*
> Popular song, sung by Gertrude Lawrence

As the LCC's architect G. Topham Forrest conceded in 1920, "the proposal to convert a tract of land, three thousand acres in extent, at present covered chiefly with market gardens, into a township with a population of 120,000 is something unparalleled in the history of housing." The Becontree estate, sprawling over the ancient east London parishes of Dagenham, Barking and Ilford, was, when it was built, the biggest in the world, with some 25,000 houses. At the peak of construction 6,000 craftsmen and labourers converted 2,500 tons of daily deliveries of building materials into a hundred houses a week. The influx of newcomers in 1928-9 was larger than the entire population of Essex's county town of Chelmsford. Five years later "the first new town in England" had a population to equal ancient Norwich.

At the level of physical planning the result was at best only a partial success. The site's lack of striking natural features denied it pleasing perspectives. Broad boulevards with central reservations for future tramways, which never materialized, proved depressing. By happenstance the short cul-de-sac, known locally as a "banjo", which planners adopted to cut down on road-making costs, happily limited through traffic, and consequently accidents, as well as fostering sociability. Newcomers initially delighted in the fresh air and the absence of overcrowding. But many missed the bustle and banter of the East End from which more than half of them had come. There were no street markets. There was only one pub per ten thousand inhabitants. Bethnal Green had twenty times as many. The new "freedom" had been bought at the price of a social emptiness and unaccustomed servitudes. In return for the comforts of inside lavatories, fitted baths, gas and electricity, tenants were expected not only to cultivate their gardens but also to scour their small-paned windows weekly and pay close attention to the maintenance of chimneys, drains and even door-hinges. Becontree's first decade witnessed the voluntary departure of no less than a third of its designated residents.

Planners had envisaged not just a garden suburb but "a township more or less complete in itself". That was not what actually materialized. Prime Minister Stanley Baldwin observed regretfully in 1934 that there was more to housing than the provision of houses. Much of Becontree's success as a community proved to be of its own making. Schools were only provided belatedly, obliging local churches to fill the gap by making over their halls for use as temporary classrooms. Thanks to the heroic and virtually single-handed efforts of the flamboyant and erudite J. G. O'Leary, Becontree developed a first-class library service. In 1930 a national institution emerged in the unlikely form of the Dagenham Girl Pipers; by 1939 they were being feted at New York's World Fair. Providence played its part, too. The gigantic Ford motor plant at Dagenham eventually became the largest employer of Becontree residents—but no thanks to the planners, who had made no provision whatsoever to create jobs or attract employers to the locality, assuming that the new residents would somehow daily make their way back to the wharves, warehouses and workshops of the industrial East End from which they had just escaped. Ford made its own quite independent decision to build there simply because there was cheap, empty riverside land with deepwater access close to London.

The LCC's second largest "out county" project was the Watling Estate of 1926-30, north of Burnt Oak station on the Northern Line, which opened in 1924. Ex-stall holder Jack Cohen opened London's first Tesco grocery store there in 1929. The 1921 population of 1,000 became 21,545 by 1931. Watling's four thousand houses obtruded on much snootier neighbours than Becontree did, provoking apoplectic accusations in the *Hendon and Finchley Times* from Mill Hill residents of constant vandalism and predations by the foul-mouthed thieving children of "Little Moscow". The mothers of the alleged offenders, however, were more often crushed by sheer social indifference, rather than hostility. "I never stopped crying to begin with," one remembered," there was nobody to talk to; I'd just stand and stare out of the window." Ironically, perhaps, the estate is now a conservation area.

It seems that the experience of "planning" Becontree as a new "community" bequeathed few lasting lessons in the locality. Between 1954 and 1960 the borough of Barking built the largest single estate promoted by a Greater London borough since 1945. Thames View, consisting of some 2,112 dwellings, was built on reclaimed marshlands, far from the town centre around Barking station. Some of the apartment blocks were nine storeys high. A clinic and library were only provided in 1960, just as the project was nearing completion, rather than at the outset, when such facilities, even if initially under-used, could have served as "tools for conviviality". Forty years later Thames View was characterized by health professionals as "an area of high need, which has suffered from a history of low investment in services and amenities. The estate itself is isolated, the community fragmented, with little access to communal facilities. Services are basic, educational attainment poor, life chances limited." Alcohol dependency among mothers of pre-school children was identified as a priority problem. With the capital's lowest house prices, lowest absolute number of graduates and its highest number of teenage pregnancies and percentage of divorced and separated adults in all England, Barking itself seemed scarcely a lifeline to a better tomorrow. Its council, however, pledged itself to yet another salvatory project in the shape of Barking Reach, two and a half miles of riverside identified as the largest feasible site for concentrated housing development in the entire capital—5,000 homes, 5,000 jobs, 15,000 residents...

Hopefully the massive redevelopment of the lower Lea Valley planned to accommodate the 2012 Olympics will have spill-over effects similar to the impact of Ford's on the Becontree estate a lifetime ago. London, as ever, promises to defy planning in favour of just happening.

OF PINTS AND PUBS
A Convivial Interlude

Just which is the oldest pub in London is a question that intrigues tourists who would not know a pint of bitter from a barley wine much more than it interests the regular patrons of the capital's seven thousand licensed premises.

The Prospect of Whitby in Wapping claims to have come into existence ca. 1520 and plays up its association with Execution Dock and pirates. Tourists lured by the Prospect's current popularity might with advantage also try the nearby Town of Ramsgate, where the notoriously merciless Judge Jeffries was apprehended in flight, dressed as a woman, and then continue eastwards to The Grapes in Limehouse, supposedly the model for the Six Jolly Fellowship Porters in Dickens' *Our Mutual Friend.* Teeny, tart, crunchy whitebait in a crisp batter, served with a squeeze of lemon, is a speciality of the house. Architecturally pinched but rich in ambience, The Grapes backs right onto the river. On the opposite bank, The Mayflower at Rotherhithe has a rear area built out on piles, enabling drinkers to sup reflectively to the gentle slip-slopping of the Thames below.

The Hoop and Grapes at Aldgate certainly has the look of an early seventeenth-century commercial building but has had a chequered career of various uses rather than a continuous history as licensed premises. The Seven Stars in Carey Street, Lincoln's Inn, is older than it looks, quite possibly from 1602, as has been claimed. Ye Olde Cheshire Cheese, off Fleet Street, was rebuilt after the Great Fire of 1666, but the labyrinthine cellars, now converted into bars, seem much older. Ye Olde Mitre Tavern, secreted down a passageway between Hatton Garden and Ely Place, quite plausibly claims to have been founded in 1546, though

The George, Borough High Street

the present building looks eighteenth-century. The front bar features a section of a cherry tree said to have marked the boundary between the gardens of the Bishop of Ely and those of Sir Christopher Hatton, Elizabeth I's "dancing chancellor". The Old Cock Tavern on the south side of Fleet Street proudly proclaims a foundation of 1549—but originally stood on the north side. The present slender pseudo-Tudor incarnation is a nineteenth-century confection. It might, one could argue, represent the ideal of a pub in a Platonic sense but the claim to have achieved that must be conceded to The Moon Under Water, an ultra-modern, ultra-fake on Leicester Square, which masquerades under the name of George Orwell's supposedly archetypal English pub. A few minutes walk to the east of Leicester Square stands The Lamb and Flag in a cul-de-sac called Rose Street, just off Covent Garden. It was outside this establishment that the poet John Dryden was beaten half to death by three thugs in retribution for some alleged literary impertinence. Responsibility for the assault is usually attributed to the dissolute Earl of Rochester.

Because, until the construction of Westminster Bridge in 1750, London Bridge provided the only means of crossing the river by road, all traffic to the capital from the south and most from the Continent converged at its southern end. Borough High Street consequently became by the seventeenth century an almost continuous strip of inns and taverns supplying food, drink, lodging and entertainment to travellers. Even today the pedestrian passing along the eastern side of the street can count eight surviving entrances to former inn-yards; and plaques mark the long-vanished sites of The Queen's Head, once owned by John Harvard's mother, and The Tabard Inn, from which Chaucer's pilgrims departed for Canterbury. Of the hostelries that remain from the days of coaching and clatter, by far the most impressive is The George Inn at 76 Borough High Street. Rebuilt after Southwark's great fire of 1676, it was already in existence by 1543. Although two sides along its former inn-yard were demolished in the 1880s to make way for the railway, what still stands is timbered and, uniquely for London, galleried, making it easy to conjure to the imagination the sort of setting in which strolling players competed for attention with the surrounding hubbub before the invention of the theatre gave them acoustic control over their surroundings. Dickens certainly did drink here and mentions the pub in *Little Dorrit*.

A few hundred yards to the west on Bankside stands the Anchor Tavern, which once took its ale from Dr. Johnson's brewer friend Thrale, and where Johnson himself drank. Nowadays a large patio attracts an *al fresco* clientele. Also dating from the eighteenth century, The Jerusalem Tavern in Britton Street, Clerkenwell, has a distinctly Hogarthian atmosphere. The Archery Tavern, near Lancaster Gate, occupies the site of the former practice-ground of the Royal Toxophilite Society. The mews just around the corner accommodates two livery stables, which assault the unwary passer-by with the unmistakable aromas of equine occupation.

From Knightsbridge passage through a former stable-block, now converted to bijou residences, is required to reach The Grenadier in Wilton Row. Masked by a positive cascade of floral embellishment, this almost too pretty Regency establishment is bedecked with militaria and boasts its own special recipe for Bloody Marys. Within staggering distance can be found the cramped, cosy, head-bumping bar of The Nag's Head on Kinnerton Street, a thoroughfare which on a summer's evening feels a century older than the streets around it. Further west still is the equally tiny Fox and Hounds of ca. 1860 in Passmore Street, at the edge of Belgravia.

Although the big brewery chains perpetrated much vandalism in the stainless-steel and formica-obsessed 1960s and 1970s, some splendiferous examples of Victorian pub architecture still remain. Out at Maida Vale, The Prince Alfred preserves a prodigious patterned plaster ceiling and the internal divisions which marked off bars of differing status in an age when hierarchy governed even (perhaps especially) the company in which one got drunk. Nearby The Warrington Hotel is festooned with the finest faience. Crocker's Folly in Aberdeen Place, St. John's Wood, is built of the most lavish materials and on a gargantuan scale. When it opened in 1898, the *Licensed Victuallers' Gazette* hailed its glowing interior as more like "the hall of some magnificent modern mansion... than the saloon of a tavern." The Albert on Victoria Street, though sadly overshadowed by surrounding buildings, is a remarkable survival for so central a location. First built in 1845 as a consequence of the laying out of Victoria Street, it was originally named The Blue Coat Boy after an adjacent charity school. Rebuilt in 1865-7, it was then renamed in honour of the recently-deceased Prince Consort. The Albert's proximity to Parliament has long made it a favourite with legislators, and it consequently possesses a Division Bell which warns MPs that they have eight minutes to get back to the Commons to vote. The stairs to the first-floor restaurant are lined with signed photographs of past prime ministers.

Other West End examples of authentic Victorian decor include The Argyll Arms, just off Oxford Circus, The Red Lion in Duke of York Street, St. James', and The Champion in Wells Street, just north of Oxford Street, which has wonderful stained-glass windows immortalizing such sporting giants as the burly, bearded icon of the Victorian cricket-field W. G. Grace and "Captain" Matthew Webb, the first man to swim the English Channel. The Cock, just north of Oxford Circus, features massive external hanging-lanterns, originally designed to lure in customers from the gloom to an oasis of warmth and laughter. Upstairs at The Sherlock Holmes, just off Northumberland Avenue, there is a complete mock-up reproduction of the legendary sleuth's study. The Princess Louise in High Holborn has tiled gentlemen's lavatories which are allegedly listed as a conservation feature in their own right.

Like The Champion, The Lamb in Lamb's Conduit Street, off Theobald's Road in Holborn, still has some of the frosted-glass "snob screens" which were supposed to protect drinkers' privacy from prying eyes. The Salisbury on St. Martin's Lane, another unrestrained celebration of brass and glass, was once a favoured hang-out of 1950s theatrical wannabes such as Terence Stamp and Michael Caine. A mile to the north, The Fitzroy Tavern on Charlotte Street, an even more massive Victorian red-brick gin-palace, was, from the 1920s to the 1940s, the rendezvous of choice for the more Bohemian end of London's literary and artistic set. Prominent among its regulars was Augustus John, the archetype of the boozy artist-rebel, who allegedly patted the head of every child he passed on the way in on the grounds that it *might* be one of his. A couple of hundred yards to the south on Rathbone Place is The Wheatsheaf, where Augustus John introduced Dylan Thomas to his future wife, the flame-haired Caitlin. At the bottom of Rathbone Place is The Black Horse, where the first ever thousand-plus break in billiards was made. The featureless asphalt parking-area at the rear, reachable through the surviving coach-yard tunnel entrance, was in the 1640s the site of Crab Tree Fort, a strongpoint on the *enceinte* of fortifications which briefly ringed the capital during the civil wars.

For decorative exuberance The Blackfriar at Blackfriars (see p.53) is in a class of its own. Flamboyantly Arts and Crafts, it boasts mosaic facades depicting beaming, big-bellied friars feasting on fat fish washed down with generous measures of good ale. Inside, the panelled and marble walls are embellished with admonitory maxims and high-relief brass depictions of the allegedly un-rigorous existence of the inhabitants of the Dominican friary which once occupied this site. A few hundred yards to the north on Fleet Street is The Punch Tavern. *Punch* magazine was founded by hacks who originally foregathered in the parlour of The Edinburgh Castle in the Strand but when its staff subsequently gave their regular patronage to The Crown and Sugar Loaf in Fleet Street the proprietor prudently changed its name to The Punch Tavern. A couple of hundred yards further west stands The Tipperary. Acquired by the Dublin brewers S. and G. Mooney ca. 1700, this is claimed to be the first ever Irish-owned pub outside Ireland and features a carefully restored period interior.

Another Arts and Crafts facade, this time ceramic, can be admired at The Fox and Anchor in Charterhouse Street, Smithfield, which also serves breakfasts of staggering plenitude. The Hand and Shears in Cloth Fair nearby, retains much interior woodwork, though of the shabby-chic variety, rather than majestic mahogany. The Viaduct Tavern, opposite St. Sepulchre's church on Newgate Street, is contemporaneous with the opening of Holborn Viaduct, the world's first fly-over, in 1869.

A number of supposedly Victorian pubs were not actually built as pubs but have been converted from other uses. A particularly fine example is The Bank of England on Fleet Street, formerly the Law Courts branch of the Bank of England, whose main bar was once a banking hall of monumental opulence. More frequently nowadays conversion is in the opposite direction, notably in the East End, once renowned for having a pub on every street corner. Noise-polluted mega-bars on major thoroughfares have siphoned off the free-spending youthful "binge-drinkers" beloved of the breweries. Tens of thousands of today's East-Enders are non-drinking Muslims. The traditional "regulars"—middle-aged married men in search of a "quiet pint"—now find their pint quieter and cheaper at home. Twenty years ago, The Seven Stars at the junction of St. Leonard's Road and Bromley High Street, was converted into flats, a pub having been on that site since at least 1603. In St. Leonard's Road, The Priory Tavern and The Imperial Crown have since succumbed to the same fate. In Bromley High Street, The Mason's Arms stands deserted and forlorn.

Less than a mile away, however, an historic East End "boozer" still thrives and maintains a unique annual ritual. The Widow's Son dates back to at least 1810 but was rebuilt half a century later. Each year the eponymous widow would bake a hot-cross bun for her sailor son at Easter and each year he would faithfully return to eat it. When, one year, he failed to return she carried on with her baking and kept up the custom until her death. Today a basket of musty, crumbling buns still hangs above the bar and every Easter a sailor is found to put in another.

Lest it be said that the above selection is too territorially biased to central London, let me briefly also commend the charms of The Windsor Castle on Campden Hill, The King's Head and Eight Bells at Cheyne Walk, Chelsea, The Doves at Upper Mall, Hammersmith, The Flask Tavern at Highgate, The Spaniards' Inn at Hampstead Heath...

SPITALFIELDS

Threatened with demolition by developers in the 1970s, Spitalfields saw them off and transformed itself into a heady hybrid of the ethnic, artistic and hedonistic, a cutting-edge kaleidoscope of curry-houses, clubs, galleries, garment-makers, bars, bagel-shops and Bengalis. Spitalfields is where a Bangladeshi hypermarket occupies the site of a vanished *mikvah*, where a flea-market, a food-court and Bubba's Arkansas B-B-Q now prosper atop a refrigerator depot for bananas. Closed in 1957 as unsafe, Christ Church, Hawksmoor's finest flight of fancy, has had its crypt cleansed, its walls washed and its soaring interior restored to a stunning setting for an annual summer music festival.

Princelet Street

Spitalfields' renaissance has stimulated authors (see p. 274), archaeologists and artists alike. Restoring Christ Church involved removing a thousand bodies, whose remains are a potent profile of the health and wealth of past parishioners. The excavation of the former site of St. Mary Spital, the medieval hospice which gave its name to the area, revealed eight thousand burials, including an intact Roman sarcophagus. This, and its occupant, a female Mediterranean yuppie, buried in silk, are in the Museum of London. Spitalfields' new standing as a "creative quarter" is based on the local residence of Gilbert and George, Tracey Emin, Chris Ofili and Rachel Whitbread. But its artistic heritage also embraces the exquisite creations of its heyday as the centre of silk-weaving. The intricate floral designs of Anna-Maria Garthwaite can be seen at the V & A.

Bricks were certainly being made in Brick Lane by 1550 but the rapid urbanization of its environs was a by-product of the phoenix-like rebirth of burned-out London after 1666. Spitalfields grew so fast that Charles II chartered a new market in 1682. Then the Huguenots arrived. Surviving Georgian houses, like that of Dennis Severs (see p.220), date from the 1720s. Fournier Street's Neuve Eglise of 1743, subsequently became a mission centre aimed at Jews (1809), a Methodist chapel (1819), a synagogue (1897) and a mosque (1976). The Huguenot home at 19 Princelet Street had a synagogue built (1869) in its back-garden, accommodated the reclusive Rodinsky and is intended to house a Museum of Immigration and Diversity. The soup-kitchen and the saveloy, oxtail soup, the caged canary and the well-filled window-box are other Huguenot legacies that have passed into cockney culture.

As the Huguenots yielded to Anglicization and silk-weaving yielded before Free Trade, Yiddish replaced French as Spitalfields' *lingua franca*. Dutch cigar-makers established a synagogue in Sandys Row. Brune Street acquired a handsome soup-kitchen for the Jewish Poor. The Jewish Free School in Bell Lane dedicated itself to replacing Yiddish with English. Pioneer Zionist Israel Zangwill, star pupil, then teacher, drew on his Fashion Street childhood to write *Children of the Ghetto* and with *The Melting Pot*, his play about the immigrant experience, gave a phrase to the language. Other local lads made good include American trade unionist Sam Gompers, Barney Barnato, co-founder of the De Beer's diamond cartel, Abe Sapperstein, creator of the

Harlem Globetrotters, dramatist Arnold Wesker and the Winogradski brothers, better known as tycoon impresarios Lord Grade and Lord Delfont. Their "Little Warsaw" has passed away. Welcome to "Banglatown"!

FURTHER READING

All books published in London unless indicated otherwise.

Introduction

Baker, T. M. M., *London: Rebuilding the City after the Great Fire.* Phillimore, 2000.

Clayton, Antony *Subterranean City: Beneath the Streets of London.* Historical Publications, 2000.

Cooper, Michael, *Robert Hooke and the Rebuilding of London.* Stroud: Sutton Publishing, 2003.

Halliday, Stephen, *Making the Metropolis: Creators of Victoria's London.* Derby: Breedon Books, 2003.

Inwood, Stephen, *A History of London.* Macmillan, 1998.

Porter, Roy, *London: A Social History.* Penguin, 2000.

Schofield, John, *The Building of London: From the Conquest to the Great Fire.* Stroud: Sutton Publishing, 2nd ed., 1993.

Summerson, Sir John, *Georgian London.* New Haven: Yale University Press, 2003.

Thomas, Chris, *London's Archaeological Secrets: A World City Revealed.* Museum of London Archaeology Service/Yale University Press, 2003.

The Survey of London: www.english-heritage.org.uk

Centre for Metropolitan History: www.history.ac.uk/cmh/

Museum of London: www.museumoflondon.org.uk

Mayor of London: www.london.gov.uk

Corporation of the City of London/London Metropolitan Archive: www.cityoflondon.gov.uk

Sights and Sites: Iconic London

Aslet, Clive, *Greenwich Millennium.* Fourth Estate, 1999.

Barker, Felix and Hyde, Ralph, *London As it Might Have Been.* John Murray, 1995.

Fox, Celina, *Londoners.* Thames and Hudson, 1987.

Nead, Lynda, *Victorian Babylon: People, Streets and Images in Nineteenth-Century London.* London/ New Haven: Yale University Press, 2005.

Warner, Malcolm, *The Image of London: Views by Travellers and Émigrés 1550-1920.* Trefoil Publications/ Barbican Art Gallery, 1987.

White, Jerry, *London in the Twentieth Century.* Penguin, 2001.

Of Bards and Business: a Poetic Interlude
Maclaren-Ross, Julian, *Memoirs of the Forties*. Sphere Books, 1991.
Vansittart, Peter, *London: A Literary Companion*. John Murray, 1992.

Chelsea
Richardson, John, *The Chelsea Book: Past and Present*. Historical Publications, 2003.
The Chelsea Society: www.chelseasociety.org.uk

London Described
Allen, Rick, *The Moving Pageant: A Literary Sourcebook on London Street Life 1700-1914*. Routledge, 1998.
Bailey, Paul, *The Oxford Book of London*. Oxford: Oxford University Press, 1996.
Cunningham, Ian, *A Reader's Guide to Writer's London*. Andre Deutsch / Prion, 2001.
Wilson, A. N., *The Faber Book of London*. Faber and Faber, 1993.

Of Diaries and Letters: a Handwritten Interlude
Queen Mary College Centre for Editing Lives and Letters: www.livesandletters.ac.uk
Samuel Pepys: www.pepys.info. www.pepysdiary.com

Dulwich
Tames, Richard, *Dulwich and Camberwell*. Past Historical Publications, 1997.
The Dulwich Society: www.dulwichsociety.org.uk

London Named
Bebbington, Gillian, *Street Names of London*. Batsford, 1988.
Harris, Cyril, *What's in a Name? Origins of Station Names on the London Underground*. Capital Transport Publishing, 2001.
Mills, A.D., *Oxford Dictionary of London Place Names*. Oxford: Oxford University Press, 2001.

Hotels and Hospitality: an Accommodating Interlude
Clayton, Antony, *London's Coffee Houses: A Stimulating Story*. Historical Publications, 2003.

Tames, Richard, *Feeding London: A Taste of History.* Historical Publications, 2003.
Brief historical details of the hotels mentioned are included on most of their websites.

Hampstead

Norrie, Ian, *Writers and Hampstead.* High Hill Press, 1987.
Wade, Christopher, *Hampstead Past.* Historical Publications, 2002.
The Heath and Hampstead Society: www.heathandhampsteadsociety.org.uk
www.friendsofkenwood.org.uk

London Mapped

Barker, Felix and Jackson, Peter, *The History of London in Maps.* Barrie and Jenkins, 1990.
Clout, Hugh (ed), *The Times London History Atlas.* Times Books, 4th edition, 2004.
Rocque's 1746 Map: www.motco.com
Greenwood's 1827 Map: www.users.bathspa.ac.uk
Booth's Poverty Map: www.lse.ac.uk

Markets, Shops and Stores: a Retail Interlude

Major store websites usually include an historical section

The Isle of Dogs

Tames, Richard, *East End Past.* Historical Publications, 2004.
Isle of Dogs Community Foundation: www.idcf.org
London Docklands Development Corporation: www.lddc-history.org
East of London Family History Society: www.eolfhs.org.uk

Intellectual Capital

Harte, Negley, *The University of London 1836-1986.* The Athlone Press, 1986.
Nicolson, Virginia, *Among the Bohemians: Experiments in Living, 1900-1939.* Penguin, 2004.

Novel Encounters: a Fictional Interlude

Glinert, Ed, *A Literary Guide to London.* Penguin, 2000.
Sandhu, Sukhdev, *London Calling: How Black and Asian Writers Imagined a City.* HarperCollins, 2003.

Islington
Cosh, Mary, *A History of Islington*. Historical Publications, 2005.
The Islington Archaeological and History Society: www.iahs.org.uk

The Blasts of War
Hewison, Robert, *Under Siege: Literary Life in London, 1939-45*. Methuen, 1988.
Van Young, Sayre, *London's War: A Traveler's Guide to World War II*. Berkeley, CA: Ulysses Press, 2004.
Ziegler, Philip, *London at War, 1939-45*. Sinclair Stevenson, 1995.
Imperial War Museum:www.iwm.org.uk

Of Quacks and Cures: a Medical Interlude
Rosen, Dennis and Sylvia, *London Science*. Prion, 1994.
Royal College of Physicians: www.rcplondon.ac.uk
Royal College of Surgeons: www.rsceng.co.uk
Florence Nightingale Museum: www.florence-nightingale.co.uk

Mayfair
City of Westminster Archives Centre www.westminster.gov.uk/archives

Sporting London
Bryant, John, *The London Marathon: The History of the Greatest Race on Earth*. Hutchinson, 2005.
Tames, Richard, *Sporting London: A Race through Time*. Historical Publications, 2005.

Of Babel: a Linguistic Interlude
Ayto, John, *Oxford Dictionary of Rhyming Slang*. Oxford: Oxford University Press 2002.
McAuley, Ian, *Guide to Ethnic London*. Immel, 1987
Merriman, Nick (ed), *The Peopling of London: Fifteen Thousand Years of Settlement from Overseas*. Museum of London, 1993.
Notting Hill
Davies, Miranda and Anderson, Sarah, *Inside Notting Hill*. Portobello Publishing, 2001.
Tames, Richard, *The Notting Hill and Holland Park Book*. Historical Publications, 2004.

The Royal Borough of Kensington and Chelsea: www.rbkc.gov.uk

Victorian Valhallas: The Magnificent Seven

Culbertson, Judi and Randall, Tom, *Permanent Londoners: An Illustrated Guide to the Cemeteries of London.* Robson Books, 1991.
Curl, James Stevens (ed), *Kensal Green Cemetery.* Phillimore, 2001.

Nicked!: a Criminal Interlude

Hobbs, Dick, *Doing the Business: Entrepreneurship, the Working Class and Detectives in the East End of London.* Oxford: Oxford University Press, 1993.

Soho

Fryer, Jonathan, *Soho in the Fifties and Sixties.* National Portrait Gallery, 1998.
Pentlow, Mike and Rowe, Marsha, *Characters of Fitzrovia.* Pimlico, 2002.
Summers, Judith, *Soho: A History of London's Most Colourful Neighbourhood.* Bloomsbury, 1989.
The Soho Society: www.sohosociety.org.uk

At Home

Jenkins, Simon, *England's Thousand Best Houses.* Allen Lane, 2003.
Wilson, Vicky, [London] *Houses :a Handbook for Visitors.* Batsford 2002

Made in London: an American Interlude

Morton, Brian N., *Americans in London.* Macdonald & Co./Queen Anne's Press, 1988.
Benjamin Franklin's House: www.benjaminfranklinhouse.org

Southwark

Reilly, Len, *Southwark: An Illustrated History.* London Borough of Southwark, 1998.
Tames, Richard, *Southwark Past.* Historical Publications, 2001.
Southwark Heritage Association: www.southwark.org.uk
Southwark Local Studies Library: www.southwark.gov.uk
Globe Theatre: www.shakespeares-globe.org

Most of London: the Suburbs

Saint, Andrew, *London Suburbs.* Merrell Hollerton/ English Heritage, 1999.

Tindall, Gillian, *The Fields Beneath: The History of One London Village.* Phoenix Press, 2002.

Of Pints and Pubs: a Convivial Interlude

Bruning, Ted, *London by Pub: Pub Walks around Historic London.* Prion, 2001.

Stuart, Donald, *London's Historic Inns and Taverns.* Derby: Breedon Books, 2004.

Pub History Society: www.pubhistorysociety.co.uk

CAMRA: www.camra.org.uk

Spitalfields

Ali, Monica, *Brick Lane.* Black Swan, 2004.

Gavron, Jeremy, *An Acre of Barren Ground, or the History of Everyone Who Ever Lived on Brick Lane.* Scribner, 2005.

Hall, Tarquib, *Salaam Brick Lane.* John Murray, 2005.

Taylor, William, *This Bright Field: A Travel Book in One Place.* Methuen, 2001.

The Spitalfields Society: www.spitalfieldssociety.org

19 Princelet Street: www.19princeletstreet.org.uk

INDEX OF LITERARY & HISTORICAL NAMES

INDEX OF PLACES & LANDMARKS